STARVED MEN, MADE DESPERATE BY COLD
AND HUNGER . . . THEY STRUGGLED ACROSS
THE MOUNTAINS, DETERMINED TO SURVIVE
AT ANY COST

"All right, Creutz, it's all right."

Creutzfeldt had the sensation of awakening from a
long, drugged sleep. It had seemed such a pleasant
sleep that he wanted to slip right back into it.

But there were interesting shapes, too. There were
three of them, clustered like petals on a flower. Because of his snow blindness, the men appeared as blurs.
And there in the middle was another blur, round as
a daisy's pistil. The others were doing something to
the blur in the middle. It seemed to Creutzfeldt that
they were playing a game.

"What are you playing?" Creutzfeldt asked.

"Just playing a game, like you wanted, Creutz."
The voice was Old Bill's.

"Can I play, too?"

There was some laughter from the blurs, but it was
strange laughter, harsh and guttural.

"Sure, Creutz, you can play," came the voice
again.

Someone thrust something into his hands.

"Well, don't just sit there, Creutz. Take some and
pass it back."

Someone forced him to raise the thing to his lips.
It was certainly a strange thing! It was long . . . and
round . . . and rough and wet at the top.

Creutzfeldt let his hands explore down the far end
of the strange, wet thing. It got narrower . . . and narrower . . . and what were these . . . ? Fingers . . . ?

The scream came uncontrollably. For a brief moment he was jolted into sanity. His eyes opened wide
and struggled to focus on the thing he was holding. . . .

JOHN FREMONT

CALIFORNIA BOUND

Michael Beahan

A Dell/Banbury Book

Published by
Banbury Books, Inc.
37 West Avenue
Wayne, Pennsylvania 19087

Dell ® TM 681510, Dell Publishing Co., Inc.
ISBN: 0-440-04221-6
Printed in the United States of America
First printing—March 1982

Chapter 1

In the gathering dusk of an early autumn day, a small cloud of white smoke could be discerned over the low-lying hills surrounding the gentle Missouri River. River boys, in sack cloth and overalls, sat kicking their heels at the edge of the Westport dock. They were waiting.

Suddenly, a distant hissing turned the heads of the boys. A faint glow of golden light was cast upon the river, a glow that grew brighter and played off the darkening banks. Finally, the steamboat's bow appeared. The whole of it came into view quickly, its great paddle wheel thrumming against the current and throwing off sheets of white water.

As the boat drew closer, its one central stack still spewing smoke, the name on its prow became visible: *The Saratoga.*

The chugging of the steam engine now drowned out the shouts of greeting from the crowd gathering at the dock. Then, as the engine sound died off and the paddle wheel came to a stop, the big boat drifted with the current toward the far end of the wharf, where dock handlers waited with ropes to tie her up. The crowd grew silent with expectation.

"Hail and welcome!" the harbormaster finally cried from on shore.

"And the Lord be praised!" came the quick reply.

Heavy ropes were cast around the dock's free-standing poles, and the boat's stern was securely moored. As soon as the boarding plank was thrown down, the passengers, easterners mostly, began to stream off, anxiously searching out familiar faces or simply gazing about in bewilderment. This rough-hewn outpost was the farthest point west that most had ever seen.

One young couple, however, seemed more sure of themselves than the others. The man especially behaved like a seasoned traveler casting about in a foreign port for a familiar landmark. He stood proudly erect and had elegantly handsome features. Wavy dark blond hair framed his clear blue eyes, high cheekbones and sharp, straight nose. His deeply tanned and weathered skin was almost as dark as an Indian's. The tall woman beside him bore herself with equal grace. Her full chestnut hair was pulled back severely, tied with a bow at her neck, and fell halfway to her waist. Though she seemed a bit too slender and a little pale, she moved with the confidence of an aristocrat, and appeared, despite the rigors of the journey, as fresh and lively as if she had just stepped out of her boudoir.

Bags in hand, the man quietly ushered his wife toward a waiting carriage.

"Colonel Fremont!" one of the river boys cried suddenly.

Others nearby stopped to look where the excited boy was pointing.

"I know it's him! I seen his picture in the paper!"

As the river boy ran brazenly up to the man, looks of recognition registered throughout the crowd. "You are, aren't you? Aren't you Colonel Fremont?"

His wife tried to gesture him into the carriage, but the man resisted with a smile. With one foot on the carriage step, he turned to face the boy and held out his hand. "John Charles Fremont's the name. I'm not really a colonel anymore."

A portly older man pushed toward the carriage. "You're still a colonel to us, sir," he shouted, and the crowd around him burst into applause. "It's a sad day when this country gives only insults to its bravest citizen."

Fremont mumbled his thanks and hurriedly joined his wife as the crowd cheered again. When the carriage had rounded a corner, he laughed with a quick look heavenward.

"Nonsense, John Charles Fremont, you love every minute of it." Jessie Fremont leaned toward her husband and patted his leg. "I wish little Lilly could have been here to see her father so admired by all those young boys."

He did enjoy the adulation, he had to admit. But after all the agony and humiliation of the last two years, who could blame him for taking quiet pleasure from the wide-eyed respect of a frontier lad? Lately he had often wondered if he was really the same man who had headed west at the age of twenty on a U.S. Army expedition to chart unexplored territory in the rugged Northwest. Back then, life had seemed so simple, a matter of pushing on, marking the trail, using the stars to survey new land, and drawing maps for the eager politicians in Washington.

Only on the last expedition, in 1845, when he had gone to Iowa and Oregon, had his world grown complex and confused. With the fervent support of expansionist senators, chief among them being Jessie's own father, Thomas Hart Benton of Missouri, John Fremont had headed deeper into Oregon than any

pathfinder had ever gone. Although his avowed purpose
had been to draw up maps of untrodden territory, he
had also been eager to prove to his backers in Washington that a railroad could be built from St. Louis
westward to the great Pacific Ocean. Secretly, he had
also planned to range south into that verdant paradise
by the sea that few Americans had ever seen—California . . . And that had been the start of all his trouble.

Pioneers, pushing westward, had by that time begun to cast their eyes covetously on the southwest
territories claimed by Mexico. Soon official protests
from the Mexican government had begun to reach
Washington, and had quickly grown into rumblings of
war when Texas voted for annexation to the States.
Finally, when Zachary Taylor pushed westward into the
Rio Grande, a conflict had seemed inevitable. In California, Mexican troops had bristled on one side, while
on the other, American settlers had spoken eagerly of
bringing California into the Union.

Into that powder-keg had marched John Charles
Fremont with half a hundred men. Although, to anyone who asked, his had been a simple surveying mission, he had sworn to himself that if war broke out, he
would ride into the thick of it and raise the Union flag
over California's rolling green hills before any West
Pointer could get there.

So it had happened, though the flag turned out to
be a strip of cloth with a bear's head painted upon it.
On his own, he had faced a troop of Mexican soldiers,
rallied the pioneers behind him and captured Sonoma
and Sutter's Fort, the twin bastions of power in the
northern reach of the state. He had then swept through
San Francisco, christening its bay, the Golden Gate,
and with five hundred armed men had prepared to
capture Monterey.

But when he pushed southward to Monterey, he

had found the flag already raised by Commodore Sloat, of the Union's Pacific Fleet. Sloat had proved maddeningly cautious about taking any military action, particularly when faced with the prospect of heading farther south to Los Angeles, a Mexican stronghold. Fortunately, Sloat had turned over his command to his adjutant, Commodore R. F. Stockton, and fled the scene. Stockton was a man more to Fremont's liking—adventurous, aggressive, and eager to hurtle California into statehood.

For a few brief weeks after that, Fremont had been possessed by the feeling that the future held nothing but golden promise. He and Stockton had marched through Los Angeles without firing a shot.

A short time later, however, Mexican insurgents had rallied to overwhelm the small party of American troops left to maintain order, and Stockton had to return for a protracted struggle. This time Fremont could not assist him, having been detached to form a California Battalion with the promise of a governorship when the fighting was over.

A governorship! He even liked the way the word felt as it rolled off his tongue. But into his shimmering vision stretched one long shadow, and then another. Stockton grew furious when Fremont proved unable to muster his battalion in time to offer reinforcements in Los Angeles, and he made no secret of his dissatisfaction. But everyone knew that Stockton was impetuous and easily angered. Far more dangerous to Fremont's dreams had been the arrival of General Stephen Watts Kearny, fresh from his conquest of New Mexico. The worst kind of army career man, Kearny was a smug, humorless martinet, a bitter old man.

Yes, thought Fremont, it was Kearny who had shattered his dream, toppled him from his hopes of governorship, dragged him like a prisoner back to

Washington and sat stone faced on a witness stand to testify against him at a court-martial!

"John? We're here." Jessie's voice brought his thoughts back to the present. The thin, bald carriage driver jumped down from his perch and opened the carriage door for the Fremonts. John stepped out first and offered a hand to Jessie, and arm-in-arm they strode into the stately Westgate Hotel. As Jessie had at first gently reminded her husband, they could not afford such plush quarters, but the hotel proprietor, a burly old fellow with a quick tobacco-stained smile, would not hear of such a thing. Waving off their proffered bills, he ushered them up to the largest room in the house, actually a suite with ceiling-high French windows which opened onto a balcony above the hotel's front porch.

Jessie touched her husband's shoulder. "Such melancholy spirits possess you tonight."

Fremont turned to face her with a wry smile. "Nothing to do with you, dearest. I'll shake them off. Anyway, soon I'll be much too busy to brood. We have plans to make."

Jessie took his hands into her own. "Then let's start now, right this minute. What's the very first order of business tomorrow?"

As always, when their talk turned to plans of the next expedition, the two young adventurers felt a kinship, a bond that went beyond love. Though Jessie never accompanied her husband on the trail, it was she who took down his vivid descriptions with paper and quill as he paced the room like a restless animal. It was she, too, who later transcribed those notes, polished his grammar and created the final reports that an eager nation snatched up to read.

Secretly, if she had had her choice, Jessie would have either headed out on the trail with her husband or seen him settle down in St. Louis, perhaps as a governmental adviser or a cartographer. The worst pain for her was the hurt of parting, or lying alone in their four-poster bed. But she endured it because Jessie knew that if John Fremont were ever forced to settle into some stifling governmental job, his heart and spirit would soon be broken.

"All right, first order of business," Fremont laughed. "I need three dozen able-bodied, experienced men who don't care about poor pay and miserable conditions."

"With you as their leader, the only problem will be keeping three dozen more from trailing along."

"I wish that were true. The best men are so damned hard to find. Even in a frontier town like Westport, with all manner of trappers and hunters about, I think it will take two weeks to recruit enough trail hands. Any longer than that, and I'll have your father and his investors breathing fire down my neck."

"My father thinks you're the most admirable young man his daughter could have married, and you know it," Jessie laughed.

"Now he does," Fremont retorted. "But I haven't forgotten how hard he tried to keep us apart. Hell, I'd probably never have gotten to go on an expedition at all if he hadn't wanted to put a thousand miles between us."

"Can you blame him? I was only sixteen, my sweetheart, and you were a dashing, headstrong adventurer of twenty-one with not a penny in your pocket."

"No one loves a poor man in this world." He frowned. "No one but you." Fremont jumped up in mock exasperation and began pacing between the balcony doors and their big, lumpy feather bed with its gaily colored quilt.

"I'll need good men and horses," he declared, changing the subject with a sheepish grin. "And enough sugar, coffee, grain and tobacco to last a month across the Rockies."

"Didn't my father mention a trader who lives near here?"

"Right. We'll look him up. And in addition to tools and tents, coats and boots, what we really need more than anything else is . . ." Fremont sighed. "What we really need is Kit Carson."

"Darling, give the man a chance to start a family, for Lord's sake. He's married hardly a month, with his fence-posts barely whittled and slotted, and already you want to take him away from his wife."

"To tell you the truth, I think he'd rather be crossing the Rockies than staying home—after a modest amount of time to, ah, work off his domestic energies." Fremont exchanged an amused look with his wife.

"I don't suppose you've built up any domestic energies of your own, have you?" Jessie slipped up behind her husband and put her arms around his lithe, tightly-muscled body.

Fremont stood still for a moment, letting Jessie run her hands up and down his chest, and then he slowly turned to face her. As her hands slid down to cup his firm, slightly rounded buttocks, he unfastened the bow at the back of her neck with a practiced touch. In another moment, she stood naked before him, no longer the innocent, pretty girl of sixteen with whom he had fallen so desperately in love eight years before, but now a mature woman, beautiful and proud. Her deep brown locks fell over strong, handsome shoulders; her breasts, dark-nippled and firm, rose ever so slightly as he caressed them.

She led him now into their bed and lay back against the coolness of the coverlet. She pulled him toward her. Her teasing good humor all but forgotten, she moaned softly once, and then again as she felt her desire arouse his own. Her breath came more sharply, in short quick gasps. Could there be anything on earth that would ever feel as good as this man, *her* man? Then, for a fleeting moment, she remembered how soon this happiness would be taken from her again.

Chapter 2

"William Jeremiah Brattle?"

A tall, gaunt southerner stepped forward in the dusty morning sunlight that filtered through the windows of Amos Tuck's Whiskey and Dancing Women Saloon.

"Yessir," he drawled.

Fremont, seated at a long table by the bar, looked the man over dubiously. "Haven't heard the name before," he said tonelessly. "Where you from?"

"Atlanta. Been with Nicollet up north."

Fremont gave a start. "Nicollet? How long?"

"Four years. I come down here this summer. Had a woman, but that didn't work out. Had a farm but that didn't work out neither. Figured it was time to push on, if you see my point."

Fremont paused, undecided. The southerner seemed a bit old to be hauling a mule and baggage over mountainous country. Still, that he had spent time with Nicollet spoke well for him. Fremont had made his own first expedition under Nicollet's command, and much of what Fremont knew of astronomy had been learned from that grizzled veteran.

"Any children?"

"No sir, not as I know of." An appreciative laugh

rippled through the crowd of men clustered around the rough oak bar.

"All right then, sign up at the door. Pay is sixty dollars a month and provisions, but not a cent if you turn back at Pueblo."

So it went. By noon, Fremont had chosen thirty-three men. He could have signed up twice as many, but he resisted his inclination to let the eagerness of the younger men impress him. Fremont knew all too well how a young fellow's courage could turn to fear when he faced real hardship. And on this expedition, weeks might pass between full rations of sugar and coffee and decent food.

Nearly all the men Fremont had found for himself had set out at least once before on an expedition west, and most could offer some special talent or skill.

Over lunch at the hotel, Fremont told Jessie the news of the morning. He thought he had picked some pretty good men. A few, including Charles Preuss, Henry King, Charles Taplin and Thomas Breckinridge were more than good. They were men who could survive in the wilderness without comfort or even much food, men who could brave icy mountain winds for days at a stretch—qualities which would be especially important on this particular mission.

"Why don't you take an artist along, John?" Jessie suggested. She always held a desire to share her husband's exploits in graphic detail.

"I hired on a fellow named Kern for that," Fremont said. "And Alexis Godey is our hunter." He took a long pull on his tankard of ale.

Jessie cut into the last of her broiled venison. "Who did you find to scout the trail for you?"

"That's where we have a difficulty. There's just no one as good as Kit. I didn't meet anybody in that crowd this morning who I'd trust my life to."

"Do you ever wonder why they would entrust their lives to you?" Jessie teased.

"For sixty dollars a month, I guess." For a brief moment, Fremont's brow seemed to knit with worry. "I'm not sure they know what they're getting into."

Jessie paused. "Do you know? Truly?"

Fremont turned his clear blue eyes to hers. For a moment he and Jessie looked at each other with quiet love and solicitude.

"I only know I have to keep exploring," Fremont said at last. "It's like a fever that's always burned inside me. I know that if I don't take this chance, I may lose what little faith our financiers have in me. You know that too, don't you?"

"Yes. But I also know that your financiers, including my father, care more about their own selfish aims than they do about your safety. They want to know that John Fremont can make it to the other side of the Rockies in the coldest reach of winter so they can feel safe in laying their millions on a train line from St. Louis to the coast. But if you don't make it, they won't lose a thing."

Fremont laughed. "If I don't make it, my sweet, sweet love, your father will have to find another suitor for you. That shouldn't be too difficult, of course."

"Now don't tease." Jessie's eyes filled with hurt and concern. "No one else has ever crossed the Rockies in December. No one knows how bad it might be, not even you!"

"Jessie, I promise that in a few short months we'll be together in California, on our own tract of land, in our very own home."

Jessie bowed her head and put down her knife and fork. Across the table, Fremont suddenly noticed the sharp glint of moisture on her cheeks and, awkwardly, he reached over to brush her tears away. "Why, the trip won't be so bad for you. You'll have a comfortable berth, Lilly for company, good food and pleasant scenery."

"Oh stop now, John Fremont!" Jessie cried. "You know it isn't me I'm aching over."

Late that afternoon, Fremont found himself in the ramshackle, rank-smelling Westport General Store and Supply House of Mr. J. Pincham Moody, Proprietor. It might have been more properly called the Westport Particular Store, Fremont thought wryly, as hardly anything in either general or good supply was to be found beneath its sagging tin roofs. Indeed, all Fremont could discover as he glanced over the inventory was a jumble of odd pipes and sprockets, single boots in need of partners and shelves stacked with crudely tied sacks of grain and coffee set against each other at random.

But to Fremont, the oddest thing of all about Moody's general store was that Moody himself was nowhere to be seen. Nor were there any customers, for that matter. Fremont, after vigorously shaking the cowbells dangling from the front door, let himself inside. The door shut with a crash, sending swirls of dust spiraling through the air. Then there was silence, punctuated only by the ticking of a captain's clock that had no minute hand.

"Hello," Fremont ventured cautiously. "Hello there. Moody?"

From behind the counter came a feeble groan. Fremont crept forward curiously. Another groan, louder, and this time a bit angry, rose from behind the counter. Then suddenly a pudgy, soot-stained hand popped up and waved the explorer back.

"Closedforlunch," mumbled a drowsy, low voice.

Fremont, bewildered, tried to peek over the counter. "Moody?" he said again, feeling a bit foolish. "What in the hell is going on?"

A mop of unkempt blond hair appeared, followed by a pair of fuchsia-pink eyes, which fastened themselves on the figure of Fremont as if he had literally walked out of the woodwork.

"Taking inventory," replied J. Pincham Moody, after focusing on his first customer of the day. "And y'know how it is, when your inventory is fine Tennessee sour mash, doncha? Gotta take it, that's all. For inventory." Moody snickered.

"Bet you never lose count," Fremont said coldly. He strode up and down the counter, his heavy leather boots resounding against the plank floor. "Here," he said. He extracted a list of needs from a pocket in his buckskin jacket and unfolded it. Moody's visage became suddenly respectful. "How soon can you round up all these provisions and supplies?"

"Not a drinkin' man, I guess," said Moody, reaching over for the list.

"Never have been. Makes it easier to go without when there's none around."

"Yes, well, maybe so." Moody peered more closely at the list, as if struggling with some great new truth. "Hundred pounds what?"

"Corn, grain, barley, peas. A hundred pounds of each."

Moody nodded slowly. "And fifty pounds of coffee and sugar."

"That is correct, sir."

"Sort of stockin' up, huh?"

"You might say so, yes."

Moody took a pint bottle of whiskey out from under the counter and drank off a good bit of it. Then he grimaced and squinted up at the tall figure across from him. "You know sumpthin' that the rest of us don't?"

"I'm not sure what you mean, Mr. Moody."

"I mean about the weather."

"No more than any other man."

"Uh-huh." Moody paused. "Bet you're wantin' all this 'cause you're goin' west, right? Goin' west with some plumb-fool peabrain easterners, right?"

"About half right."

"Half right, indeed." Moody took another swig from his bottle. "Well, sir, maybe you got the dates mixed up, or the month mixed up. Or maybe you even got your directions mixed up. Maybe you're really headed east."

"Mr. Moody, I don't have all day. Can you fill my order, or shall I go somewhere else?"

"Hold onto your britches, boy. Ain't nowhere else to go, for one thing, and I don't mean you no disrespect, understan'? What I'm tryin' to tell you is that you're too late for goin' west. You're gonna get stuck in the snow, sure as I'll be sittin' right here by this potbelly stove warmin' my hams."

"I'm looking forward to some snow along the way. I'd be very disappointed to miss it."

Moody drank off the last of his bottle and cast it out an open window. It landed with a loud smash on top of a pile of identical, pint-sized bottles. "In that case, mister, all I have to know is if you're payin' cash on the barrelhead. I'll be doin' no business on credit with a crazy son of a bitch who wants to cross the Rockies in the middle of the winter."

"And your receipt, Mr. Moody?" Fremont said, fishing out a sealed stack of crisp, freshly minted bills.

Moody eyed the stack with awe. "Receipt, yessir. Yes, indeed."

"When do you suppose you'll have my supplies rounded up and neatly set out on the front porch, sir?"

"Midday tomorrow, you can bet on that." Moody hurriedly wrote up the order and signed his own name with a drunken flourish. "Now all's I need is your name sayin' you gave me the money and want the goods."

"Of course." Fremont took the quill from Moody's pudgy fingers and signed his name in a practiced, elegant script.

"Tomorrow, then," he said, tipping his hat, and turning sharply, he strode out the door.

Moody burped after him.

Fremont had called the men to a meeting at sundown in the genteel lobby of the town hotel, with the proprietor's eager permission. Jessie kept quietly to herself upstairs until the meeting was over and the men had dispersed. Her husband would not have asked her to leave. Indeed, he was so confident in her judgment that he would not have cared if she sat right beside him as the men trooped in. But Jessie knew these rugged men would consider it an odd gesture, and some might even snicker thinking Fremont a sissified dandy who clings to his wife's petticoats. On an arduous expedition, when men's wills and energies would be taxed to the limit, leadership would be hard enough to maintain without a bad first impression to live down.

When the men straggled in, doffing their wide-brimmed hats as they walked through the hotel portal, Fremont sat alone at the far end of the room in a red velvet wing armchair. He kept his papers beside him on the threadbare rug, and, to his other side, a sheet of slate propped up on an end table. He sat there as confidently as a nobleman. His long blond locks hung down to his buckskin jacket, and his features—strong, lean, and proud—seemed naturally to command respect.

He was keenly aware of his power to lead men like these. The ability had always been there for him even when he was a child leading his friends at play. Sometimes his own forceful presence seduced him into haughtiness, but he tried never to let himself give in too much to such temptations. A proud leader, he always told himself, was a leader doomed to failure.

Fremont remained seated, yet such was the anticipation with which the men awaited his words, that when he leaned forward slightly to speak, the room fell silent immediately.

"Gentlemen, good evening," Fremont began. "Many of you already know each other, though as yet you are strangers to me. I can assure you that in the next three months we will all come to know each other very well—too well, I'd wager."

An appreciative laugh rippled through the room.

"Those of you I do know can attest to that. Alex Godey, there, was with me in '43. He's a good man and a good hunter. Creutzfeldt was along that year, too. That's a man who knows his plants. I think he's given surnames to every prairie bluebell and mountain rose from St. Louis to San Francisco. Charles Preuss was with me on the '45 expedition. Now he knows his rocks. Geologist. He can tell you how the Rockies were made in the first place."

Fremont reached in his pockets for chalk. "But what you want to know first, before all that, is what this trip is about. One fellow I know has already called us a plumb-fool bunch of peabrain easterners."

Again there was quick laughter. Already the men were growing comfortable. Most settled back easily into the formal, ornately carved chairs that filled the room, though a few insisted on leaning on their saddle-bags on the rug.

"Well, first off, we're not taking the route south of the range, down through New Mexico. It's straight out west, along the thirty-eighth parallel, from Pueblo over the middle of the range and into California."

Fremont pressed on, over the general murmur of surprise. "Two reasons, gentlemen. First, no one—no white man, at least—has ever crossed that range and lived to report on it. No one really knows what's out there, besides snow and ice, that is. So we're going to learn a few things that might help some other folks to get across the mountains easier.

"Most important of all," Fremont continued, "we can fill in this map." Here he took a large map from the floor by his chair and unrolled it to its full length. Over the region between most of Colorado and Oregon extended only cursory lines, and hardly any names. "Most of you probably know already that a map can't be drawn without readings—astronomical readings—and that to take those readings you have to travel the territory. No word of mouth or Indian tale will do."

Fremont set the map down. "That's half of why we're going," he said. "But there's another reason. Some of you may be aware that I'm no longer a soldier of good standing in the U.S. Army. That's of no account now, except that it means the government isn't bankrolling our trip. A group of private investors is. Most of them are back in St. Louis, and they're not of a mind to hand out their money just so we can all head west by the easiest route. They want to know whether they can run a railroad directly west to California from St. Louis."

Fremont raised his hands to quiet the outcries of amazement. "I know it sounds crazy. But who of us can really say for sure it's not possible? Who's been across to tell?"

One man raised a tentative hand. Fremont nodded toward him and the man stood up with some embarrassment. "Colonel, ah, Fremont, sir, I been on the trail in winter up north toward Canada, and over northwest, too, and I wonder, sir, if you're acquainted with conditions down around the south range into New Mexico in winter?"

Fremont smiled. "I've seen the same view myself, and in winter, too. All I can tell you is that I'm ready to go myself, and that anyone else who's ready is welcome to join me. Anyone who's not had better bow out now. It'll be a mite more difficult to turn back at twelve thousand feet."

The questioner shrugged. "I trust you, Colonel. Just askin' is all."

"And how about the rest of you men?" Fremont coolly appraised the group. "Anyone want to change his mind and spend a warm, cozy winter in Westport, curled up beside a good woman, eating well and drinking whiskey?"

No one moved.

"Well then," Fremont said briskly. "Time for a few details. We leave in four days." He drew an X on the slate to mark Westport below an arc that indicated the thirty-eighth parallel. "I want to reach Pueblo in three weeks." A circle for Pueblo, zigzag lines for the Rockies. "After we rest up a few days in Pueblo, I want to strike out northwest and head up the eastern flank of the first range to look for a pass. That should put us into late November."

"How about the pack animals?" came a query at the far end of the lobby. "How they goin' to get through the snow and such, bein' the mountains is steep and all."

"They'll just have to make it," Fremont replied. "Because if they can't, we probably can't either."

"We got horses and mules to take enough food to last us?" The speaker was Brattle, the southerner.

"Might depend on how much you eat, there, Brattle," put in another southerner, a bearded fellow named Taplin. To the rest of them he added, "I seen that cracker eat forty flapjacks at a sitting without a belch."

"Eat that way atop the Rockies," Fremont said, "and you might roll right back down the mountain. So I'd bet on eating less, Brattle. But if the snows don't hit us too hard too soon, we should have enough food to make it."

There were other details to be established, but Fremont saw that the crowd was growing restless. If he continued speaking the men might listen. But they would not listen well. It was best to let them go. There would be time in the next few days to pull each man aside and tell him his duties.

"All right then," Fremont said, surveying the room. "Now I have only one more thing to say. You all know there are no saloons out on the trail past Pueblo, and you may be fixing to remedy that by bringing your own spirits. Don't bother. I'll be sure there's a bit of whiskey packed for medicinal purposes, but that's all the liquor we'll take. It doesn't do a damn thing for a man who's got to ride twenty-eight miles over rough terrain every day."

Fremont waited patiently for the grumbling to die down. "However, we're not on the trail yet, and while I'm not a drinking man myself, I can appreciate that most of you men do like a shot now and then. So what I propose, gentlemen, is that you all adjourn to the hotel saloon and have a drink or two on me."

An enthusiastic cheer went up, and as one body the men charged out of the lobby, across the foyer and into the hotel's long, narrow saloon. It was still early in the evening, and only a half-dozen regulars had already clustered down at the far end to belt back shots of bourbon and joke with the ample-bosomed, middle-aged barmaid who went by the name of Rose.

"Set us all up a round, my sweet-smelling Rosie!" Taplin cried as three dozen others tumbled into the bar behind him. Rose was slightly annoyed at the sudden intrusion, but the drinkers at the far end positively bristled. Trappers all, they wore deerskin shirts, hand-stitched leather jackets and coonskin hats. Behind them, on rough pegs driven into the wall, were hung their roughhewn coats of beaver and bear fur. Not one of the trappers was under six feet tall, and not one looked weaker than a full-grown bull.

With sultry slowness, Rose began setting shot glasses up along the bar in a long, crooked row. Rather than count them, she simply took out a fresh bottle, pulled the cork and carelessly filled glass after glass straight down the line. Amber colored whiskey splashed over the rims, between the glasses and onto the bar. To the waiting men it was a grand display and they whistled and catcalled their appreciation. To the trappers watching, it seemed a show of contempt by the woman, and they exchanged disdainful, knowing glances. But no one knew for certain what Rose intended. In all the years she had spent behind frontier bars, she had long since developed an inscrutable cast, letting all of her customers see and hear what they wanted to, but revealing to none anything at all.

"To Colonel Fremont and the Rockies!" one man cried.

"Here, here!"

Gradually the group broke into smaller clusters, which ranged along the bar and back against a wall hung with framed sketches and political cartoons clipped out of big-city newspapers. One man, younger than most of his new companions, leaned against the wall away from the others. This was Charles Kern, the artist, who had traveled with Fremont before. He usually kept to himself, preferring to watch and, sometimes, to sketch a scene in the notebook he carried everywhere.

Now, indeed, he pulled his notebook out and began to sketch the trappers. With quick, deft strokes, he captured their rugged features and heavy frontier clothing. After every few strokes, he looked up quizzically toward them to refresh his memory and to search out the next salient detail.

As Kern worked feverishly on the sketch, one trapper nudged his partner and nodded slightly toward the artist. His partner nudged the next man. In a few moments, all of the trappers had turned their cold eyes on Kern, who worked obliviously on.

Suddenly his notebook was snatched out of his hands. His charcoal had zigzagged a line to the bottom of the page before Kern realized what was happening.

"Hey!" he cried out, and looked up into the angry, heavily whiskered face of the tallest man he had ever seen.

"Hey what, boy?"

"What the hell did you do that for?" Kern managed, more annoyed than frightened.

For an answer, the trapper gave Kern a tremendous push that sent him sprawling.

"We'll have no prissy-faced drawer makin' pictures of us," the trapper bellowed as the rest of Fremont's men turned toward him. "And we'll have no school of prissies in our saloon either."

The trapper stepped menacingly forward as Kern scrambled to get off the floor and out of the way. The trapper's drinking partners slid off their barstools, and formed into a phalanx of muscle and grit, then drew and cocked their long-barreled pistols.

"Just a minute now, friend."

The calm voice came from over near the swinging saloon doors.

As Fremont moved forward, his men stepped aside for him. He had slipped off his gunbelt and now, wearing no arms at all, he stopped five feet away from the closest trapper.

For a moment, neither spoke. Then Fremont smiled almost imperceptibly and fixed his clear blue eyes on the other man. "Long way from Calgary."

The trapper made an effort, unsuccessfully, to mask his surprise. "Do I know you, brother?" he said suspiciously.

"No."

Another silence passed. Then the trapper felt compelled to speak again. Fremont had figured that he would.

"How do you know Calgary, then?"

"Never been," Fremont replied. "But I had a friend from Calgary."

Now the trapper felt both curious and slightly ridiculous. "Who?" he asked finally.

"Andre Pelletier. Know him?"

The trapper, with a look of disbelief, jerked his thumb over his shoulder at one of his friends behind him. "That there's a Pelletier."

As the trapper spoke, Pelletier stepped forward. His gun was still drawn and cocked, but he lowered it as he approached. "How do you know my brother?"

Fremont turned his gaze to the second trapper. "I was with him for a spell in Oregon. Fine hunter. Saw him take a squirrel out at fifty yards."

Incredibly, Pelletier's face broke into a broad, toothy smile under his bushy brown mustache. "That no good son of a bitch couldn't hit a cow at twenty feet."

"Word down in Oregon was that no one could best him," Fremont smiled back. "The year I was out, he took eight hundred beaver down from the hills in spring."

Pelletier pushed the hammer forward on his gun and shoved the big barrel into his belt with good-natured disappointment. "Eight hundred beaver? Shit. I done taught him too good."

Fremont laughed, then turned to the first trapper. Calmly, so as not to set to twitching any trigger-happy fingers, the explorer held out his hand. "We owe you an apology, friend. No man should draw another man's likeness without his permission."

For an instant, the big trapper hesitated, as if he had a glimmering that he had been defeated. But here was this stranger holding out his hand in apology. The trapper shook his head and took Fremont's hand in his own massive paw.

"Now, madam," Fremont said, turning to Rose, who was waiting with a bored look behind the bar, "set these hard-working men up with another round of whiskey. And put a nickel in that player piano."

Fremont joined the trappers at the far end of the bar. The clinking notes of a bawdy Spanish love song came from the battered player piano in the corner, and Rose took down another full bottle for the crowd, this one compliments of the portly hotel proprietor. As she filled the trappers' glasses, Rose glanced up at Fremont with a curious look. He studied his glass for a moment, then allowed himself one small sip.

Chapter 3

A crowd assembled soon after sunrise on Westgrove's wide Main Street. A festive mood prevailed, as though the people were awaiting a marching band or a holiday fancy-dress parade. Many of the men wore dark suits, and the women all sported sun-dresses, bonnets and parasols. Many storefronts had been decorated with Union flags for the occasion, and the mayor of Westport, a pompous strutting politician named Julian Baskerville, had prepared a speech.

"Good citizens of Westport," Baskerville began as he stood on a small wooden platform amidst a chorus of catcalls, "this is indeed a day of great historical importance for our little frontier town."

Hoots of laughter greeted this pronouncement, but he pressed on bravely. "In our midst, we have with us for a brief while, the country's most renowned explorer, a man of noble mane and even nobler accomplishments, a trailblazer and great explorer, John Charles Fremont."

"Get him back to jail," came a voice in the crowd. Baskerville had once been imprisoned in the Westport jail for poaching. "Somebody better shoot him before he talks us all to death," the voice cried again.

Baskerville, crimson-faced, was about to respond

when he was spared further indignities by the sudden appearance of Fremont leading a long procession of men, horses and mules up dusty Main Street.

Every man in the parade was handsomely outfitted with a pack containing a bedroll, cooking utensils, toiletries, a few extra layers of clothing and a Hall breechloading carbine, as well as a pair of Colt revolvers slung about the waist. The mules, tied together on a long rope harness, followed behind. Some carried sacks of flour and campfire kettles. Others bore sacks of sugar or coffee, or the khaki-colored tents that the men would use until they reached Pueblo.

The last mule carried Fremont's instruments, which were more important to the explorer than arms or provisions. Here, stashed in carefully padded, curiously shaped packs, were chronometers, sextants, a syphon barometer, thermometers, compasses and even a refracting telescope. With these vital instruments, Fremont would take his daily measurements and jot them down in the ledger he always kept with him. Though he thrilled to the adventure and challenge of the expedition, Fremont was more greatly moved by a sober pride in compiling scientific facts. His own expedition, he was determined, would accomplish more than any other man's ever would.

As the party rode up Main Street, the eager spectators on either side fell strangely quiet. The grandness of this ceremony blinded no one to the critical dangers these men were about to face. Yet, ironically, the men seemed far less perturbed than the onlookers. In fact, to a man they seemed proudly resolute, even high-spirited, as if the hardships and deprivations that awaited them were more tempting than frightening.

As Fremont reached the edge of town, he reined in his horse and leaned to the side in his saddle. From amidst the strange faces in the crowd, Jessie emerged.

Her hair streaming behind her, she ran up to her husband and pressed his outstretched hand against her
lovely, pale face. She squeezed back her tears, and
smiling up at him, whispered, "I'll miss you so much,
my darling, so very much."

"I'll miss you too, Jess, all of every day and all
the more at night."

Abruptly steeling herself against her own sentiment, Jessie let her husband's hand go and bade him to
ride on. In a moment, she had slipped back into the
crowd and disappeared. Fremont spurred his horse,
and the whole party quickened to a canter, kicking up
dust and breaking the spell that hung over the crowd.
Applause broke out, and Baskerville, who had never
relinquished the rostrum, took the opportunity to finish
his speech.

For Fremont, the most poignant and memorable
time of any expedition was always when his home
slipped out of sight behind him. He had seen Westport
dip away out of sight behind the rolling hills only an
hour after leaving, and though it wasn't really his
home, his wife would be waiting there. Now, across
the gentle Missouri grasslands, the men could no longer
turn back in their saddles and see the faint, hazy out-
line of rough wood houses and storefronts.

Ahead stretched the autumn prairie. A beautiful
pageant of lavender astors and shimmering goldenrod
reached to the far horizon. Only a decade ago, most
men had thought this wide stretch of land to be a
barren and forbidding obstacle to reaching the West.
Fremont, in fact, had been among the very first to dis-
prove that illusion. His journals from the trailblazing
expeditions of 1843 and 1845 had offered, to an awe-
struck public, elegiac descriptions of the prairie's beauty, of its flowers and fertile soil. Now, as he rode into

that lovely vision again, he could not help feeling a deep surge of pride and affection for the land and the life it had granted him. It was a gift, he knew, to be alive in this time of adventure and exploration.

By midday the men had traveled nearly ten miles. For much of that distance, Fremont found himself riding alongside a young Georgian named Micajah McGehee. A scion of a wealthy tobacco family, McGehee had chosen to abandon his life on the plantation of tending the slaves and selling tobacco. To his father's consternation, young McGehee had struck off on his own. First, he told Fremont, he had gone to St. Louis, but he had found society there as starchy and prim as it had ever been at home. So he had pressed westward, hoping to join up with a wagon train headed for California.

"The trouble was," McGehee said in a slow southern drawl, "none of the wagonmasters seemed to know a whit about which trail to take, or where in California they'd finally end up. I had a most distrustful feeling about every one of those parties, and my feelings of intuition have saved my life more than once."

"So now you're headed across the Rockies in winter."

McGehee laughed. "Well, it does seem passing strange, but I had two good reasons. The first one was you. And the second was that my feeling about this trip was different—my special feeling, that is."

Fremont smiled and said nothing. Long ago he had learned it was better to listen to a man than to talk him down. In fact, he had come to the point of hardly commenting at all to the men he rode with, preferring to hear them tell about themselves. They were usually happier that way, and in a strange way they respected Fremont more for his interest in them than for any words he might have spoken.

"So what do you hope to do out West, McGehee?" he finally asked.

"Oh, I suppose I'll find a good, honest woman, first of all. There's a shortage of those down South, you know," McGehee laughed. He had a quick, engaging laugh, Fremont had observed. A good man. "I mean, they're honest as the day is long until they learn you're sitting on a pot of money. Then suddenly it's 'honey' this and 'darlin' that, with a lot of talk about the children they'd like to have someday, right down to their names." He fanned himself with his broad-brimmed hat and continued. "A good woman would be the finest thing, along with a stretch of land and a good horse or two. And then, well, I do have one outlandish dream."

"What's that?"

"I'd like to start my own newspaper. Be an editor, I mean. The way I figure, there's a half-dozen settlements out West, and they'll be growing like wildfire over the next ten years. Every new town ought to have a newspaper, don't you think?"

Fremont nodded. "I reckon so, though you're talking to the wrong man about newspapers."

McGehee colored. "Oh, yes, I suppose there were a few that lit into you, weren't there?"

"Doesn't matter now," Fremont replied. "They can't shoot you, they can't scalp you, and they can't starve you to death."

"I suppose that's so," McGehee replied as Fremont tipped his hat and spurred his horse on ahead.

The sun was still hours from setting when Fremont gave the order to pitch camp. Those men who had traveled under other leaders found it odd to stop so early on this first day out, but they soon recognized the wisdom of the decision. Instead of waiting until dusk to settle on a campsite, Fremont secured a wider margin of safety by setting up camp in daylight, when you could still see a far distance.

On this first day, Fremont established a routine for pitching camp. First, the horses were unsaddled and brushed down, hobbled and set loose to graze under guard. Packs were opened, tents unfolded and stakes hammered into the ground. When the tents were up in a wide circle, bedrolls were laid down inside them, and a half dozen campfire pits were dug. Only then, as the big copper cooking pots were filled with water for beans and set over the fire, could the men begin to ease their tired limbs.

"Whatcha doin' there, son?"

Brattle, the southerner, took a seat beside Kern, stretching his lanky legs toward the nearby cooking fire.

"Just what you see," Kern replied cheerfully. He showed Brattle the sketch pad, with a half-completed drawing of the tents, a few figures clustered around the campfires, and in the distance, the already recognizable figure of Fremont.

"Now what's he doin'?" Brattle asked.

"Best I know, he's looking at the stars."

At that moment, Fremont was, in fact, beyond the tents, peering toward the heavens through a telescope set on a tripod. After taking several sightings, Fremont would translate them into readings of longitude and latitude, which he would then set down on a map.

In conjunction with these readings, Fremont had to take a magnetic bearing of every new hill or valley, even during the day. Only in this way could an accurate map be drawn of all the rivers and mountains the expedition would pass over. It was an undeniably onerous task for him, but Fremont, so restless to get on the trail and eager to journey ahead, took all the minute detailing as a matter of daily routine.

Presently the camp cooks called the men to dinner, and just as the sun was beginning to set over the wide prairie, they all lined up with their cooking gear in hand.

"What you done to all that good meat?" jibed the bearded southerner, Taplin, who also went by the nickname Doubleback, given to him because of the courage with which he had once slipped from a wagon train through an attacking line of Sioux to go for help.

"Here we have *boeuf bourguignon,*" announced the cook in a heavy German accent. He grinned at the thick brown glop that bubbled merrily over the flame. "It is *Français,* if you know what I mean."

The cook called himself Captain Cathcart. A towering, burly man whose knitted black eyebrows belied a gentle soul, he had fought with the eleventh Prince Albert Hussars against Napoleon's advancing armies. That, he decided, had been all the fighting he ever wanted to see. Leaving his country and royal title behind, he had worked his way to America on a big merchant three master ship, bought a horse in Baltimore and traveled westward. He had taught himself how to trap and to shoot, and had promptly fallen in love with the rugged frontier. Now, though he carried no regrets about leaving his home country, Captain Cathcart still hung onto a few emblems of his heritage: his accent, for one, his captain's rank and uniform and his love of fine cuisine.

"Buff, what was that, cook?" demanded Doubleback.

"*Ach, mein Gott!*" Captain Cathcart moaned. "Eat what is on your plate, okay, you bearded baboon?"

When the men had been served and had gathered around the campfires, they fell to their stew, thick black bread and whipped butter, cider and black coffee, with such a ravenous appetite that hardly a word passed among them.

Fremont, who had not yet served himself, took the opportunity to briefly address his men.

"Uh oh," muttered Doubleback to Brattle. "I didn't know we was gonna have entertainment."

"Men, those of you who've been out on the trail before know what I mean when I say the food's always better at the beginning. You might do well to remember this dinner long after it's gone, because there might come a time when the memory of good hot food is all that's being served.

"Now, I'm not suggesting that we'll run out of food, exactly. But I am suggesting that the way to conserve what we've got in the days to come is to be on the alert for any appetizing varmint that pokes its head up over the prairie grass. I'm not just talking about prairie dogs, either. I mean buffalo, because the meat we're eating tonight is all we've got. Couldn't have packed much more anyway. It would have spoiled. And there were other provisions needed that can't be found roaming around the prairies. Like tobacco . . ."

Here a great cheer went up.

". . . and coffee and sugar. Tonight's meat is a gift, a way for me to say I'm glad we're off, and I'm glad that each and every one of you is with me. Tomorrow night . . ." Fremont raised a tin cup of cider. "Tomorrow night fresh buffalo."

By the time the sun had melted into the horizon and the blue of the sky had deepened to violet, the men had finished their first-night feast and washed their plates in a nearby creek, which was swollen with the autumn rains. In the remaining hour of dusk, Fremont let the campfire stay lit, albeit low. Doubleback pulled out a harmonica, Brattle a Jew's harp, and the two commenced to play together, softly at first, then more boldly as the other men gathered around to join in a verse or two. In the gentle chill of the October evening, as the sweet music wafted from the campfire light into the surrounding darkness, not a man there would have chosen to be anywhere else.

From the circle of tents around the snuffed-out, smoking campfire pits rose a chorus of ungodly snores that might have sounded, to a stranger, like a chorus of clamorous, drunken grizzly bears.

Above them hung a full harvest moon, bathing the prairie grasses in a soft, ethereal, ochre light. But off to one side, wrapped in his bedroll, John C. Fremont, holding a cup of cold black coffee in his hand, sat brooding.

The snores of his sleeping men helped to calm him, for he had grown to love that sound. It meant all was well, that a long hard day of traveling was over and that he had gained two dozen miles on the trail. But burning in his mind's eye as vividly as gold against black velvet was the image of Jessie, holding his hand softly to her face and whispering farewell. She must be lying awake right now, thought Fremont, alone in that four-poster hotel bed. It was hardly conceit to imagine, he decided, that she was also thinking of him, for the two of them had always had an understanding they carried with each other, even when they were apart. For all the passion they shared, this understanding was as calm as a gentle sun shower. They knew, with complete conviction, that each was the other's perfect lover and mate.

Ever since he had first lain eyes on her in the drawing room of her father's home, John Fremont had known that Jessie was the only one for him. And she had known every bit as surely that John C. Fremont was the man for her.

As he sat there brooding over his Jessie and all the miles that separated them, an idea suddenly possessed him. He knew his weakness. On more than one occasion his stern self-discipline had given way to a reckless, childlike exhilaration that swept him off on some half-mad gambit, just for the risk of it, or perhaps for the fun of it.

Without a thought to the aching fatigue he might feel the next morning, Fremont slipped, fully dressed, out of his bedroll, pulled on his coat and boots, and stole quietly over to the guarded horses and mules. With a low greeting, he approached the bleary-eyed guard on duty.

"Too eager to sleep, sir?" asked the guard, a young Missourian named Thomas Martin.

"Sort of," Fremont whispered back. "I thought I'd take a little night ride."

The guard looked blankly at his leader. "A night ride?"

"You ought to try it sometime."

Fremont unhitched his horse and swung a saddle over its strong chestnut back. "Martin, do me a favor and keep this to yourself, all right?" Fremont cinched up his saddle. "Wait a few minutes till I'm far enough away, and then end your shift early if you like. Kern'll take over."

"Yessir!"

In another moment, Fremont had eased up onto his horse and ridden slowly away from camp. As soon as he judged that he was out of earshot, he pressed in against the horse's flanks until it was moving at a gallop straight back toward Westport.

"That's it, my beauty, take me home." Fremont

crouched low in the saddle, and the wind whipped up his golden hair, making him squint as he urged the horse on. A gift given to him by an Indian chief in Oregon two years before, Man o' War, as Fremont had christened him, had roamed wild as a colt and had grown into this proud, dark stallion, sixteen hands high. Man o' War was as vigorous a horse as he had ever seen.

The moon had risen high enough to cast a brighter light over the prairie grasses, which enabled Fremont to see his way clearly and to race headlong back to town. With all the mules and baggage, this had been a day's distance. But unencumbered on an eager horse, it was only an hour's ride. Up ahead loomed the familiar silhouettes of Westport's wooden homes and storefronts. Here and there a gaslight still burned in a bedroom window.

Reining in his horse as the trail gave way to Main Street, Fremont rode at a canter down the four long blocks, then one block left, past the jail, the general store and the Indian Agency to the three-story Westgate Hotel. With a whispered admonition to keep still, he left his horse at the hitching pole and tiptoed in his big leather boots up the rickety porch stairs.

The kindly old proprietor, snoring gently in a lobby chair, slept with a newspaper unfolded on his lap and a gaslight still flickering. Fremont crept over to him, took the paper aside and turned the light off. Then he crept out to the main stairs, removed his boots and stealthily ascended to the second floor. Jessie's door was closed tight, but a pencil line of light shone from the crack at the top and bottom.

Fremont knocked once, very softly, then again. There was no response from within. Then he tried the doorknob. Locked. This was a fine predicament, he mused. If he knocked loudly, he might awaken the

other guests. If he tried to pick the simple lock, he
might wake up Jessie in a panic and set her shouting
for help. What to do?

At the end of the hall, a window overlooked the
street in front of the hotel. Upon closer inspection, he
found it was within an arm's reach of the balcony at
Jessie's own windows. Without a moment's hesitation,
Fremont eased the window open, straddled the sill and
took hold of the balcony railing. It held firm.

Now came the difficult part. With one hand gripping one of the balcony struts, Fremont swung outside
and dangled precariously over the street, not high
enough to risk a deadly fall, but certainly high enough
to break an arm or leg, and visible enough to earn a
bullet in the back from some law-abiding citizen out
for a nocturnal stroll. He could imagine the headlines:
JOHN C. FREMONT, GREAT WILDERNESS EX-
PLORER, SHOT WHILE HANGING FROM WIFE'S
BALCONY.

But Fremont managed to get one leg up, and then
the other, without falling or disturbing the sleeping
town. The sight that met his eager eyes made the risk
seem worth taking. There, dressed in a nightgown and
curled up on the quilted coverlet, was his beloved wife.
She had fallen asleep while reading the published report
of his last expedition.

Gently, Fremont slipped the window latch up and
pushed open the balcony doors. The October night
breeze that swept by him into the bedroom seemed to
invade Jessie's dreams, for she moved slightly and
frowned, but did not awaken. The next touch she felt
was that of her husband caressing her cheek. Jessie
seemed to know, even as she rose out of sleep, that the
intruder was her beloved. Her eyes delicately flickered
open, and her arms encircled her husband.

For a while neither spoke. Then Jessie, still blurry

with sleep, pushed Fremont away and looked at him in disbelief. "What's the meaning of this?"

"Oh, just got to thinking of you. Too cold in my bedroll, you see."

"Don't tease!" Jessie laughed.

"Well there's nothing wrong. I really did get cold." Fremont leaned over to kiss her. "And I thought you might be, too. And you were only a few miles away. And here I am."

"Oh John!"

Jessie wrapped her arms around him again and ruffled his hair. "Would you like some tea, my sweet?" she whispered. "You must be cold from your ride."

Fremont nodded his head in the crook of her shoulder.

"But then I shall have to get up to make it," she giggled.

"Then I can't have it." This in a muffled voice with his head still buried.

Jessie's laughter sparked his own. Across the bed they rolled, laughing in each other's arms. Finally Jessie made him stop, and got up to heat water on the tiny gas stove in the corner.

Fremont settled into a pine rocker to drink from the steaming mug Jessie had given to him while Jessie, like a small child waiting for a bedtime story, sat on the edge of the bed.

"So," she said. "Tell me how the first day went."

Fremont, hesitant at first, began to describe the rapturous beauty of the autumn prairie, its flowers still in bloom, its grasses just now turning sere with the chilling winds. He told how eagerly the men had ridden, how many were truly disappointed to stop so early in the day. It was a good group, he said. But he still wished Kit Carson were scouting the men.

"In Pueblo you'll surely find someone," Jessie

consoled him. "Didn't you say that town's populated by men who have crossed the Rockies?"

"That's what I'm hoping, though I know Pueblo's passed its heyday. As the trapping trade dies, that town dies with it."

After a pause, Jessie brightened. "Oh John, guess what? I got my passage confirmed to Panama. A week from Monday I leave on the *Saratoga*, pick up Lilly in St. Louis and board a boat called the *Merryweather* bound for Panama. Richard's coming, too."

This was good news, indeed. Richard, Jessie's uncle, had traveled with Fremont on his last expedition. Though a somewhat timid man, he was at least a man who could act as a guardian for Jessie. Richard had promised to go with Jessie to San Francisco, where he would put his savings into farmland, but privately Jessie had her doubts. Richard had grown to love all the luxuries St. Louis had to offer—wonderful food, good port wine and fine cigars.

But if he said he would go, Jessie would take him at his word and hope for the best. Otherwise she would face an arduous passage with only her daughter for company. The southern route west, around the Gulf of Mexico and down along the Chagres River through Colombia to Panama, was certainly less grueling than the overland trip through Texas and New Mexico. And it would be nothing like the awesome ordeal Fremont faced along the thirty-eighth parallel. Still, it had its own dangers and discomforts. Tropical diseases, pestilence and a brutal sun all contributed to the risks.

"Think of it, Jess," said Fremont with shining eyes. "In three, four months time at most, we'll be together in San Francisco. We'll get ourselves some coastline land and make a life for ourselves—just Lilly and us."

Jessie bowed her head. "I truly hope so, John, I

truly do. But you can't just trade the land you already bought for some other plot, can you?"

"I'll find a way, even if it means taking only ten acres on the coast instead of forty-three thousand God-forsaken acres in the mountains. I mean that land's not worth a plug nickel, at least not to us. What could we possibly do in the mountains, hundreds of miles from the nearest store?"

"Well, my sweet, we could lead a very primitive life," Jessie teased. "We'd go around in loincloths. Don't you think I'd look good in a loincloth? And we'd plant our vegetables and sow our fields. And we'd probably be perfectly content, even Lilly." There was a silence between them. "At least, darling, we've learned from this whole horrible business, haven't we? You can't let friends buy land for you, take your hard-earned money and invest it where they like."

"I told them exactly what I wanted," Fremont snapped. "And I hardly had the choice of staying around to choose my own land with Kearny prodding me back like a pack horse."

"Hey, now!" Jessie set her cup aside and put her arms around her husband's neck. "That's enough. Anyway, you could do worse than owning forty-three thousand acres of beautiful mountain country in California. Ten years ago, you would have been delighted. Who knows? Maybe it will work out better than you think."

"Maybe," Fremont grumbled. He too put his cup down and surrendered to his wife's embrace. He removed her nightgown and let it fall to the floor around her feet. Naked, with a ripple of goosebumps from the night air, Jessie knelt down to take off his boots. Slowly, firmly, her hands moved up his legs with the loving, unabashed caress of a woman touching the man she loves.

She unbuckled his big brass army belt, the one he had been unable to part with even after his court-martial. He tugged recklessly at his shirt buttons, then stood to pull off his shirt and worn leather pants.

Jessie fell onto the billowy, four-poster feather bed, spread her flowing brown hair over the goose-down pillow and held out her arms to her husband. John came to her. He cradled her in his arms and gently kissed her, each time with more passion. Their tongues met, and with a stab of ecstasy, Jessie softly moaned.

He made slow, sweet love to her, bringing her over the edge again and again. And then, with a sudden rush, it was over. Fremont turned over on his back, his golden-haired chest gleaming with sweat. To cool him, Jessie blew against him, until he lightly pushed her away, laughing at her effort.

"So, now you're going to leave me, is that right, John Fremont?"

"I'm afraid so, my lovely."

For a long while they lay silently together, Jessie with her head against her husband's shoulder. Together they gazed out of the hotel windows at the blackness of the sky beyond as it slowly, almost imperceptibly, began to lighten to a dusty grey. When Jessie noticed the night ebbing at last, she nudged Fremont gently and propped herself up again. "Time for you to go, crazy man."

Fremont lingered on the bed for one last passionate kiss, then sighed and shook himself to wakefulness. He dressed quickly and tucked the covers snugly around his beloved. "You get some sleep now," he whispered.

With one last backward glance of affection, he closed the door behind him. Careful not to wake the still snoring guests in the adjacent rooms, he crept quietly down the stairs only to discover the startled proprietor standing out on the porch.

"Jumpin' Jehoshaphat, when did you come in? I thought you was gone, Colonel. Hell, I saw you go myself."

The proprietor edged away before Fremont could speak. "Now wait just a goldarn second here. You ain't no ghost, are you? Maybe some goldarn Injun killed you, and now you come back to haunt us."

Fremont clapped the panicky man on the shoulder. "I promise I'll go for good this time," he smiled. "You just do like you promised and take care of that woman."

"Yes, yes indeed I will," the proprietor mumbled uncertainly.

"One other thing," Fremont said as he swung up on his horse.

"Yes, what's that?"

"That four-poster bed—I think it needs a new mattress."

Chapter 4

The next morning brought blue skies and wind-blown grasses and the rhythmic clip-clopping of horses and mules as the men rode along in single file. They surrendered to the rock and sway of their powerful horses as the mules plodded along behind them, harnessed by a braided rope.

At the head of this slowly weaving procession rode Fremont, eyes bleary from lack of sleep, but too happy from the previous night to feel his fatigue. When the column reached the only rise of land in sight, he signaled a stop and dismounted to take measurements. Kern immediately began to sketch a landscape, and the naturalist, a veteran of other Fremont expeditions named C.Z. Creutzfeldt, went about collecting specimens of flowers and insects for examination under his most treasured possession, a German microscope.

It was Creutzfeldt who first heard the faint thundering sound. As he bent close to the ground to study the stem of an unusual purple and black prairie flower, he cocked his ear to the earth for a moment and heard what he at first mistook for an earthquake.

"Buffalo!" he cried out suddenly.

The others cast quick glances around them at a clear, unbroken horizon. Brattle jumped off his horse to put his own ear to the ground, but he heard nothing. "What in the hell . . ."

"I'd know that rumble anywhere, Creutzfeldt exulted. "It's buffalo coming straight out of the northwest."

Fremont pulled his rifle from its saddle holster. "How far you figure, Creutz?"

Creutzfeldt put his ear back down. "Twenty miles, maybe more."

"Strike me dead if he ain't right on the money!" Brattle called out.

Every pair of eyes followed his pointing finger. There in the far distance, like the hazy, hovering smoke of a cigar, rose a tiny cloud of dust.

"All right then," Fremont shouted. "That's our dinner out there. If we bag it right, that is. Now for anyone who's never seen a stampeding herd of buffalo before, I better explain a few things. First of all, it looks scarifying as all hell."

Some of the older men laughed. McGehee wet his lips, torn between curiosity, excitement and a sudden, twisting pang of fear.

"The most important thing is to stay calm," Fremont continued, "because the only thing dumber than buffalo are rocks, trees and frightened men. Now, we'll want to see exactly what direction they're headed in. When I give the signal, you follow me at full gallop. We'll likely veer right as they come at us veering left. Then we'll aim to cut off a dozen or so from the end, riding right into them. Then, and only then, we'll start shooting."

Fremont gave Man o' War a friendly slap on the rump, headed him around and took off without a backward glance. With a chorus of whistles and battle cries, his men tore off after him, spurring their horses and waving their hats.

Steadily now, the distant cloud of dust grew larger. In what seemed only the passing of a single exhilarating moment, a line of dark movement, nearly as long as the horizon itself, could be discerned under the cloud. Individual buffalo now became recognizable shapes in the heaving mass of rugged brown humpbacked fur. Kern, desperately holding the reins of his galloping horse, strained to see their heads clearly—their whiskered chins, flaring nostrils and panicked, searching eyes. Other riders yelled for him to get out of their way. He seemed lost in a dream, perhaps struck by the awesome power of the herd.

He was finally aroused from his reverie by the frantic shouts of Fremont, who was gesturing wildly up ahead. The words were lost in the roar of the stampeding animals as they approached—three thousand yards, two thousand, then only one.

At first, Fremont led his men toward the middle of the herd. With a shrewd, experienced eye, he had judged that the buffalo would turn to the left, scared and confused by the small cadre of horses and humans ahead of them. Had he led the men too quickly toward the right flank, he would have risked missing them altogether. Now, no matter how sharply the bison might turn, he could be sure of riding into the herd.

The men, racing on into this deafening stampede, choked on the dust swirling all around and tried to shout to each other above the roar of hooves and the bleating cries of fear from the buffalo.

Fremont seemed to merge with the buffalo. Then the huge woolly creatures were on either side of him, terrifying his horse and ramming his legs against the horse's side.

"Please God, don't let me fall!" Kern shouted as his horse wheeled about in the dust cloud.

Another of the men, a half-Indian named Gregorio, appeared suddenly out of the dust swirl, grinning demoniacally. "You holdin' on, boy?" came the hoarse shout.

Kern nodded without speaking, his two hands tightly gripping the horn of his saddle.

A patch of daylight then appeared and gradually broadened. They had passed the herd and separated out four terrified buffalo as the rest thundered away. Fremont, followed by Doubleback and Gregorio, spurred his horse frantically around these few. Flustered by the line of horses and men that now blocked their path, the animals veered off even farther from the herd. That gave Fremont, Gregorio and the others the time they needed to catch up with their prey's outside flank.

As Fremont came close to completing a circle around the buffalo, he raised his rifle as a signal. Then, wrapping his reins loosely around his arm, he took aim at the massive, lead bull and squeezed off a shot. The animal stumbled and fell, as if suddenly tripped by a hidden rope.

The others now dislodged their own guns and fired into the bleating, flummoxed animals. Another buffalo crashed to the ground with a resounding thud. A few of the badly wounded struggled to regain their footing, only to fall again under their own crushing weight. Finally they lay still, in four rough heaps of twitching fur, flesh and blood.

An eerie stillness returned. The great galloping herd of buffalo retreated farther and farther, the roar of their hooves now becoming indistinct, their hulking bodies once again merging into a long brown line against the horizon. Kern, still in shock, looked from the escaping herd back to the carcasses behind him. An expression of grief passed briefly over his features, followed by a shifty, embarrassed glance at his comrades.

The mules were still struggling along in the distance under the hands of a few wranglers supervised reluctantly by a half-Indian named Joaquin. The men nearby slid eagerly off their horses and set to hacking the limbs off their dying prey. Two of the buffalo fought feebly to escape, straining up awkwardly on their forelimbs and snorting in desperation. These the men dispatched with a coup de grâce from their rifles. Soon the ground was awash in blood, intestines and great hunks of raw, red meat. The severed heads of the dismembered buffalo were propped up and staring blankly across the prairie.

"Hey there, Kern," cried Doubleback to the artist. "How about a sketch of this, huh?"

Kern smiled wanly, but made no move to take out his sketch pad.

"Come on, Kern, what about it? How about a few sketches for the womenfolk?"

Glancing up, Fremont took one look at Kern's ashen features and immediately set down his knife, wiped his hands clean of blood and ambled over to the artist.

"Tiring business," Fremont said as he sat down.

"It certainly is that."

"Bloody too, eh?"

The artist eyed Fremont's blood-smeared clothing. "I guess you could say so."

They sat in silence for a moment, then Fremont spoke again. "The Sioux have a saying about hunting— 'a fresh kill is the greatest affirmation of life.' "

"How do they figure that?" Kern said drily.

"A freshly killed steer or buffalo that lies gutted and bleeding on the ground shows us how complicated a living thing is inside."

"So you go out and kill it."

"Kern, you're acting like a child who's seen its

first tough bit of luck in this world. Tell you what I think. I do believe you're more disgusted by all the blood than truly sorry for the animal."

"All right, sure, the sight of blood and guts is hard to bear," said Kern. "But I am sorry for these poor dumb buffalo. Hell, it seems to me there should be some other kind of food around."

Fremont laughed. "So what would you do, brother, kill some other creatures instead? Rabbits maybe, or prairie dogs? You wouldn't like that any more than you did this. Suffering doesn't look pretty in the eyes of any of God's creatures."

"I guess you just don't think much about killing when you sit down to a Christmas turkey or a steak or a leg of lamb."

"Of course you don't. It's easy to forget where all that food came from and how it found its way to your table, when you've got your Sunday-go-meeting clothes on, and there are candles on the table, and fine linen and silver, and a freshly cooked, mouth-watering bird on the plate. That's as it should be, Kern. No need to look at the blood and guts if you don't have to. But it doesn't hurt to just think about it once in a while, to put the image of a live turkey up against what's sitting in brown sauce on the plate. Helps you when you're out here and you've got to do it the other way around— looking at the kill, while you're dreaming about that fancy tablesetting!"

Now it was Kern's turn to laugh.

"There's another side of that old Sioux saying, Kern. Not a living thing in this world lives without something else dying. So instead of sitting here and brooding about four dead buffalo, learn to think like the Sioux. Celebrate. We're going to fill our bellies, so that life can go on—our life."

Kern nodded without looking up. Then he smiled

sheepishly and reached for his saddlebag. "Just had an idea." He pulled out his sketch pad. "Maybe I'll draw this after all, before the meat's cut up and carried off."

Kern chose a sharply whittled pencil from the silver case that had been passed down to him as a family heirloom. Then opening his sketchbook, he studied the men carving the meat, and was soon so absorbed in his task that he failed to notice when Fremont left his side.

In the days that followed, the last cool breezes of autumn gave way to a bitter chill. The blue skies clouded to grey, and the grasses seemed to fade to a dull sere brown before the men's eyes. Winter was sweeping out of the north, tugging at the last stiff leaves on the trees, billowing across Oregon and Idaho, Kansas and Oklahoma, and farther south.

Along the Santa Fe Trail, Fremont and his men met only a few eastward-bound parties, mostly merchants headed for St. Louis. These were not at all like the stooped, meek-mannered proprietors of stores, but men as tough as any trappers. If their appearance was not enough to mark them as tough customers, the garrison of guns they carried to ward off Indians and bandits who might want to divest them of their newly earned lucre was. Outside of a curt nod or tipped hat, they offered no greeting as they slapped the reins against their horses and rode on.

Any hope of a few more temperate days was dashed on the blustery grey morning the party reached the Arkansas River. For two days the river had glittered in the far distance like a serpentine diamond necklace. Fremont, with his telescope, had been the first to discover that the water was frozen, but he had made light of it, hoping there would be ice only on top. Now, as the men dismounted at its bank for a better

look, they discovered the bitter truth. The river was
frozen solid.

Not that this would have any effect on the future
of the expedition. Fremont would still lead his men west
along the river and hope to reach the small supply outpost at Bent's Fort in a few days' time. But visions of
fresh trout sizzling over the fire had been playing in
the men's minds more than they cared to admit. And
with the party's own Spartan water supply limited to
drinking rations, even a quick bath in an ice-cold river
had begun to seem preferable to no bath at all.

"Tell me something," McGehee said, riding alongside Doubleback as the disheartened men resumed their
journey. "What happens if you go without bathing for
a couple weeks or more? I mean, do you start growing
things? Lice or something?"

"Shoooeee, boy," Doubleback slapped his leg in
amusement. "This the first time you ever been dirty?"

"Uh, no, not exactly. When I was a young boy I
used to get muddier than a hog when I went swimming
or riding around. But there's a difference between soiled
for one day and being dirty for a month."

"Oh boy, that's rich. Yes, indeed." Doubleback
leaned over toward him with a leering grin. "On that
plantation of yours you couldn't go dirty for more'n
one day, could you? Cause your little mama would say
you had to get washed for dinner and scrub behind the
ears. And you had two darkey women, I'll wager, to
soap you down real thorough."

At this, the men within earshot turned around to
laugh at McGehee's discomfiture. He was not well
liked by most of the others. On more than one occasion,
as everyone sat around the campfire after dinner, he
had thrown in some remark that made it quite clear
he had never been forced to struggle for money. "When
my daddy and mama used to come back from Rich-

mond, they'd be all laden down with new clothes and such . . ." he would say, and, "Once, one of our slaves ran off and stayed hid for two weeks right on the plantation, in a giant stretch of cottonwoods." McGehee had no idea he was painting himself as a southern rich boy, but his comments, together with the soft, sonorous Georgian accent they came wrapped in, had already betrayed him.

"Matter of fact, McGehee," said Doubleback, "I'll bet your daddy made you go out and get dirty with all those peach-and-cream sisters of yours, just so's you'd all know what dirt was. I can see it clear—all of you sittin' 'round the mud hole, and them sayin', 'Ooh lawdy, brother Mica, can we touch your little thaang? You can touch our little thaangs as long as we're all just bein' dirty.' "

"I did not!" McGehee said hotly. "And I bet I worked every bit as hard as you did—every summer!"

"Every summer!" Doubleback whooped with laughter. "Every summer, boys, you hear that? I guess the rest of the year he was wearin' his lilly-white hands raw turnin' school book pages! And the teacher in all her pretty petticoats would turn and say, 'Mica, you stand up here and read poetry to us all. And then you show us your little thaang.' "

"Shut up, you ignorant fool. If you never learned to read and write, it's no fault of mine."

"I can read all I need to read," Doubleback shouted at him. "A lot of good your booklearnin's goin' to do when you're freezin' your ass off up in them mountains. See what all the books in the world will do for you then."

Fremont was too far ahead to notice the raised voices, but Captain Cathcart, riding behind, heard clearly and knew there was trouble. Not only did McGehee and Doubleback appear close to blows, but the circle of men around them, none of whom appeared to be the slightest bit friendly toward McGehee, had drawn closer. The rich kid's too blind to see it coming, Cathcart thought grimly.

"So what's this, eh? Are the ladies having an argument?" Cathcart drew abreast of the men, his figure stark and imposing in his Prussian army uniform and heavy black boots.

"Butt out of it, General," Doubleback snarled. "This is between Miss McGehee and myself."

The other men snickered. Cathcart sat rigidly in his saddle, and glared down at Doubleback. "In the Prussian army, when the men have a little disagreement, they have to follow a little rule," said Cathcart, cutting off his words sharply as he spoke them. "Each man must first fight the biggest fellow in the company. Then, if they can still stand up, they are free to fight each other."

"Well this ain't the Prussian army, General," Doubleback said, looking around nervously. "This here's America, and this here's the West, and if a man don't like what another man says, he settles it how he wants to, without no one else buttin' in."

"How strange," said Cathcart. "The weather must be making me crazy. I swear I feel like I'm in the Prussian army right now. But then I can never remember for sure where I am."

There was a pause, then Doubleback angrily spurred his horse and rode on ahead, followed by the others. Cathcart and McGehee were left riding alongside each other.

"That stupid cracker," McGehee raged. "He deliberately set out to pick a fight."

"Shut up, McGehee," Cathcart growled.

McGehee turned to him in shock. "I thought you were on my side!"

"I'm on nobody's side. I just don't like to see a stupid cracker like you get the crackers punched out of him."

"You must be kidding, I'm nearly a head taller than he is." McGehee slapped the dust from his trousers as he rode.

"You also a head taller than Colonel Fremont? Maybe you want to tell your pretty little wife you crossed the Rockies washing cups and plates."

"I guess I hadn't thought about that."

"You know, boy," Cathcart said in a fatherly tone, "I heard that whole argument from start to finish, and I'll tell you something. You're right to be angry. He was baiting you, and you was only trying to be friendly. But when you get so old and wise as me, you stop taking things only for what they look like on the surface, you know? Tell me, do you know what made him say those things?"

"Hell, I don't know. He doesn't like me, I guess."

"You are wrong. He doesn't even know you. If he did, he'd like you a great deal."

"You think so?"

"Sure. You're a good man, and so is he. But you talk like you've got all these fancy airs about you. And Doubleback, he's a poor man, but he's very, very proud."

"So what should I do?"

"Well, here's what you *don't* do. You don't go riding up now to say you're ready to sign a peace treaty, because he's still hot under the collar, and he's still got his friends around him. But sometime today, after we pitch camp, you go to him and somehow apologize." Cathcart held up a hand at McGehee's remonstrance. "I know, I know, he was wrong, too. But you asked, so I tell you what you should do."

In the late afternoon Fremont announced that camp would be pitched two miles ahead.

Doubleback, as it happened, was the cook that evening. That day near the river, one of the men had bagged a thin, weakened deer, so venison stew, Doubleback's specialty, was the order of the evening. On one other occasion, he had served up his special Cajun recipe, and been roundly applauded for it. When Fremont asked what made the stew so flavorful, Doubleback had sheepishly admitted that he always brought spices with him on the trail.

After the men had hammered their tent stakes in and set the horses out to graze, they gathered round to wait, with undisguised eagerness, for the now famous Doubleback stew.

"Just get back, get back all of you," the cook demanded as he sipped from the ladle.

"Hey now, c'mon, Doubleback, stop hoggin' it all to yourself and serve it up," cried an anguished voice.

"Ah, hold your horse a damn minute," Doubleback retorted, but not without a bit of culinary pride.

Finally, when he announced the stew was ready, the men crowded up, tin plates in hand. As each one was served, he would elbow back through the crowd and, not even waiting to find a seat, would plunge a hunk of stale bread into the steaming concoction. When McGehee held out his plate, Doubleback grimaced, then slammed a ladle full of stew down hard enough for it to splatter on McGehee's shirt.

As the men around him guffawed, McGehee fought down a desire to throw the plate back into Doubleback's face. Instead, without looking up, he made his way back with the others to eat alone and in silence.

The men ate so quickly that the meal was over almost as soon as it had begun. Two of the cooking pots had been filled with ice, which had now melted to water. As the men filed over to wash their gear, McGehee quietly sought out Doubleback, who was sitting away from the fire's light as he always did, in case of sudden attack.

"Hey there, Doubleback."

Doubleback stiffened and scowled. "What do you want, rich boy?"

"I only have one thing to say to you."

"Oh yeah?" Doubleback put his plate and spoon down, tensing for any move McGehee might make.

"That stew of yours."

"What about it, rich boy?"

"It's real good."

Doubleback peered at him suspiciously through the shadows. "What do you mean by that?"

McGehee smiled and held out his hand. "I mean it's rightly good stew, that's all."

Doubleback looked suspiciously from the extended hand up to McGehee's eyes, then down again. "Oh for cryin' out loud," he muttered and took the hand in his own. Then he added with a trace of a smile under his bushy whiskers, "Now go on and read yourself to sleep with some damn book and leave me in peace."

Chapter 5

Bent's Fort looked to Fremont very little like any other fort he had ever seen. It was neither square nor high. It was not protected by any heavy front gates or look-out towers, and though it was made of wood, it seemed hardly strong enough to withstand the onslaught of a children's battalion, much less a phalanx of attacking Indians.

Fortunately, the local Indians were so busy warring with each other that they had little time or energy left for the whites. Most, in fact, were delighted when the affable George Bent, trapper and failed magician, traveling doctor and dispenser of tonics guaranteed to cure all bodily ills, had found himself compelled to leave several states in haste and had established his modest supply post here.

So it came as no surprise to Fremont, who had stopped in at Bent's Fort on three previous westward journeys to find George Bent drinking amiably with a half-dozen Mojave Indians.

The men who were new to the place were shocked, but not by the presence of Indians. At the front door, a peephole flap had slid away to reveal a large, unblinking eye that darted back and forth, inspecting them. The door was then opened to reveal an African monkey chained to a wooden ledge. The monkey, trained to pull the flap and eyeball visitors, was but the first of George Bent's practical jokes.

Ushered inside by an Indian youth, the men found themselves in a narrow room that looked out onto the fort's dirt-packed atrium. There, ranged around its four sides in close proximity, were small wooden booths where doleful Indian women stood leaning on counters, obviously waiting for customers to buy their wares. One booth offered leather goods; from the railing of another hung woven baskets and macramé shawls. And in the middle of the atrium, at the head on a long oak table, sat George Bent with his drinking Indians.

"Fremont!" he shouted as soon as he saw the explorer. "By God, if it isn't Colonel Fremont!"

The two men embraced heartily, and engaged in a special handshake that Bent employed only with his favorite customers: a vigorous downward push, a little flick of the pinky fingers, then up again.

"Fremont, you old cadger, how you been keeping yourself?"

"Pretty well, George, pretty well. And you?"

"Bent clean out of shape as usual," said Bent, patting his considerable girth. "Someday I'll straighten out, heh?"

As genially corrupt as he might be, Bent had always been a favorite of Fremont's, partly because Bent's deceit, his town-to-town con tricks and trumperies, were to Fremont like so many juggling acts and carnival gambits. True, he usually ended up with someone else's money, and he almost always tempted some local posse into angry pursuit, but no one was ever hurt, and everyone, even the gullible who stepped forth with their money, was always entertained. As Bent was fond of observing, he gave ordinary folk extraordinary stories for next to nothing.

"So what do you need this time around, Colonel?" asked Bent.

"Let's start with some food. The men could do with a hot meal."

"You're as generous as always, Colonel. It's your one shortcoming. Well, sit you all down," Bent called out to the men. He turned to wave the Indians away from the table. "Cooling Bird! Princess Water Moccasin! Let's have more tables for these fellows!"

Two tall Indian maidens with deep brown eyes and shining long black hair, appeared from the shadows, bowed low before Bent, then vanished in search of two more long tables. As the men milled about warming themselves, Kern wandered over to the selling booths, where he found one woman displaying enchiladas.

"You like?" she said meekly, pointing to the buckets of batter, tomatoes, onions and green peppers from which the enchiladas were made.

Kern, of course, had no money in his pockets, but he reached deep into his pack and came up with a bit of change.

"Enough?" he said, holding the money out to her.

She looked carefully at the coins, then shrugged.

"More?" Kern reached again in his pack and located a stale cigar, which someone had given him as a farewell gift.

The woman's eyes glimmered, and she eagerly snatched it from him. Taking a box of matches from the recesses of her skirt, she lit up the cheroot with practiced ease. "Red sauce or green sauce?" she asked, reaching for her ladle.

A few of the others, observing Kern's success, came over to stand behind him. Soon the shrewd Indian had collected a fist-high pile of trinkets: penny whistles, foreign coins, love letters and other good luck tokens.

"Hey now, don't ruin your appetites," Bent called out. "Sit you down, boys, sit you down."

Before long, a tempting feast had been placed in front of the hungry men: venison, rabbit stew, maize, fresh bread, whipped butter and, best of all, frothy ale brought in from the new settlement of San Francisco.

As the men fell to their meals, Fremont explained to his host the purpose of the expedition, only to be met with looks of astonishment.

"Colonel, it sounds kinda crazy to me." Bent poured ale from a metal pitcher into his cup.

Fremont smiled grimly. "My friend, if we don't know whether the railroad can run through the Rockies, we'll never build one. And if we don't build one, there's a whole sweep of the country that may be left unsettled—wasted."

"Railroad or no railroad," Bent replied with a sage smile, "this country's goin' to fill up fast. You watch, Colonel. It's mathematics. What expands, keeps expanding. Two people have three babies, three babies grow up to have three more babies each, and each of them has three babies, and then what have you got? Thirty-six people, who all have to live somewhere."

Fremont leaned toward him. "But none of those thirty-six people will go and do something new, move somewhere new, unless people like you and me blaze the trail for them."

One reason Fremont liked Bent, he realized, was that the man was courageous in his own way. After all, he was situated way out here in the middle of nowhere, unafraid of Indians or wilderness.

"Perhaps," Bent said thoughtfully. "Perhaps."

After dinner, Bent stood up, tapped his glass with his fork and waited until the voices had died down. "Men," he said finally. "I'm proud to be your host, and I'm proud to know you all." Bent raised his glass.

"A toast to your fearless leader, a man of true honor and courage."

The men raised their glasses with a round of cheers.

"Now I have a special show for all you folk," Bent went on. "It's a bit of magic, a little razzle-dazzle —and maybe a few dancing girls, if the colonel permits."

Fremont could not suppress a frown at the suggestion. What tolerance he had for magic tricks did not extend to the exhibition of scantily-clad women, even Indians. But he knew it would be better this time to let his men have their way—as long as they didn't get the idea he had given in to them.

"Well, I don't see the harm in a little magic," Fremont remarked. "As long as you're all prepared for bad magic. This fellow is an incorrigible charlatan."

Bent took the ribbing in the best of spirits, and clapped his hands loudly for his Indian servants to bring out his props. First he performed a standard bit of *trompe-d'oeil*, whisking handkerchiefs from his sleeves to his pockets and mysteriously back again, making red ones out of blue ones, finding four where there were only two before.

Brattle, the lanky southerner, sat beside him transfixed. Brattle had never seen any magic tricks before, and Fremont, with a sidelong glance, realized that the poor man was utterly taken in. Soon a few of the others also noticed it and nudged each other down the line.

None of this was lost on Bent. Rapping a magic wand against the table, he called for volunteers and chose Brattle as soon as the southerner raised his hand.

"Your name, sir?" said Bent with a flourish of his wand.

"Brattle. Uh, William Brattle." This seemed not to be sufficient. "From Tennessee. Oak Ridge."

Still Bent stood silently, imperiously. The men began to laugh. Brattle looked around him in near panic.

"Very well, Mr. Brattle. Take this hat in hand, sir."

Brattle hesitantly took the top hat offered to him.

"What do you see in that hat, Mr. Brattle?"

Brattle looked inside. He saw nothing.

Bent first instructed his nervous volunteer to put the hat upside down on the table, then ordered him to close his eyes, to walk in a wide circle and finally to repeat verses from Leviticus, all of which contributed to the general hilarity of the situation.

"Now sir, open your eyes and inspect the hat!"

This Brattle did.

"Nothing in the hat, Brattle?"

"No sir, nothing at all."

"Then put it on, Brattle!"

Gingerly, Brattle reached for the hat. It felt slightly heavier than before, but it still appeared empty. With mixed feelings of dread and curiosity, Brattle put the hat on his head and immediately felt the strangest, most startling sensation of his life. There *was* something in the hat, by God, and now it was sitting on his hair —and now it was moving!

With a sudden shriek, Brattle tore the hat off, batted furiously at the top of his head and leapt back in terror. There, writhing on the ground in front of him, was a live rattlesnake! As the other men gathered around, unsure whether to howl with laughter or sympathize with their friend, the beaming magician stepped forward and deftly picked up the snake with his bare hands. "Not to worry, gentlemen. Not to worry. This genuine timber rattler has been defanged for safety. It cannot bite. It cannot harm."

Fremont pushed his way through the others, angrily snatched the snake from Bent and threw it off to one side. "That was a lousy trick, George."

"But why?" asked Bent, taken aback. "It's a great illusion. No one's ever figured it out yet."

"That's not what I meant, and you know it. Any trick that scares a man half to death is lousy."

"Okay, okay." Bent put his hands up in mock surrender. "No more snakes."

Then, turning to the stunned southerner, Fremont gave him a healthy slap on the shoulder. "And you, Brattle, ought to learn not to be duped by carnival magicians. There isn't any magic in this world, boy, but the honest magic of sweat and struggle."

Hardly a man to be bothered for long, Bent turned to a quartet of Mexican musicians who had been standing in the shadows, awaiting his cue to come forward. With a rapid drum roll and a strumming of Mexican guitars, they launched into a festive song that brought three young Mexican women out to dance.

The women were modestly attired in long, flowing dresses, with shawls draped over their gaily colored native blouses. But their propriety was due, it turned out, more to the cold than to the nature of the entertainment. With darkness falling fast, and the air growing chilly, Bent ushered his guests into a cavernous, two-story-high hall where a wide hearth crackled with burning cedar logs. As the men sat on soft leather pillows close to the warming flames, the mariachi band and the dancing women struck up a raucous, pounding rhythm with their guitars and castanets. Then, at the host's urging, the women began to disrobe. First one, then another let her shawl slide off, and threw it to her

audience. The flowing skirts followed, revealing black
lace stockings and garters stretched out around dark,
slim legs.

With a sigh, Fremont sat back in the shadows. He
felt the deep stirring of indignation and personal af-
front that such sights always provoked in him, the result not only of his mother's solicitude and stern teach-
ings, but also of his own sensitivity. He had never been
comfortably able to watch a woman behave in a bawdy
fashion. He was too concerned for the modesty and
respectability of their kind.

Of course, he thought, most men never pondered
such issues and perhaps they were better off having no
moral questions to plague them.

After all, if a woman wanted the attention she received, who was he to judge her? And certainly, Fremont mused as he gazed at the rapt expressions around
him, he should not presume to judge his own men.
They wouldn't even understand his feelings.

Only Jessie understood, and in all likelihood, she
was the only person to whom Fremont would ever confess such sentiment. Even Kit Carson, who could grasp
so many things so quickly and so cleverly, would never
bother with such notions. Kit was a simple, strong man
who had frankly and directly propositioned any woman he met before his marriage. He had set himself free
of any such moral concerns.

Suddenly, Fremont's reverie was broken by a delicate touch on his back. He quickly turned and tensed,
instinctively ready to duck a blow, only to find himself
staring into the most exquisite limpid brown eyes he
had ever seen. They belonged to an Indian maiden, no
older than eighteen, Fremont reckoned, but she possessed a calm self-assurance that he found entrancing.

"You are Colonel Fremont?" the girl whispered.
Her full bronze lips seemed to moisten as she spoke.

"Yes, I am. And you are . . . ?"

"I am called Twin Willows. For many months, I have heard your name spoken, always with the greatest respect, even by the warriors of my tribe."

"I am honored." And a bit suspicious, he might have added. Twin Willows leaned close to Fremont's ear so that her soft voice could be heard over the thrumming music of the mariachi band. As she did so, she gently touched the explorer's knee. He looked down to see her full breasts rising and falling gently under a beaded, loose-fitting leather shirt.

"I have heard many stories of you," Twin Willows continued, "of your great journeys over the mountains and plains, and I have often found myself dreaming of you."

Fremont felt her hand caress his knee. His mind raced, and he tried to summon his resolve to resist her temptation, but his ruminations of a few minutes before already seemed distant, if not silly and prudish. Why should he not spend the night with this beautiful maiden who wanted him? It would have nothing to do with his love for Jessie. He would love Jessie for the rest of his life. As long as half a country separated them, and she would never discover this small infidelity, why should he not indulge himself?

He realized, as he looked around the fire–lit hall, that many of his men were already tasting the charms of other Indian women. No one would notice him slipping out a side door with this girl who, he noticed with some measure of pride, was far more attractive than any of the others.

But what if desire were not her only motive? The other men might not stop to ask such a question, but Fremont was their leader. He had to keep his sense of caution working constantly.

"I have a room here. You would like to come?"

The words, coming after a long stream of compliments he had barely heard, startled him. Suddenly he found himself replying, but not with the words he had thought he would say. He felt as if someone else were speaking for him.

"Yes," he heard himself say. "Let's go."

Outside, the night was cold and clear. Twin Willows led him by the hand across the atrium, into a narrow doorway and up a rickety, planked staircase. On the fort's second floor were cramped bedrooms that looked over a balcony onto the square. The room was only large enough to contain a single army cot, a handmade wooden dresser topped with candles, and Twin Willow's one luxury, a large, round mirror.

Fremont stood by the balcony windows and watched Twin Willows, in the reflection, light the candles. She looked demurely into the mirror and saw Fremont's reflection in the window. She caught his eye, and across two reflections, she and Fremont exchanged a smile.

"What do you do here?" he asked, turning toward her.

"I work in the kitchen," she said. "I help the cooks."

"What does Bent pay you?"

She shrugged. "Nothing. Room and board."

"Why do you do it, then? Why don't you stay with your tribe?"

"I do not like the tribe. Women grow old too quickly in my village. It was better to come here and see all the pioneers and soldiers."

Fremont looked hard at her. "Tell me, Twin Willows, do they pay you? To spend the night with you?"

The beautiful Indian maiden blushed. "No. Only sometimes."

"I can't offer you any money."

"And I would not take it if you did. Though I know you would not offer because you are an honorable man. I just . . ." She searched for some way out of her predicament.

"But why did you seek me out?" Fremont took a seat on Twin Willows' bed. His desire to sleep with her seemed to have vanished. It was not that she sometimes took money. It was that now she seemed more like a flesh and blood woman, with dreams and passions and regrets, and Fremont felt a wave of compassion for her obvious unhappiness.

"I told you. I have heard that you are a great man, and I wanted you."

Twin Willows spoke with such simple dignity that Fremont was touched. Still, he did not entirely believe her.

"You're a beautiful woman, Twin Willows. You are also a very experienced woman. I'm surprised to hear that a woman who has spent the night with so many different men would feel a desire for a stranger she has never seen."

Again Twin Willows blushed, but this time with anger. "I am young," she said stiffly. "I have desires. Is that strange to the white man?"

"No, not so strange. But I think you have something else on your mind."

There was a pause. Finally, Twin Willows sat down next to Fremont on the bed. "Yes," she said quietly. "There is another reason. I want to go to a white man's city. I want to become a lady, not just an Indian. I want to wear lace and carry a parasol."

"But why, Twin Willows? I've never heard of an Indian woman wanting such a thing. You have great beauty, and you know the pleasures of the wilderness. Why would you want to give up your Indian pride and family and customs?"

"I hate being an Indian," she spat out. "I hate my family and my tribe, and I hate living here with that snake you call your friend."

"Bent? What's wrong with him?"

"He sleeps with a different Indian girl every night. And if you don't let him in, when he knocks, out you go, into the cold."

Fremont nodded slowly. Bent, for all his affability, was a born conniver. The story fit him perfectly. "All right, that's George. But what about your family and your tribe?"

Twin Willows bowed her head. Her long dark straight hair swung out from behind her shoulders. For a moment she was silent, then Fremont noticed tears falling to her leather skirt. "I have a bad family," she said at last. "I have a very bad family."

"What do you mean? Are they not held in great respect by the rest of the tribe?"

"The whole tribe is bad! They used to be the happiest tribe in all the valleys. They fished in the most plentiful rivers, they hunted the fattest deer, and their soil was the most fertile. Then came the white trappers with their firewater."

"What happened?"

"The trappers wanted our rivers, and our woods and our soil, but they were not strong enough to attack us or scare us away. They were only a dozen, and we were many powerful braves and strong women. So they came in peace with their firewater, and they gave it to us for free. They wanted only a chance to fish and hunt on our ground. This they swore.

"But soon our braves were drinking firewater every day. They could not have gone hunting and fishing even if they wanted to. They were too drunk! All winter the trappers collected furs. And in the spring, they left with many, many furs piled over the tops of their wagons. Of course, they were very clever, and they left at night, after giving our tribes enough firewater to last three days. By the time our braves got over their headaches, those trappers were gone."

Fremont shook his head sadly. "I have heard that story before, from other Indians and other tribes. The trappers are not always good and honest men. And when the Indians are new to whiskey, they don't know how powerful it can be, and how quickly a man can build a steady thirst for it. But how did all this affect you so much? Didn't the braves stop drinking when the trappers left?"

"They stopped, all right," Twin Willows said bitterly. "They stopped until the very next year, when the trappers came back with more firewater, and the men once again spent the whole winter drinking. My father, my brother, and then even my mother sat around our tepee drinking firewater every day. And when my people drank firewater, they became angry and cruel. This was five years ago, when I was only twelve years old."

Fremont whistled softly. "So you're only seventeen years old now?"

"Yes, and now I can take care of myself. But then I was very young, and very weak, and I could not imagine leaving my tribe, and they all drank. So at night, when my family grew sick with anger from firewater, my father would yell at me, and my brother would laugh at me. But my mother was the worst."

Fremont grimaced. "What do you mean?"

"She would take me out and hit me. And then she would keep hitting me until I pretended to sleep. And I hurt very much then, all the time."

"But surely she would wake up in the morning and

see what she had done to you?" Fremont insisted. "Wouldn't your father and brother at least keep her from hitting you?"

"They didn't care. And my mother, she would be sorry in the morning, but soon she would be drinking firewater again and she would forget. Besides, she was already a woman with demons in her head. She had always had demons, and so had her mother before her. That was because many generations ago one of my mother's ancestors killed his wife's secret lover, a man from our own tribe. So forever after, there will be demons in our family. Even in me, I think."

Fremont leaned forward intently. "What sort of demons?"

"Demons that make you crazy. Demons that make you afraid of animals and shadows, and make you hurt your own children."

"Tell me," said Fremont, "how does your mother act when her demons possess her? Without the firewater, I mean."

"Her eyes become glassy and wide." Twin Willows trembled as she spoke. "She cannot remember who her friends are. She thinks they are all her enemies. And she gets very angry, and she does strange things."

"Like what?" Fremont pressed her. "What exactly does she do?"

Twin Willows held back a minute, then reluctantly whispered, "Once, when I was young, she tied me down to the ground with leather and sticks that I could not defend myself. Then she . . . she would burn me, put a hot stick from the fire against my skin, or she would take a knife and . . ." Twin Willows choked on the words, "she would stick it into me. Here." She pointed to her lap. "Then when it hurt so much that I screamed out in pain, she would talk crazy talk, about how I had to be a good daughter to her, and how she had to teach me not to be bad."

"Good Lord in heaven," Fremont murmured. "How did you survive?"

"I had to run away, alone, in the night when all my family was asleep from the firewater. I took some food in a bag and a knife to hunt. For two weeks I went through those woods, far, far beyond the trees I knew."

"You must have run out of food," Fremont said.

"Yes, oh yes, I did. And then I ate berries and other fruits from the forest, and finally I met a trapper on the trail who seemed friendly. He gave me food and blankets, and nursed me until I felt better. He also made me sleep with him. After a short while, I could stand him no more. And so when he brought me here, I went to Bent, who seemed so good then, and I pleaded with him to let me stay. He gave the trapper a horse to leave without me."

"You were traded for a horse?"

Twin Willows smiled thinly. "For a little while I felt better. But then Bent, the ugly snake, wanted to sleep with me, too. So now I must leave." Twin Willows looked earnestly into Fremont's eyes. "You will help me? White men do not treat their city ladies this way."

"I don't know how I can," Fremont exclaimed. "If we were going east, perhaps you could come with us— or even if we were going west by a southern route. But you see, from here we go directly west, into the snows. The trip would be too rough for you. Much too rough."

"No it wouldn't! I am tough, too. I could even carry a pack, or cook for you. Anything would be better than this place!"

Fremont threw up his hands. "You cannot, you simply cannot. I would give you money, but I barely have enough to buy more rations for the men. There is nothing I can do for you, Twin Willows."

At this the girl broke into tears, cast her arms around Fremont and buried her head in his shoulder. For a long while they sat on the bed, Twin Willows' slender body wracked by sobs, Fremont's strong arms encircling her.

Beyond the balcony windows, a cold white moon shone down, bathing the fort in a quilt of silky light and grey shadow. The music had stopped, and now and then a boisterous voice could be heard singing an Irish drinking song. A set of heavy boots, followed by the almost imperceptible padding of bare feet, made their way down the hall. A door creaked open, and a man mumbled something and laughed with lecherous anticipation.

Sometime later, Fremont discovered that the girl had fallen asleep in his arms. Deftly, he stood up without a sound, slid the blanket out from under her tightly muscled body and spread it over her. She stirred and shook her head like a small child, but she was too tired now to shake free of her dreams. Fremont tiptoed to the door and turned to look at her once more before leaving. Lying there, she seemed happy at last, free for a few hours from her cruel circumstances. Fremont closed the door behind him. There was nothing he could do.

Chapter 6

As a bright November sun burned off the night's hoar-frost, Alexis Godey was one of the few men feeling fit enough to get out of bed. An American of French descent, Godey was a brilliant hunter and rugged frontiersman who had accompanied Fremont on previous expeditions and had ridden with him into California, serving as a lieutenant in the California Battalion. He stood six feet tall, with a full beard and curled mustache, and he moved with a nimble grace that belied his raw strength. Next to Kit Carson, he was the man Fremont most depended upon and respected on the entire frontier.

"You get some sleep last night?" Fremont asked him, riding alongside as the group, two hours later, finally set out from Bent's Fort.

Godey chuckled. "Bit of it. Had a friend for a while." Ahead of them, on this crisp, clear morning, rose their first glimpse of the Rockies, the snow-topped Spanish peaks and Pike's Peak.

"Pretty, aren't they?" Fremont observed.

"Like most pretty women," Godey replied. "Inviting, but mighty cold, too."

They rode on silently for a while, so accustomed

to traveling together that they had no need of conversation.

"You remember the Sierras?" Fremont said finally.

"I sure do. They were some pretty mountains, so pretty I never thought we'd get through them."

"And that first look out over the green valleys . . ."

"You could look out over them one way, then look behind and see nothing but snow and ice," Godey remembered. "It was like standing between two worlds as different as night and day."

Who could have imagined how it would all turn out, Fremont mused. To descend from that glorious peak into the verdant valleys of California, only to end up the prisoner of some arrogant West Point army man.

Already the court-martial seemed like a bad dream, an awful and unreal intermission from the real business of being westward bound, with new challenges ahead. The cold-eyed, sharply chiseled face of General Stephen Watts Kearny blazed in his mind's eye, and with it, the face of Commodore R. F. Stockton. Like opposing symbols of good and evil, they hovered, neither one able to overcome the other.

So it had been in real life. After Fremont had taken Los Angeles with his California Battalion, he had met Stockton and immediately taken a liking to him. Stockton, who had been given command of Monterey, possessed all the traits that Fremont admired in a man. He was strong, daring, full of zeal for the American cause. Stockton also understood and appreciated Fremont's military maneuvers. Because he was the government's representative in the territory, Fremont gladly accepted his order to move the California Battalion north and made no complaint when Stockton reprimanded him for his tardiness.

Then Stephen Watts Kearny, from Santa Fe, New

Mexico, came into California with only a fraction of his soldiers because he refused to be intimidated by a scattered band of insurgents. And, of course, his men had been nearly decimated by battles long before they reached Los Angeles. Only the daring of Kit Carson, whom Kearny had pressed into service when they met in Taos, had saved the day. Carson had sneaked across enemy lines at night and alerted Stockton, who returned with a brigade of reinforcements.

But when Kearny had then followed Stockton into Los Angeles, he had immediately put away his gratitude. Soon, in fact, he had declared himself the ranking officer not only in Los Angeles, but in the entire territory. A chill between the two men had deepened into open confrontation, with each claiming to be in command, and each maintaining his own headquarters in town. Into this tense situation had entered Fremont. Who should he obey? He wrestled with his dilemma, but only briefly. To him the matter seemed clear. Stockton had arrived in California first, had saved Kearny's neck, and was recognized as the civil governor. He had also been Fremont's friend, even though angered over Fremont's late arrival. Kearny, on the other hand, was anything but friendly.

What Fremont had not known was that Kearny, not Stockton, had the President's blessing. When the first orders from Washington arrived, admonishing Fremont to follow Kearny's orders, the tight-lipped West Pointer had cleverly withheld them from Fremont. Fremont, of course, had continued to assert his loyalty to Stockton, and imagined it would only be a question of time before Stockton's command was confirmed and Fremont was made a civil governor of the north. Thus Kearny had eventually ordered Fremont's arrest on the charge of mutiny, and had forced the explorer to accompany him east.

Nothing might have come of it, even then, if Fremont had been able to swallow his pride and endure the military reproval that might have followed. But he could not bring himself to do it.

Neither could his father-in-law, Senator Thomas Hart Benton. Wrathfully demanding that Fremont be granted a court-martial to clear his name, Benton had sought a hearing with President Polk. But Polk had quietly demurred. It was not worth the trouble, the President had said. Better to leave the entire episode quietly buried. No, Benton had insisted, there had to be a court-martial. As one of the country's leading senators, Benton's had been a voice to be considered seriously, for his support in the forthcoming election would be important. More than a little annoyed, Polk had finally given in, and the court-martial had been convened. Across a crowded courtroom, Fremont had faced his nemesis.

Oh that damnable face! Fremont still remembered it—rigid, unyielding, with cold eyes concealing deep jealousies. Kearny had taken the stand to deliver his version of events in a clipped, authoritative voice. Fremont, he had testified, had refused to obey his orders, had tried to abrogate his command, had shown an utter disregard and disdain for the spirit and the letter of the military rule. To which Fremont had responded, in his own carefully prepared case, with his own very different report, that he had acted with caution upon entering California and had only been drawn into the fray when the lives of American settlers seemed imperiled by Mexican troops. Then he had moved swiftly and surely, losing remarkably few men as he swept into one Mexican-held city after another. Kearny, on the other hand, had straggled into California when the fighting was nearly finished, had required Commodore Stockton to rescue him from a ragged line of insurgents and had only then moved on the crutch of Stockton's military assistance into Los Angeles. What hubris to then declare himself commander of all troops! What insolence to belittle Commodore Stockton's generous aid and to then refuse to honor Stockton's appointing Fremont as civil governor! And what an insult and an outrage for Kearny to drag Fremont back to this courtroom!

To outsiders, the blame seemed due to fall on Kearny's shoulders. Fremont had been the victim of blatant jealousy. Most of the newspapers had defended him with vigor—all, that is, except those taken in by the propagandizing of one W.H. Emory, a West Point officer under Kearny's command, and as much a skunk, Fremont thought, as any man could be. Emory had made it his business to circulate fraudulent accounts of the affair to any newspaper that would print them. He was a man Fremont was not about to forget.

Unfortunately, while observers and commentators championed Fremont's cause, the court, under heavy influence from West Point, had reached an incredible verdict. Fremont had been judged guilty of all three counts brought against him. Thereupon the case was sent up to the Cabinet, whose members declared, after due deliberation, that the explorer was perhaps guilty of disobedience, and of conduct prejudicial to order and discipline, but certainly not of the third charge, mutiny. And, in any event, so brave and valuable an officer as Fremont should hardly be dismissed from military service. President Polk had been urged by some members to set the entire sentence aside, while other members counseled that he dismiss only the charge of mutiny and waive Fremont's dismissal. He had decided to adopt the second solution, so Fremont was duly declared guilty of two charges, then reinstated and ordered to report back to duty.

For a man like Fremont, whose pride was apparent to all at a glimpse, the President's decision had been intolerable. To go back to the Army now would have been to admit both guilt and the justice of the verdict. This Fremont would never do. As far as he was concerned, the Army had held him up to gross humiliation and disgrace, after he had single-handedly delivered so much of California to Union rule.

Godey's voice penetrated Fremont's bitter reminiscence and pulled him back to the present.

"Take a look." Godey was pointing. "Look like Kiowas."

Riding behind the men were perhaps three dozen Indians. Judging by the casual pace at which they rode, they hardly seemed intent on attacking.

"Kiowas all right. You can tell by the silver in their hair," Fremont remarked. He spurred Man o' War around. "Get your rifles cocked and ready," he ordered the men. "But no one is to raise a gun to fire. If they're Kiowas, they'll be harmless enough."

Rather than ride on and wait for the Indians to catch up with them, Fremont had his men rein in their horses. This way, they would seem to be meeting the Indians from a position of strength, and indeed, they would be in a better position to fend off an attack.

As soon as the men turned their horses around, the Kiowas halted their own and stared across the half-mile that separated the groups.

"Dumb Kiowas," Doubleback grumbled. "Dumbest Indians alive."

"You mean they aren't dangerous?" McGehee asked. Since his apology, he and Doubleback had begun to get along almost as friends.

"Nah, boy, they ain't any more dangerous than a

garden snake in a flowerpot. Just dumb is all. Like leeches."

After a few minutes of this staring contest, Fremont ordered the men to turn forward again and ride on. Sure enough, the Kiowas followed coyly, cautiously, never getting nearer than half a mile from the last pack of mules.

Twice more the pattern was repeated. Finally, as the sun began to sink in the late afternoon, the Indians drew closer.

"Dumb Kiowas," Doubleback grumbled for the fifteenth time. "Now's their tea time. They're always coming up to say howdeedoo 'bout now."

The Kiowas rode right up to the men, and Fremont waved to them in greeting. They looked little like the savages McGehee and Kern had expected. Rather than beaded leather garments and moccasins, these Indians wore ragged clothes, obviously bought or taken from white men.

"Where they get those duds from anyway?" McGehee asked.

Doubleback spat in disgust. "Mostly from corpses lyin' by the trail," he informed the astonished southerner. "Everythin' else they steal, they sell to buy silver for their hair."

This, indeed, was the strangest part of their attire. Bits of silver hung in their long, matted hair, each piece apparently hammered around a lock in such a way that only by cutting the hair could it be removed.

"You have silver?" the Kiowa chief demanded of Fremont.

Fremont shook his head slowly. "No silver."

The Indian's features contorted in anger. "You are on our land. You give us silver to pass."

"No silver. And this is not your land," Fremont

added. "I know where your land is. You should be up north now, hunting food for your squaws, not troubling white men from the fort."

The Indian sputtered some unintelligible obscenity. In response, Fremont turned his horse and ordered his men to ride forward.

"We got guns, you dumb Kiowas," Doubleback shouted as they rode. "You go botherin' someone else."

The order to pitch camp came early, and Fremont posted two men as guards over the horses. After a dinner of roasted antelope meat, the men turned in for the night. Fremont stayed wide awake, both out of a sense of responsibility for his men and because of a premonition that the Indians they had met that day might attempt to steal their horses under cover of darkness.

For almost four hours, all was quiet. Fremont and Henry King Kern took the watch at midnight. The night sky was completely clouded over, threatening some snow in the next few days. Here the land was more rugged than it had been around Bent's Fort. Rolling prairies often gave way to sharply rising hills and high plateaus. To the west were the jutting dark silhouettes of the Sangre de Cristo Mountains, the highest visible range of the Rockies.

Suddenly Fremont stiffened and listened intently for a long moment. Yes, there it came again. The dull sound of clinking silver was unmistakable. With a warning wave to the other guard, Fremont picked up his loaded rifle and pulled back the hammer. One of the horses whinnied, then another. More clinking. More whinnying. There was no doubt about it. The Kiowas were indulging in a bit of horse rustling.

Fremont crept toward the sounds, motioning the other guard to follow a parallel course. A dark shape moved no more than fifteen yards away. Fremont's gun blazed, and in the same instant an anguished howl went up.

In another instant, the camp was aroused, and shouts filled the air. Horses scattered everywhere. As the Kiowas instantly beat a desperate retreat, Fremont's gun, a breechloader, blazed again. Then the other guard took aim and squeezed off a shot that brought another howl of pain.

It was over in another minute, even before most of the men had rushed to Fremont's side. The Kiowas' ponies could be heard galloping furiously away, their riders whooping and yelping to urge them on.

McGehee found one Kiowa lying with a bullet in his leg near the horse he had tried to untie. Bleeding profusely, he was dragged into the circle of tents, where his wound was bound up. He was then set loose.

"Why'd you do that?" Doubleback asked Fremont. "Hell, they done set all our horses loose. At least we could have had one Indian to play with in return."

"We'll ride the mules," Fremont replied taciturnly. He would miss old Man o' War.

Two more days of rugged travel brought the expedition to the mud wattle encampment of Pueblo at the foot of the Rockies. Progress was slowed by the first snowstorms the men had encountered. Like some supernatural warning from the mountaintops, a fierce wind swept down with the snow to blanket the last stretch of prairie and hide the Rockies from view. For the longest time, it seemed the world had become a tableau of swirling white on grey. For nearly a day, Fremont was forced to pitch camp in the midst of it all, with only the Arkansas River to show him he was still headed in the right direction.

To compound his troubles, the Kiowas doggedly

followed behind, always keeping a respectful distance, but nevertheless posing a continuous threat and obliging Fremont to post a heavy guard by night. In fact, Fremont knew he was drawing close to Pueblo only when the Indians, who knew every rise and fall of the land, abandoned their pursuit.

Finally, on the morning of November 21, as the wind and snow abated and the grey sky grew clear, a small cluster of log cabins became visible at a turn in the river. Beyond, across the Arkansas at the mouth of a tiny tributary called Fountain Creek, was the adobe settlement of Pueblo. Once a busy trading town for local trappers, Pueblo had recently fallen on hard times. The beaver, mink and ermine in the area had been hunted almost to extinction. Now only a few grizzled old-timers and a handful of Spaniards remained.

"Looks deserted," Godey observed as the men approached the cabins.

"I don't remember these particular buildings," Fremont said suspiciously. "They weren't here in '45. But why would someone build them now that Pueblo's a ghost town?"

"Hotel maybe," Godey grinned. "The Hotel Pueblo."

The mystery was short-lived. Carved in the door of the nearest and largest cabin was the word TABERNACLE and this exhortation: "To the Glory of Jesus Christ the Savior, Signed Brigham Young, July 12, 1846."

Godey whistled softly. "Yeah, I heard about those folks. They call themselves Mormons."

The cabins were indeed deserted. This strange new band of Christians had traveled west two years before, led by an irascible demagogue named Brigham Young, in search of a home for their church. Fremont had heard they had journeyed up to Utah and settled there. In fact, Young had used Fremont's own written report on the region, and then had berated the explorer in a bitter letter. Young had insisted that Fremont's report on the Great Salt Lake described it as partly salt and partly fresh water. But as anyone who had read Fremont's description closely could attest, this was simply not true.

"I'd say Mr. Young owes me," Fremont said drily to Godey as the group passed down to ford the river. "Perhaps we'll make some use of his cabins."

A few men were reclining on crude wooden chairs outside Pueblo's adobe walls when Fremont arrived. Heavily bearded, with battered, wide-brimmed hats, these trappers could hardly be distinguished from one another. Only their eyes, sharp and darting, let out that they were not stuffed decoys.

"Morning," Fremont said easily.

"That it is," one returned in a disinterested monotone.

"Reckon we'll use the cabins across the river," Fremont said.

There was no response from the seated trappers leaning against the wall. Fremont waited for a moment out of courtesy, then withdrew to shout instructions across the water. In a short time, the air was filled with the raucous, joking voices of men and the braying of thirsty mules as the packs were unloaded. Fremont ventured into Pueblo first, accompanied by Godey and Kern, and found the place just as malodorous and poorly repaired as he remembered.

"I can't believe the stink!" Kern muttered to him.

Godey overheard the remark and grinned. "That's what happens when there's no women around to do the cleaning."

Like Bent's Fort, Pueblo's gates opened into an atrium surrounded by balconied walls with small, shuttered windows. Unlike Bent's Fort, however, its dirt-packed ground was strewn with garbage and the offal of butchered livestock, as well as the droppings of chickens and mangy dogs.

"Thank God we don't have to stay here," Kern murmured fervently.

"I stayed here last time through," Fremont said. "It's awful at first, but you get used to it. Gets so you can't tell the difference between stench and fresh air."

Now a bearded old trapper detached himself from a group at a far table, tucked his flapping shirttails into his grimy pants, and sauntered unevenly over to the men. He seemed, at this early hour of the day, to be already inebriated. "Welcome," he called out with a burp. "How you be?"

"Well and good," Fremont returned. "Who's in charge here these days?"

"Who's in charge?" The bearded trapper looked up at Fremont with a mixture of shock and amusement. "Why, there ain't no one in charge here, unless it be me. That's 'cause I'm the only one who ain't too lazy to come on over and say howdee." He turned back to his comrades. "Ain't that the truth, boys?"

They responded with derisive chuckling.

"There was someone in charge when I was here before," Fremont said stiffly.

"Well, now, when was you here?" the old trapper inquired.

"Three years ago."

"Three years ago! Well sir, three years ago was before the Arkansas got trapped out, and before all the other rivers and streams from here to New Mexico got trapped out, too. No more furs, no more people. They done moved on. And we just stayed 'cause we're tired, and we're gettin' old, and a man's gotta settle down sometime. Though damned if I know why I should bother tellin' this to a stranger."

Godey felt obliged to step forward now. "I have the honor to introduce Colonel John Fremont," he said. "And who are you?"

The trapper's eyes bulged in awe as he stood back, tipped his hat respectfully and held out his hand. "Cornelius Whiting's the name, and it's a real pleasure."

The trapper then announced to his comrades, in a voice loud enough to be heard by everyone in Pueblo, the name of the tall, blond stranger who stood before him. In a moment, two dozen trappers, Spaniards, and squaws tumbled forward to gather around Fremont. The diminutive Mr. Cornelius Whiting rapidly called out orders to the women to clean the place up and to set out the nearest thing to a royal meal that could be mustered. One man was sent across the river to greet the rest of the expedition with three flasks of whiskey. Another began to fix a fire in the charred but serviceable hearth at one end of the atrium. By the time the rest of Fremont's men had warmed their innards with a swig or two, and ventured over to the Pueblo Hotel, a merry fire was crackling in the hearth, while another smaller fireplace was put to use for heating bathwater. A long banquet table was laid out with large bowls of steaming beans, rice and milk, and a carefree, festive mood took hold of the place.

In the midst of all these preparations, as the trappers bustled vigorously about, Fremont began to notice one man in particular—a decidedly odd character, who was easily sixty years old, but who seemed to have a greater reserve of youthful energy than any of the others. Age had lent a stoop to his figure, but he still stood taller than the rest, with a lean, hard frame that gave evidence of long years in the wilderness. His features were most peculiar, too. He had squirrel-like, roving brown eyes, set in a sharply drawn face with a strong, hooked nose and large, almost pointed ears. The most peculiar trait of all about him, however, was a walk that soon attracted the curiosity of Fremont's men. Though the fellow moved quickly as he helped others set the table and clean the place, he did so with a quirky, awkward gait, heaving from side to side as he stuck one long leg out in front of the other.

A smile touched Fremont's lips. He knew of only one man in all the West with that kind of walk.

"Old Bill Williams, if I don't miss my guess."

"Why ain't I too Old Bill, yessir, I am. And it is a pleasure to meet you, Colonel, yessir, it is."

Fremont rubbed his stubbled chin as he took the full measure of the man. "You look as tough as they say you are, Old Bill. You still go out trapping?"

"Nary a bit of it. No more. Not me. I had my fun. Took me a few furs, bought a few drinks. That's it. Now it's time to stretch out."

In fact, Fremont knew that Old Bill had done more trapping, taken more furs and bought more drinks with his earnings than any other man on the whole frontier. Legends of his prowess had spread far and wide, and rare was the trapper who would fail to come up with his own Old Bill tale around a campfire.

Old Bill had started out as a backwoods preacher in his home state of Missouri, and then a missionary for the Osage Indians. But that was long, long ago. Always a crack shot, he had drifted into the bitter, lonely life of hunter and trapper, staying holed up in the wilderness, alone, for months, even years on end before emerging. Such a somber recluse might have been expected to pack away his earnings and grow rich in time, but Old Bill had a fatal weakness. As soon as he had traded his furs for stacks of crisp green bills at the old Pueblo or the Taos Trading Post, off he would traipse with his odd, rolling gait, to the nearest saloon to buy a drink for everyone in sight. Sometimes, for the Indian squaws who lingered outside in the square, Old Bill would purchase long rolls of calico and lace. Always he would stalk out to the street and unroll his merchandise, then howl to the squaws to come and take it all home.

He had also done his share of Indian chasing, and on more than one occasion Old Bill had come away with a scalp hanging from his belt, a practice that Fremont found abhorrent.

No matter what his sins, however, Old Bill knew the Rockies better than any man alive, better even than Kit Carson, and that was why, when the assembled men sat down to eat, Fremont made a point of sitting next to the old trapper.

"When's the last time you went over the mountain?" he asked casually.

"Whoah now, take a bit of figurin' out. What you mean by that?" Old Bill had a way of talking in questions, ending even his most emphatic opinions with a sudden upward lilt. "I mean I been up in the mountains even this last fall, and I took to 'em last year to trap a bit, for old time's sake."

"No," said Fremont, between bites. He was discovering he had a sharper appetite than he had realized. "What I mean is, when's the last time you crossed the mountains to the other side."

"Well, that takes a bit more figurin'," Old Bill mused. "I guess it be three years back this last spring. Three years back."

"Ever gone over this time of year?"

"Good God and golly no!" Old Bill exclaimed. "A month ago, maybe so. But no later than the end of October, and no earlier than April."

Briefly, Fremont explained his mission.

"Lordy, lordy, you must be plumb crazy!" Old Bill cried. "I thought you was just headed south, maybe down through Taos."

Fremont shook his head. "That wouldn't be the point now, would it?"

"But hell, Colonel, you seen the snow already. It's worse now than I seen it in any of the last twenty Novembers. There's one hell of a winter comin'. Ain't that the truth now, Whiting?"

Whiting had been listening gravely. "Colonel Fremont, I fear you don't know the lay of the land up this way. There's not a man in the world ever tried the Rocky Mountains in the middle of November. Ain't no one's ever done it, and no one ever will."

"I will," Fremont said with quiet determination.

"But you don't even have a scout there among you," Old Bill stated incredulously. "I mean, those mountains'll eat men alive, swallow 'em up and never spit 'em back out. Ain't I right, Whiting?"

"You're right, Old Bill," Fremont interjected, "I don't have a scout—not yet." He looked ironically at the older man and smiled.

Suddenly, Old Bill understood. "Whosh, no, if what you're thinkin' is to take me along. Thank you kindly, but nossir, I got to say."

"I need you, Old Bill. You're the best, and that's what I need."

"Whosh, no," Old Bill shook his head vigorously. "I seen it in the sky this year, aurora borealis, and that's a sign, doncha see? It's a sign that any man in his right mind best cut himself a cord of wood, pack up some vittles and whiskey and settle in for a long, cozy winter inside his own house and home."

Fremont leaned forward. "You don't understand, Old Bill. We need you. And this is no ordinary expedition. This is for the entire country, not just a few trappers. There's never been a trek like this one. When we get to the other side of those Rockies, we'll have proved you can connect one side of this nation to the other with tracks and trestles. And if you come with us, if you can find the way, when that railroad is laid down and settlers start riding out to the coast you'll be the man they thank."

"Listen Colonel, I don't know." Old Bill spat a quid of tobacco on the floor. "I mean, what if we all freeze our skinny butts up there?"

"We won't," Fremont declared evenly.

"Well, but, how you fixin' to go?" Old Bill asked.

"Due west," Fremont replied.

"But that would mean the Robidoux Pass! You can't take the Robidoux Pass! That's just askin' to get yourselves killed. Nossir, you got to take the Sangre de Cristos, down south of the Robidoux. Ain't no other way at this time of year."

Fremont shrugged. "We can decide when we get there, and see how much snow has accumulated. Maybe the Robidoux will turn out to be hopeless, but the main point now is to get started with you as our scout. Pay is sixty dollars a month and a place in history. What do you say, Old Bill?"

Old Bill paused, looked down at his beans and rice almost as if he were bidding them good-bye, then glanced truculently up again to Fremont's waiting eyes. "I'm a damned fool is what I am," he said, "but you talked me into it."

"This whole expedition . . ." He paused. "It's madness, Colonel Fremont. You're about to lead three dozen men to their deaths, but you're so hungry for glory, you don't seem to care."

The room fell silent. All eyes had fixed on Fremont and Billedoux.

Fremont's eyes blazed with barely contained fury. "This is my fourth expedition," he said. "And the third that I have led. In all those trips, I have lost no men to the elements. If you doubt my ability to lead my men safely across these mountains, perhaps you should reconsider going yourself."

"That's exactly what I have done, Colonel Fremont. I'll take no part in this madness."

Billedoux turned to face the other men. "And to any of you who would call me coward, I say you are the cowards. Not a one of you has had the courage to stand up to that madman. Before he leads you all to icy graves, I suggest you search your own hearts. Ask yourselves if you have not been bullied into a mindless mission or whether you're too afraid to admit that you have."

Billedoux glowered proudly around the room, and each pair of eyes he met fell away.

Finally Fremont spoke again. Now he, too, addressed the entire group. "Are there any of you who feel as Billedoux does? Any of you who feel it's time to turn back?"

There was no rancor in his voice, no threat, but only silence remained after he spoke.

"You seem to be alone, Billedoux."

"God strike me dead if I am," Billedoux returned. "Not a man in this room will speak up now, for the same reason that they never have before. They're all scared to death of looking like cowards to you and to each other. Deep down, that's what they're all thinking.

You can say they're free to turn back a thousand times, but not one of them will take you up on it. And you know it."

"Very well, then," Fremont said. "We'll try it the only other way I know. Because if there's a man in this room who's got second thoughts about this expedition, believe me, I'd rather see him turn back than keep him on. So we'll take a vote. A vote is fair, don't you think? If you want me to stay on as your leader, knowing if you do we march out into those mountains this morning, raise your hands. If you've lost your faith in me, keep your hand down. Fair enough, Billedoux?"

"You do what you like."

When the vote came, a string of hands rose as every man at the table showed favor for Fremont. For an angry moment, Billedoux scowled at the lot of them. Then he stormed out of the dining hall. Through the windows, the men could see him hurl his pack onto his mule, swing a leg up and over, then brutally spur the startled beast back in the direction of Pueblo.

Fremont made a silent prayer of thanks. Without a firm hand over the men, even a vigor and determination as steadfast as his own could not propel him over the Rocky Mountains.

As the explorers set off from Hardscrabble that day, their pack mules laden down with bushels of corn, their own stomachs full of hot food and their hands and feet still warmed by a crackling fire, their spirits were vaulting high. This was adventure, after all! And not a man among them did not want adventure, did not crave it even, and recognize that along with it came always a stinging presence of danger.

The sun was brilliant and warm, lighting a summery clear blue sky. The tall pines along the way arched up above a fine crust of snow. Doubleback broke out his harmonica, and the men sang along, their voices ringing out joyfully in the clear mountain air. Fremont led the way, accompanied by Old Bill, who looked a strange sight, walking with his awkward, rolling gait, his shoulders heaving back and forth as he went.

"Snow's deeper'n even I bet on," he informed Fremont.

"But it's dry."

"Here it's dry. Wait a bit more and see if it stays that way."

The steeper the ascent became, the deeper the snow was. They began trudging as if they were climbing any hill, but by midafternoon every step required a strong push up, and the incline, together with the rapidly thinning air, wore the men down considerably. Fremont was forced to call a halt every half hour, which made their progress slower than it would have been had he come on his own. For some reason, the rugged climb seemed only to invigorate him.

They finally pitched camp on a gentle slope and gathered whatever wood they could find at this altitude. When they had found enough to build a fire, Captain Cathcart, melting snow for water, concocted a thick corn chowder. As night fell and they burrowed into their sleeping sacks, a poignant, tranquil beauty seemed to hover over the world. From this height, they could see the distant settlement of Hardscrabble, from which thin wavering columns of chimney smoke wafted up grey against the blue-black night.

Next morning, the weather turned sharply colder, and as the men climbed higher, the firs gave way to aspens. Once they crossed bear tracks, and often they startled a deer or mountain rabbit into sudden retreat. But despite the occasional signs of life, the steep escarpment appeared gradually more pristine, more remote, and more inaccessible.

That afternoon, the first mule died. The snow was six inches deep here, and the ground underneath was turning rockier. Here, too, the men were beyond their first view of Hardscrabble. They had climbed one ridge to find yet another, then a narrow cleft that led up through two imposing, icy mountain faces.

So far, the remaining mules were still all laden with bushels of corn, so all the men walked alongside them, each man tethering three mules. Like the others, Kern had fallen into a kind of daze, his head turned down to ward off the wind, his eyes on the freshly fallen snow. Only the occasional tug of a recalcitrant mule jolted him out of his thoughts.

Suddenly a tremendous pull from behind nearly yanked Kern's right arm out of his shoulder socket, and one of the tether ropes snaked loose. At the same time, one of his mules let out a high-pitched whinny of terror and plunged headlong down the side of the cliff. The other two mules scrambled frantically to keep their footing, and it was all Kern could do to keep from losing them too. Falling backward into the snow to prevent himself from being thrown off balance, he caught only a brief glance of the ill-fated animal as it slid down the icy pass, flailing with its hooves at the unyielding crust, and finally becoming entangled in its own tether as it plunged to the bottom with an awful, resounding thud against the snow-packed ground.

"Here, I've got them," came a voice at Kern's ear.

It was Fremont, his face ruddy with cold but looking otherwise unruffled.

"I'm sorry, I don't know, I . . ." Kern found it difficult to speak.

"Forget it, it doesn't matter now."

"What should we do?" Kern asked.

Fremont looked down at the fallen mule, now so

far below them that it appeared no larger than a protruding rock through the snow—but a rock that moved, for the mule was not yet dead. Fremont took Kern's rifle from its long leather holster on one of the other two mules. "Best to put that poor bugger out of its misery," he muttered.

Kern watched, fascinated, as Fremont took a firm stance in the snow, raised the gun and nestled its cold wooden stock against his cheek. Fremont squinted down the sights only long enough to draw a bead on the target below, then calmly squeezed off a shot. The echo rebounded through the pass as if the bullet itself were ricocheting from one side to the other. Then all was still. A brief, grim smile touched Fremont's lips.

Down the line of men and horses, Doubleback let out a whoop. "You got him, boss!" he cried. "You got that son of a bitch right in the head, I'll betcha."

Fremont replaced the rifle in its leather holster and looked pensively down at Kern, who remained lying in the snow. "Next time, boy, pay some attention to your mules. Else we'll find we're shouldering those bushels and packs ourselves."

By the time the cold grey light of day began to give way to dusk, Fremont had led his men to the top of the second ridge. Spirits that had flagged during the arduous climb were resuscitated as the men struggled up one last steep slope, crusted over with a half inch of ice in parts, to get their first glimpse of the other side.

Stretching out before them like a heavenly blanket of eiderdown was the flat white valley that led to the tremendously imposing Sangre de Cristo Mountains to the west. That valley could not have looked more inviting if it offered up a thousand twinkling lights from a thousand warm homes and hearths. Just to see proof that the entire journey would not be one long painful ascent cheered the men mightily and even brought a grin of delight to Fremont's stern face.

To escape the fierce winds that swept across the peak, the men broke protocol and pushed over to the leeward side to pitch camp. Here, nestled in bedrolls with their rations of mashed corn and water, they felt a warmth and comfort they had sorely missed for the last two days. Before turning in, Fremont, as usual, took his daily measurements. With a fascination instilled long ago by his old mentor, Nicollet, he computed the longitude and latitude, the nighttime temperature and barometric reading, and then sat awake, watching the appearance of the stars with enchantment.

Captain Cathcart, intrigued by Fremont's obsession and too restless to sleep, sat up with him.

"How do you find the strength, Colonel?" he asked, raising himself up on one elbow.

"You know, Cathcart, what I find myself wondering is why other men don't find it in the natural world around them. Why they don't seem to care much about the sun and the moon and stars except to know they're always there."

"That's all most men need to know."

Fremont shook his head. "I think if a man could sleep all day, then stay awake all night and do nothing but watch the stars and record their movements, his life would be redeemed."

"Maybe if he had a *fräulein* beside him," Cathcart laughed.

"Or even if he didn't. I tell you, Cathcart, I love my wife as much as any man could love a woman. But sometimes, out here at night, with the sky full of such wonder, I feel a different kind of love, one that's . . . almost stronger, somehow."

"Ah, now that would be a fine set of affairs, to have your wife learn she was being two-timed by a star."

Now it was Fremont's turn to laugh. "All right, fair enough. But I do feel a little guilty about it sometimes, strange as that sounds. I mean, a man is supposed to feel different kinds of love—for a mother, for a daughter . . . and his love for his wife is supposed to be the greatest of all. But to tell you the truth, Cathcart, I think my love for this view, and this sky right now, is at least as great as my love for Jessie."

"You just think too much, my friend. Your love for the stars doesn't make your love for your wife shine any less brightly. It only makes you a good explorer, that's all."

"I don't know, Cathcart. This is the fourth time now. The fourth time I've taken off and left her alone, the fourth time she's had to worry day and night whether I'm alive or dead. That's selfish of me, Cathcart. It's really selfish in a way."

"But it's always that way between men and women."

"Is it?" Fremont mused. "I wonder."

Fremont had been gazing up at the stars all this time, and after a pause he said, "You see up there? To the right of the moon?"

Cathcart followed his finger and nodded.

"That's it. That's Mercury."

As the men watched, the tiny dot of light seemed to kiss the moon and then be absorbed by it. For perhaps half an hour, the tiny orb remained obscured behind the larger one. Then, like a mischievous child peeking out from its hiding place, the smallest planet inched once again into view.

"There it is, Cathcart, you see it?"

There was no response from Cathcart's hulking form. Fremont started to speak again, then cocked an ear and heard the soft, regular breathing of the older man. He was fast asleep.

Chapter 8

As if the men had crossed instantly from midwinter to the first blush of spring, they began their descent into temperatures growing so mild that the snow began to melt into rivulets. These fed into streams that in turn converged into rushing torrents of sparkling clear water bound for the valley below.

Though their progress was far more rapid now than it had been climbing up, the men were far more exhausted by the work of constantly straining against stumbling down. They had to move so carefully, in fact, that their leg muscles became almost paralyzed with tension. Even Fremont, who showed little strain in any circumstance, was observed shaking out a leg more than once.

By noon the group had reached a more gradual slope, and by midafternoon, men and mules were on flat ground again. Old Bill, leading the way with his odd, rolling gait, paused to do an impromptu jig of celebration, sloshing around in the wet snow and whooping like an Apache. After taking his bow to applause and catcalls, he resumed his lead, and the men pushed on, slogging through slushy snow that soaked boots and pants.

The weather continued warm, but the ground and

available wood were so wet that the men were forced
to do without a fire that night and to camp on wet sod.
By morning, every man's bedroll was soaked through,
and the entire party shivered until the warm sun dried
them off. As the day progressed, however, the warmth
gave way to a cold wind that swept down from the
Sangre de Cristos in the west. With no trees in sight
anywhere in this wide, flat valley, the men could find no
shelter, and the wet snow rendered them colder still.

By late afternoon, one of the men, Julius Ducatel,
the slight, mild-mannered son of a Baltimore doctor,
had become dangerously chilled. The other men were
cold as the sun sank lower, but Ducatel was convulsed
by shivering, so much so that he could barely keep one
foot moving in front of the other. McGehee, marching
behind him, gave a shout when Ducatel collapsed.

"What in the hell is the matter?" Old Bill shouted
back. When he saw the answer to his question, he came
bounding awkwardly through the slush. "Froze, is he?"

"He's been doing poorly all day," McGehee returned, slipping a blanket under Ducatel's violently
shivering form.

"Well, get him up on the mule, boy. Don't just
leave him in the snow."

McGehee helped Old Bill pick Ducatel up, slip
the pack off the nearest mule and put the man, like a
bushel of corn, over the animal's warm body.

Fremont called an early stop to the day's progress
and dispatched a half dozen men to search out greasewood and sage to make a fire in a cleared patch of
ground. With the wind still whipping fiercely against
them, the men huddled to shelter the tiny flame until
it grew into a strong, healthy blaze. Then they curled
Ducatel next to it, buffered him with blankets and set
about cooking some corn chowder. By the time the
chowder was ready, Ducatel was resting more comfort-

ably, though he was fairly embarrassed to be the one man who had weathered the day so poorly.

"Colonel, I'm truly sorry to have caused so much trouble," Ducatel said, as Fremont walked over to see him.

Fremont looked him over with a wan smile. "Happens to us all one time or another. Don't worry about it."

"It's just that I've never faced that much cold and wet in one day, sir. I expect I'll be more used to it now."

"I expect you will, Ducatel. Eat some chowder while it's hot."

"It won't happen again, sir."

"That's right, son," Fremont replied curtly. "It won't."

It seemed no more than a few minutes after the weary men had laid their heads down to sleep that Fremont's shouts awakened them again. In fact, it was just after midnight.

"The mules!" he shouted. "Get the mules!"

A great tumult of cries filled the darkness as the men stumbled blindly out of their bedrolls and groped about for their boots. Lit matches stirred the shadows and briefly illuminated startled, sleepy faces.

"The mules have gotten loose!" Fremont cried again.

By now the braying of mules came from every direction. Apparently the guard had fallen asleep, and a few hungry mules had chewed through their tethers, releasing all the rest. Soon the entire train had taken off in the vain search through the snow for grass.

"Over here, over here!" Fremont ordered the men to the still-glowing embers of the greasewood campfire. When they had assembled, he quickly dispatched them in four groups to plunge off in all directions. Soon there was a rough chorus of human voices mingled with braying as the men shouted their progress and called to one another for help in the darkness.

With nearly a hundred mules to round up, two hours passed before the men collected at the campfire pit to take stock. A half dozen mules were still unaccounted for. Resolutely, Fremont called an end to the search.

"Brattle!" he called out grimly.

Brattle stepped forward, as guilt-ridden as a schoolboy caught stealing penny candies.

"Brattle, you were guarding the mules tonight, were you not?"

Reluctantly, the tall southerner nodded. "Yes sir."

"Could you explain why the mules got loose?"

Brattle struggled to spit out the words. "I . . . I was asleep, sir."

"Asleep." Fremont pondered this for a moment. "You were asleep, you say?"

"Yes, yes sir, that's right," he mumbled timidly.

"And interestingly enough, Brattle, we are all now awake."

"Yes sir." Brattle scowled uncertainly and shuffled his feet.

"Well then, we owe you a few hours of wakefulness, and you owe us a few hours of sleep. Wouldn't you say?"

Brattle nodded miserably.

"Fine. For the next two weeks, you'll take the midnight watch. Alone." Fremont turned to the rest of the men. "We've got four more hours of darkness. I don't know about the rest of you, but I'm going to get some sleep myself. McGehee, you've got the two to four shift; Doubleback, you've got the four to six. Good night."

Too tired to make any response, the men sought out their bedrolls. Within five minutes, nearly all were snoring fitfully. Only McGehee remained awake, posted by the mules with a rifle across his knees.

On another night he might have cursed the luck of the draw that had him assigned to guard duty after slogging through the wet snow to round up the mules. But tonight he actually felt content to sit alone in the darkness.

Why was that? he wondered. Perhaps he needed some time to sift through his thoughts. Yes, perhaps that and more. The truth was, he felt a hard ball of resentment toward Fremont deep down in his gut. It was partly how Fremont had just now dealt with Brattle. The colonel didn't get mad, really, didn't lose his temper, but he had shown such a silent contempt for the poor southerner. It didn't square with the sympathy he had shown when Bent had made such a fool of Brattle with the rattlesnake trick. Now, out on the march, Fremont seemed almost another man altogether —distant, cold, even arrogant. Did Fremont think his men would not obey if he appeared less rigid? That was conceivable, of course, but not likely.

So why, then, did Fremont stand so unyielding in every situation, from the most trivial task to the whole expedition in general? McGehee began to wonder how rational Fremont really was about making this winter passage. Already they had endured some brutal weather. Would it not get worse? And if that were the case, why should they risk their lives to soldier on? Because some rich easterner dreamt about laying down a railroad to make his fortune?

That was it, all right—maybe not Fremont's only reason, but the most obvious one. The less obvious reason was only now becoming apparent to McGehee. He wondered how many of the others suspected it too. Although recently reinstated, Colonel John Charles Fremont had been stripped of his rank and humiliated in public. He had fallen from the hero's pedestal. McGehee wondered just how desperately the man hungered to regain that pedestal and seek a hero's vengeance from the man who had toppled him.

Not that McGehee begrudged his leader the right to feel angry, bitter or disillusioned. But what if that anger was blinding him now to the hazards of this mission? Would it affect his ability to make sound decisions? Perhaps he was indeed capable of leading his men into a wintry grave.

Another day's slogging through the snow brought the men across the rest of the Sangre de Cristo Valley. They now faced the awesome range of mountains, which ran directly from north to south and separated them from the verdant California coast beyond. The Sangre de Cristo Mountains were often traversed by wagon trains of westward pioneers, but always in the warmer weather of June or July. Some peaks, snow-capped and ringed with grey clouds, stood as high as fourteen thousand feet.

Wagon trains followed the Robidoux Pass, hardly a sea-level route, but considerably lower than the mountains that banked it on either side. This was also the most central passage for settlers coming from Missouri and points northeast. The only other choices were to simply travel more than a hundred miles, either north or south, and skirt the mountains completely.

This was what Old Bill proposed. Ever since he had agreed to join the party, he had counseled taking a southerly detour around the Sangre de Cristos, heading southwest into New Mexico, then through Arizona and on to the coast. This Fremont yet again refused to do as the party reached the foot of the Robidoux Pass.

"But I'm tellin' you, Colonel," Old Bill argued, "I knowed folks to try Robidoux even in early October, and they ain't had a chance. I mean they mighta done it, but it just weren't worth the trouble. You be best off turnin' south."

Fremont remained adamant. "You don't seem to understand. If we head south, we'll defeat the whole purpose of this expedition. There's no doubt a railroad could be laid down south of the Sangre de Cristos. But that's as much a detour for a train as it is for men and mules. The question is not *should* we, but *can* we make it?"

Old Bill threw up his hands in defeat. "Yeah, sure we can make it. It's just a matter of how comfortable it'll be."

Fremont shook his head in frustration. He was growing to dislike Old Bill more and more each time they spoke.

The group began its ascent of the snowbound pass. Compared to the mountains they now faced, climbing those behind them seemed like child's play, a jaunt over gentle hillocks. Not only were the Sangre de Cristos forbiddingly high and icy, but the peaks were densely clustered, as if a dozen mountain ranges awaited the men in quick succession.

The pass began as a mild slope for a few hundred feet. Soon, however, it grew precipitously steep, a winding, tortuous trail that narrowed as it snaked around the lowest mountain peak, then dipped sharply, only to sweep back up again around the next rugged peak.

Fremont stayed up at the front of the long party of men and mules, just behind Old Bill. He was at least relieved to see that the scout really did know the trail as well as he claimed. Often on that first day of climbing, Old Bill steered the group from wandering off the snow-covered trail into snowy ravines.

Their only mishap that day was the loss of two mules. The animals had managed to chew through their tethers and wander back down the pass out of sight before any of the men noticed. One of the mules had carried the group's only remaining sack of coffee, which put many of the men to such grieving that a stranger would have thought they had surely lost their entire families.

That night they camped in a stand of junipers and pines, built a roaring fire, and ate the best dinner they had tasted in days—roasted elk meat, courtesy of Godey's marksmanship. Then Fremont directed several men to beat the remaining meat into pemmican. Well-salted and wrapped in fat, it would offer sustenance on days when no game ventured into sight.

A heavy snow fell before morning, and not until noon could the men assemble the mules and packs and start on. That day they made only five miles and lost three more mules. But this time, the mules collapsed in their tracks, dead from exhaustion and starvation, for as the provisions had dwindled, Fremont had ordered a drastic cutback in rations for the beasts. As the party climbed higher into even more remote territory, the same corn that had filled a mule's stomach was now welcome fare to the men's stomachs, too.

Because provisions were quickly dwindling, the men could do without the expired mules. Their packs were loaded onto others, though none of the remaining mules were doing well either. A dozen times that day the men stopped to coax one of the poor beasts up from its knees. And almost constantly, the mules had to be kept from chewing each other's tails for food, or from chewing through their own leather reins.

This was a baneful enough task, but it was all the more annoying because the men were so battered by the cold. The wind whipped the falling snow into the men's faces and it adhered to their whiskers and froze in ever-thickening carapaces of ice.

The temperature was now dropping steadily toward zero. One man, Harry King, had frozen toes. Upon inspection, Fremont found they had turned greyish blue, only a few hours from complete frostbite. King's problem was painfully clear: his boots had nearly lost their soles, and the man owned only one pair of thick socks. Fremont, calling an early halt to the day, put King by a fire and then cut off a long strip of his own blanket, which, when severed in half, provided King with another thick layer of woollen warmth.

"He oughta be thankful it's his toes that froze," Doubleback said to Cathcart.

"What do you mean?"

"Well, you know the man's just got married. If he'd froze his pecker, he'd likely lose his wife, too, doncha think?"

Cathcart grinned. "Is that what your wife would do?"

"Oh, I got me no wife I'd worry about." Doubleback grinned ironically.

"But then what do you do for women, boy? You just go to the cathouses?"

"Hell, no, Cap'n," Doubleback exclaimed. "I just marry a new woman every time I get to a new town. I got four of 'em now, one in Westport, one in St. Louis, one in 'Frisco, and one in Santa Fe."

Cathcart failed to hide his astonishment. "But what happens if they start having babies? Do you leave them high and dry?"

"Well now, Cap'n, I don't put it that way. And I don't know if they got any kids, 'cause I don't stick around long enough to see. Most fellows, they get into town with a little money, and they head straight for the local saloon, where they just buys themselves a woman. The next thing they know, they find out they bought more than a memory—they bought a disease.

"And jumpin' Jehoshaphat, what kinda woman they got for their hard-earned money anyhow? Just a tired old whore—pardon the expression—who's probably lookin' to rob 'em blind. So I don't do that. Nossir, I don't do that at all. What I do is, I buy one good Sunday-go-meeting suit, and I go to the barber, and I get my hair cut and my whiskers trimmed, and I take a room in the hotel. You follow me so far?"

"I'm afraid I do."

"Then what I do is, I go to church! And I'll tell you the truth about something, Cap'n, though I'll swear up and down the plantation that it's a lie if you tell anyone. Fact is, I know I'm a pretty decent lookin' fellow. Not the best, you understand, but I'm all right. And when I get to that church, lookin' all scrubbed and clean and handsome, well strike me dead if the purdiest little girls in town don't all start dyin' to know who I am."

"So what do you tell them?"

"Well now, Cap'n, there's the beauty of it, yessir, the God-blasted beauty of it. Because you see, Cap'n, you are talkin' right now to a gen-u-ine, legitimate, ordained preacher of the gospel."

Cathcart's jaw dropped.

"Now I'm serious about this, Cap'n, I'm an ordained preacher in the Worldwide Church of the Savior Jesus. That's a local church, actually, though the name throws you off a bit. Local to the town of Freshwater Springs, Georgia. Which also happens to be the town where I growed up."

"It sounds like a local church," Cathcart observed drily.

"Why, yes it is. It's exactly that, Cap'n," Doubleback replied. "Matter of fact, I started it m'self with two other fellows. We're just in it ourselves, just the three of us. And we do the whole works, you know what I mean? Savin' souls, blessin' babies. Savin' babies, blessin' souls. That's the main thing, really. Why, at one time, we had a congregation of a hundred believers."

"What, if I may ask, does your church hold to be true?"

"Why, just about anything I guess, Cap'n. We're not uppity. You believe that the good Jesus Christ gonna come down another time, fine with us. You believe that all sinners'll go to fire and damnation, fine with us. I tell you, Cap'n, you believe in a life after death, we'll go along with that, too. That's why we had so many believers in Freshwater Springs. 'Cause we could accommodate everybody."

"Including, I gather, all the local women."

"Why yes, exactly so, Cap'n. Which is what I started to say. You see, when I begin tellin' all the womenfolk in some new town about the Worldwide Church of the Savior Jesus, they just get down on their knees and near to die with religiosity. And I bless 'em all. Then I take the very purdiest one into the church itself, which is to say, into the holy covenant of my hotel bed. And there they do get blessed and blessed again."

"Don't their parents or their families ever recognize that your ministrations are a bit unorthodox, Doubleback? I mean, didn't you ever get tarred and feathered?"

"Ain't come close once." Doubleback pulled his beard with an air of great self-importance. They were sitting now in Doubleback's tent, after a dinner of leftover elk. The tents, which protected them from the fierce snow-laden wind outside, were large enough to fit two men comfortably.

"Well, maybe once I did. It was in Santa Fe, a couple years back. I was passin' through, as usual had a pocket full of jingle from sellin' my furs, and I was gettin' mighty restless. Well, I ran up against the absolutely most purdiest woman, half-Indian, half-Spanish, and she was all desperately willin' to enter the World-wide Church of the Savior Jesus, which she proceeded to do, with my blessin'. Turns out, though, her father is a real important Spaniard, and he's real close to old General Kearny, that man who was such a friend to Colonel Fremont. So Kearny hears about me, and he and his soldiers come fetch me from the hotel where I was stayin'. I got dragged over to the Palace of the Governors, where Kearny keeps his military headquarters, and he makes me come in my Sunday-go-meeting suit and all, and he says . . . 'Well, Mister Murphy—'cause that's the name I was usin' at the time—I hear you are a righteous man of the Lord.' To which I say in my most churchfelt voice, 'Yessir, that's exactly what I am.' And he says, 'Well, then, Mister Murphy, you'd like as best start prayin'.'

"Before I knowed it, I was dragged into the garrison and thrown into a jail cell. But here's the most amazin' part, Cap'n, and the part that made me a true believer in the church. That night, my beautiful lady comes up to the window, and she got a handsaw. Before long, don't ya know it, she gets that window sawed out, and I creep through. And that night, I have to tell you, I commenced to baptizin', confirmin', and takin' into the bosom of the church as a lifelong member that wonderful child.

"Of course, the next mornin' I got goin' pretty fast."

"Ever consider going back?" Cathcart asked. He was curled up now in his bedroll.

"Go back? Hell no, Cap'n. In my church the members have to do the seekin' out. And when the church has up and left them, it's their righteous duty to follow along."

Chapter 9

Though the sky was brilliant and clear, the men awoke to find nearly six inches of newly fallen snow shimmering white on the steep embankments and dusting the cedars and pines. Even the mules were covered, with some showing only their steaming, flared nostrils. As they struggled up to their feet, prodded by sympathetic slaps on the flanks from a muleteer, they barely had the strength to shake it off. Some of the men helped to brush them. If they didn't get the animals dry quickly, the morning's bitter wind would turn that snow, mixed with the mules' own sweat, into a coating of ice.

When the mules were finally loaded up, the party pushed resolutely onward, driven not only by their need to keep warm, but by the clear view of the summit ahead. Old Bill, as usual, led the way. Behind him trailed Fremont and Godey. Then came the others in a long, ragged line.

Kern found himself walking alongside McGehee and Ducatel. The latter was fully recovered from his freezing spell of the other evening, but he still felt badly about it.

"I tell you," he said to the others as they made their way slowly up the mountainside, "this whole blasted expedition is fast approaching lunacy."

"Where'd you think you were going to be when we all set out, man? Florida?" Kern smiled ironically.

"You know what I mean, Kern. We haven't even gotten into the thick of this trip, and already there's not a man who hasn't all but had his toes frozen off his feet. Now you figure what another month of this weather'll do, and then you add on the fact that the San Juans are a hundred times worse than the Christos. I'll tell you what it adds up to, Kern. A cold grave, just like Billedoux said."

"Maybe you ought to do like Billedoux, too, and tell that to the colonel."

"That's just the point, Kern. We're not dealing with a rational man. We're dealing with a man whose pride has got the best of him. You saw him the other night when I got the shivers. He talked to me like it was my fault. I'm telling you, Kern, it's going to get a lot worse. That man's going to march us right into hell if it kills him, too."

"Ducatel, I'm not going to hell, and neither are you. I knew what I was getting into when I signed up with Fremont. I also know that he'll get us through. Ain't that right, McGehee?"

McGehee was hunched over, his breath steaming up from under his wide-brimmed hat. "Guess so, Kern."

Kern squinted against the brilliant white of the snow. "You got doubts, too?"

"Not doubts, exactly. I think we'll make it, though I've made better bets. But Ducatel's got a point about the colonel, if you ask me. I think he's got more pride than is good for him. And Kern, you know he's in this for more than the damned adventure, and for more than helping his backers to make a case for laying down a railroad track. He's in this to show Kearny and all those other West Pointers who did him an unfairness that he's better than they are. Revenge, pure and simple. Once you're way up there as a hero, you don't much like coming back down."

"Exactly my point," Ducatel broke in. "Which is why I say we ought to recognize that if something started to go real wrong, we should be ready to show him we're not going to be led to perdition."

Kern looked at Ducatel in amazement. With the wind whipping his hat against his thin, bony face and freezing the whiskers of his bushy mustache into brittle strands of ice, the man bore more than a passing resemblance to a scarecrow. "Are you saying we should prepare to mutiny?"

Ducatel wiped his raw, red nose. "Not mutiny, damn it, don't get me wrong, Kern. I mean that as rational men we ought to be ready if we come up against an impossible situation. If that were to happen, then maybe we might change our course a bit, that's all. And because the colonel's got his whole pride and reputation at stake, there just might come a time when we're of a better disposition to make that decision than he is. Am I right, McGehee?"

Under his wide-brimmed hat, McGehee nodded.

Kern shook his head. "If it happened, if we really did come into a bad way, that's when we'd have to be all the more ready to take his orders. That's when having a good leader is most important. It wouldn't do at all for everybody to be turning around and deciding they've got a better idea."

Ducatel turned a sudden, stabbing glare at Kern. "Now listen, Kern, what we're saying here is nothing but opinions, you understand? And a man ought to respect another man's opinions and not go spreading them around. Do you catch my drift?"

"Don't you worry," Kern scowled, "I catch it."

The column marched silently onward.

Speaking was becoming difficult, for the air had thinned considerably since the start of the day's march. In the clear morning light, the summit ahead loomed enticingly, as though it were only a few hundred yards beyond reach, but not until noon did the men finally get there. Old Bill struggled up first over the final hundred feet of windswept rock, to be followed immediately by Fremont and Godey.

"Now, there's a gift from God," Godey gasped in awe.

It did truly seem so, for to the west a breathtaking panorama extended across the San Luis Valley to the San Juan Mountains beyond. By straining an eye, it appeared that the faintest blue on the farthest horizon was actually the Pacific, but this was a delicate illusion. Still, the view exposed hundreds of miles of the snow-bound West, all framing the towering mountains that hid the Continental Divide and marked the Rockies' highest elevation.

Fremont promptly set about measuring the elevation of the peak they stood upon. At close to ten thousand feet, it was the highest point of land he had ever reached.

"Well now, Colonel," Old Bill said above the wind, "there's your mountains. And there's the way we go."

With a long, gnarled finger, he indicated one of the gentler peaks toward the southern end of the range. "That there's the pass I found back in '32."

"Laroux Pass, you mean?"

Old Bill did a mock jig of anger. "Hell no, Williams Pass, after me, goldarnit. That ignorant cotton-head Laroux was still playin' with hisself when I went through that pass."

Fremont grinned. "So why'd he get all the glory?"

"Because he's a trickster and a showman is why!

You ask any trapper who's old enough to be your grandpappy, and he'll tell you the same."

When the last of the mules had straggled up and over the peak, Fremont waved the men on. His hope was to get most of the way down the Sangre de Cristos by day's end, but this proved impossible. As the men stepped gingerly past the windswept ridge to the steep snowbound mountainside, they found their way impeded by treacherous fallen logs hidden under the drifts. Sometimes a gentle hump in the snow warned the men, but much of the fallen lumber was completely obscured, and the men ended up stumbling again and again.

For the mules, the going was even more arduous. Even though the men ahead cut a rough passage through the snow and exposed the fallen logs, the mules had to be pulled over them by a tether.

In this halting fashion, the men had traveled only a third of the way down by nightfall and were forced to camp on a hillside so steep that, to keep from rolling down to the bottom of the canyon, they made their beds of boughs padded in against pine trunks that cantilevered out from the hill.

McGehee, who had never seen such a lean-to, watched with awe as the others fashioned their own. One of the men, Lorenzo Vincenthaler, set about the task with a bustling earnestness that McGehee found quite funny.

First he measured his own height in axe-handle lengths. He determined that he was exactly three and a half axe handles tall.

Then he began measuring the fallen logs around him, after which he chopped four to accommodate his height. With McGehee's help, he banked them into the snow, two below the space where he would lie, and two above it. Two shorter logs followed, each measured to stretch across the head and foot of his little bed.

"Now you see, McGehee, that way you're guaranteed to keep from falling down, falling up, sliding out, or in any other way confounding yourself in the act of sleep. Like I always say, you make your bed, you lie in it."

Because he so loved to lecture, Vincenthaler was no one's favorite comrade. An Ohioan by birth and a merchant by choice, he had seen his small fabric business totter into bankruptcy just a year before. Now, with dreams of a new life in California dancing under his bald pate, he had come to Missouri, desperate to join a westward-bound party.

Now he proceeded to clear the snow from the enclosed space, to cover it with pine boughs, and to set a pack at one end as a pillow. Gathering his coat around him, he then stepped in and lay down.

The bed, as McGehee had already surmised, was too small.

First Vincenthaler tried stretching out his back, with his head against the pack pillow. No luck. His feet stuck out. Then he tried turning on his stomach, as if this might make some crucial difference. Again, his big booted feet protruded over the bottom log of his bed.

"I don't understand it, I don't understand it at all," he fumed.

"If I may offer a small suggestion," McGehee said, with a less than successful attempt to suppress his laughter, "the next time, you might want to cut the logs a bit longer than your height, so that when you place the short logs within their length, you'll still have room to lie down."

"My only problem," Vincenthaler snapped, "is you, McGehee. Too many cooks spoil the broth. If you had just left me alone, I'd have done just fine and dandy, thank you."

McGehee was laughing too hard by now to offer an argument. Instead, he went off to cut his own bed, taking care to benefit from Vincenthaler's mistake, and by nightfall, he was lying in it comfortably.

Soon he dozed off into a fitful sleep riddled with dreams. At first, his dreams seemed pleasant—he saw himself lying in his own warm bed at home on the plantation, nestled in the best cotton blankets money could buy. But then his dreams began to trouble him. He awoke once with a vivid image of starving in the snow. He felt terribly hungry for a long while. Then his hunger and coldness gradually diminished until he felt quite warm and content. At that point, he dreamt of falling off to sleep and having a sudden, awful realization that he was about to die. This tore him out of his imaginings and sat him up blinking in the cold night air.

He fell back asleep after midnight. At about two o'clock in the morning, he began to dream that he was a boy again, floating on a raft down the Mississippi River. All was very calm, very still, and he felt happy just lying back with his eyes closed, feeling the sun's warmth and light against his closed eyelids.

Then, somehow, the river became a raging torrent. One minute he was floating gently, the next he was being swept downriver toward a roaring sound that had to be a waterfall.

McGehee awoke to find himself tumbling out of his pine log bed. The logs had given away. He reached out desperately for something to grab onto as he fell away, but his hands clutched only air. He tried to halt his sliding, to dig his heels into the snow, but he skidded inexorably downward, his arms and legs swept around him, his head pounding against hard ground.

The worst pain came a split second later. His eyes wide open in terror, McGehee saw a darker shape through the swirling of snow and darkness. Helpless to steer himself, he slammed headlong into it, his right knee hitting first and exploding with blinding pain. Then his body crumpled against it.

Though he could feel the bark digging into his face, he was relieved he had stopped moving. Fighting the incredible pain that shot up his right side, McGehee grabbed blindly for the tree trunk as his body began to fall away again. His hands took hold of it, slid, dug in, slid again.

It was gone! McGehee was falling again with that same awful helplessness, compounded now by his terrible pain.

Another dark shape loomed, this one not so tall, but wider. A boulder! Wrenching his elbow around desperately, he managed to hit the shape with his upper arm and shoulder, then he bounced away. More pain rocketed through him, but a duller pain this time. Compared to the sharp throbbing of his knee, this new ache felt almost soothing, a diversion to take his concentration away from his other hurt.

The last pain smacked into his chest. It was another tree trunk, wider than the first and breaking his fall, but also breaking something inside of him that felt nearly as bad as his knee. For what seemed like forever, McGehee could not breathe at all. He lay wrapped around the big tree, his cheek ground into the cold stinging snow. His right side pounded. He could not distinguish the feeling of one leg from the other. There was just throbbing, exploding pain that seemed like a living thing, a demon, utterly merciless and vengeful, that took shape in his mind as a vivid color—a molten orange-red, like volcanic lava, but alive, billowing up and engulfing him.

His breathing came back to him finally, though he had to fight for each breath he took. What would it be like, he wondered, if we had to fight for every breath we took every day of our lives? What if we had to pay for each breath, pay this cruel orange-red demon? Then we would look at living as if every day were an unendurable lifetime. And how grateful we would be at last to fall into a sleep every night, as if falling into death.

Sleep. He seemed to be sleeping now, drifting in and out of sleep. With a start, McGehee realized he was fainting from pain. He looked down with tremendous effort, and the orange-red of his mind was darker there. It was blood, a rich dark blanket of blood creeping gracefully across the virgin snow.

A voice so distant that it might have been coming from the rim of the world called down to him.

"McGehee! McGehee!"

Again the voice came down to him. McGehee tried to raise his head. His own voice was so feeble that it frightened him. "Help!" he rasped.

What was wrong with the voice up there on the rim of the world? It seemed not to hear him. Other voices joined it, like an eerie chorus of seagulls. They were calling his name. They were calling for him, but they could not hear him answer. He would die down here at the bottom of the world. He would die and the demon would win.

Chapter 10

"Get rope from the mules. Tie the lengths together and make the knots tight. Kern, get a blanket. Godey, find me something I can use for bandages. And somebody get me a flask of whiskey."

Fremont's blue eyes were sternly set as he rattled out the orders. While the others appeared still groggy, he moved among them like a general rallying troops on the front lines.

In another moment he had stuffed what he needed into a small pack slung over his back, and he strapped onto his boots a pair of bentwood-and-leather snowshoes.

"But Colonel, how are you going to keep from falling yourself?" Cathcart asked anxiously.

"We'll just have to hope it's an easier hike down when you're awake than when you're asleep."

As the other men watched from the tiny ridge of their camp, Fremont began his careful descent. Once he appeared to stumble and lose his balance, but just as quickly he recovered. Soon he was a dark form silhouetted against the tall firs beyond. Then he disappeared from view altogether.

It was a bitterly cold night. As he carefully made his way downward, Fremont searched the darkness of the canyon below for a telltale plume of steamy breath. There was none.

Nor, though, was there any doubt where McGehee had fallen. Zigzagging down the bank of crusty, glistening snow was a rough, wide trough. Fremont followed the trail, reaching with some effort the first tree McGehee had hit. A trail of blood extended from it.

The way was even steeper from here on. Fremont, crouching back on his snowshoes, slid from one tree to the next, stopping at each to regain his balance. Finally, he saw it—the plume of white steam. "McGehee!" he cried out. "McGehee!"

There was no answer. Fremont pushed on, drew closer and called again. In another moment he was at McGehee's side. McGehee had fainted once more. His body was twisted unnaturally, and his right leg was pinned up at an awkward angle under his rear. One arm hung loosely downhill and the other was bent behind his back. A stream of blood had spread out from under his lower torso and legs, but what bothered Fremont most was the thin trickle of crimson at McGehee's mouth.

Fremont knew that moving the body right away could be disastrous. Better to bring McGehee back to his senses and have him describe the pain. Fremont slipped his pack off and took out a vial of smelling salts, which he opened quickly and slid under McGehee's nose.

McGehee sniffed and scowled in confusion at the sharp smell. His eyes fluttered open. He raised his head and tried to focus on the kneeling form in front of him. "Colonel?"

"How do you feel?"

"Not real good." McGehee tried to locate his pain. "My right knee's hurt pretty bad."

"What else? Any teeth knocked out? Your jaw feel broken?"

"No, uh, no. I don't think so. My arm hurts, and my chest pains me something fierce. Not as sharply as my knee, but as bad in a different way."

Fremont held the flask of whiskey to McGehee's lips and eased a long draught down his throat. "Tell me, can you move your toes?"

McGehee tried. "Left foot, I guess. Can't feel anything but pain in my right."

"All right, then. First thing is to see if you've got any broken bones there. And let's hope especially that your knee's not broken because there's no way to set it properly way out here."

As gently as he could, Fremont cut off the bottom half of McGehee's right pant leg. His knife blade was dull, but what hindered the task more was the incredible swelling around McGehee's knee. It was easily three times normal size, and with its violently black and blue coloring, it reminded Fremont of an eggplant's skin.

"Can you move that thing at all?"

McGehee tried. Wincing with the pain, he managed to bend his knee just a bit, first one way, then another. "It's broken, I know it is," he groaned.

"I'm not sure about that," Fremont returned. "If you can bend it, you may only have a king-sized scrape or a sprain. Or maybe a hairline crack in the kneecap."

With a gentle but firm touch, Fremont felt along McGehee's injured arm and shoulder. Here, too, the swelling was ample, and the skin had turned a sickening purple-black. But McGehee had managed to hit the boulder exactly as he should have, with the muscle and fat of his upper arm, rather than his elbow or shoulder or collarbone. In a week or so, Fremont could see, there would be nothing left of the injury but a shrinking bruise.

"I'm worried about your chest," Fremont said when he had finished inspecting the arm. "What does it feel like? Hurt anywhere special?"

McGehee nodded slightly. "Feels right close to the heart. Rib cage, maybe."

Fremont passed his hand slowly up McGehee's chest along each rib, right and left. McGehee gritted his teeth in pain. Finally, he cried out loud, and Fremont stopped.

"My guess is you got two ribs either cracked or broken. You might have some bleeding inside too."

"Bleeding inside?" McGehee's eyes widened in terror. "What am I going to do?"

"We'll sit out the night here. No point in trying to move before the morning. Then the others can cut a trail down close to here."

McGehee was still frightened. "You're going to leave me here till then?"

Fremont passed him the flask again. "Of course not. I'm going to sit right here with you, and I'm going to break my usual rule of abstinence and share the rest of this whiskey with you."

McGehee sank back into the snow with a sigh of relief.

"Tell me," Fremont continued when both men had taken a generous swig from the flask. "What name have you chosen for that paper you want to start in California?"

"There are several, I suppose." As McGehee grew calmer, his voice slowed into its usual lazy drawl. "My wife likes *The Sentinel*. If we started it in San Francisco, it would sound especially pleasing, don't you think? *The San Francisco Sentinel*."

"Yes, it would, by God. With Mr. Michael Mc-Gehee, Editor-in-Chief."

The two men finished off the last of the small whiskey flask. Fremont remained seated in the snow, his pack beside him. McGehee slipped off into a sleep. Once he began to cough, as if trying to clear his throat. The effort woke him, and he raised his head to spit out a gob of thick bloody phlegm. Then he settled his head back in the snow and, still breathing laboriously, slipped out of consciousness again.

Sometime after that, in the last reach of darkness, Fremont dozed off, too. He was awakened by the sharp, insistent call of a hawk, and it was that call, in a strange, inexplicable way, that made him realize Mc-Gehee was dead, even before he turned to look.

They buried McGehee right by the tree where he had died. There was no other feasible place. The mules were too weak to support his limp body all the way down to the bottom of the mountain, and as Double-back observed quietly, one piece of land was every bit as good as the other.

The men took turns digging a shallow grave. Mc-Gehee lay close by, a blanket over his stiffening form. Dark blood still spread out around him. When the grave had been dug, Doubleback stepped forward to scoop up his friend, still covered by the blanket, and placed him tenderly into the upturned earth. He stood up, crossed himself, and in a strong, clear voice, recited the Lord's Prayer. The others joined in with him.

Fremont knew the men were devastated and fright-ened. Death had found them here. Now it could come again at any time. He also felt this fear, but in a differ-ent way. He had been close to death too many times. He had seen it take friends, had even dealt it out him-self to attacking Indians.

Death was a darkly familiar presence to him, a nemesis he could only hope to shake for a while. It had always seemed to him that life was best at just those times when death was about to strike, that is, when it had been quiescent for so long that its sting had faded from the minds of men. It was at that moment that it returned, and all of a man's freshly blooming illusions of peace and permanence were dashed.

On an expedition, this was especially true. Until someone died on the trail, an expedition always possessed a carnival gaiety. Men and mules paraded forth; the air was crisp and the sky was blue; vaulting, buoyant joy was everywhere. But when a man died, so did the carnival. And though all the others might make their way and reach their goal, the taste of death always remained to sour the conquest. Only when those men were set free of each other's company, only when they hit town and dispersed, would the taste of that dark, familiar presence be forgotten.

It took another day's descent to reach the San Luis Valley, and another long day after that to cross it. A haunting aura of unreality seemed to surround the men as they made their way through the unbroken silence of the snowbound valley. Not a bird or coyote could be heard, nor even a rushing brook. And not a single tree could be seen across this wide, flat plain. Instead, in the bracing cold and brutal wind, the men were treated to the strange, ironic sight of huge sand hills, almost as white as the snow, but snowless, for the wind had swept them clean.

"What in the Goddamn hell is that sand doing here?" Doubleback asked Cathcart.

"Been here longer than you, my friend. The Bible says the whole world was covered with water for forty days. Every here and there you see a few signs of that flood, just to remind you."

Despite the cold, Fremont decided to stop and examine the sand hills. He called an early halt to the day's march, much to the others' relief, and he set out, carrying his instrument pack, accompanied only by Godey.

From the top of the sand hills, he felt a deep peace come over him. It was strange, in a way, to be distanced from the others, to see them clustered around a small greasewood fire half a mile away. Yet he felt relieved, too. For a short while, he could shake off the feeling that he must lead these men, that he must always be more aware than they of all the dangers that lay before them. As their leader he was a different man from the one Jessie knew. He couldn't let out a shout just for the thrill of hearing his voice bouncing back across a canyon.

"Cold?" he asked Godey.

Godey had pulled his buckskin coat more tightly around him and folded his massive arms across his chest.

"A bit. Not so bad."

"Be nice to have a steaming hot bath right now, wouldn't it? A good hot bath, and a robe and slippers, and a fire roaring in the parlor hearth."

Godey laughed. "But then we wouldn't be looking out over all this, would we? We'd just be bored sitting around with all the womenfolk."

Fremont took out a compass and his record book. "I wonder if the others still feel like you do."

"Sure, I guess. No one's turning back, eh?"

"No one could, now. That's what gets me thinking. There always comes a time on an expedition when the food's running low and it's cold and the men could use that hot bath, and maybe they're halfway between where they started from and where they're going to. That's when they begin to get really quiet, you know what I mean? Just real quiet."

Godey nodded. "Best to ignore them. Hear them out, and before you know it, you've got a mutiny on your hands."

"But if you do ignore them, you may get caught unawares. There's some who'd say the best idea is to keep an ear cocked for all the gossip and griping that goes on, so you can have a plan worked out."

"Maybe so. But I seen it go wrong the other way, too, in Utah, half a dozen winters back. I was with a wagon train of settlers from Boston and thereabouts. All greenhorns except for me, I guess. I was supposed to be scouting, but I wasn't the leader exactly. Another fellow was, a big bragging merchant from Boston who had his whole family with him. See, he'd organized the group. And they brought so much equipment you could have built a town—when they started out, that is. Soon enough, of course, they found it weighed them down, and summer was runnin' out, and they began to throw off whatever they could so they could make it to California before the winter."

"Didn't make it?"

"Not by a damned sight. I'd warned them about traveling light from the very start, but that Boston fellow wouldn't listen. Seemed all he cared to hear was every piece of gossip floating in the air. Before we were halfway there, he was shaking in his boots from worry that the others might try to take charge from him. Not that it mattered so much who was in charge, but with all these greenhorns you needed some kind of leader. The short of it was that he got to seeing conspiracies all around him, and he'd take to every side he saw, badmouthing one fellow to someone else, then bad-mouthing that one back to the first. It finally got so everyone knew what he was up to, and no one trusted him as far as they could throw him."

"That's true enough," Fremont said. "A man can't start taking sides unless he plans to stick to the same one through the entire battle."

"Well, this fellow didn't. So when the snows came and we were out of food, he couldn't make the others do a damned thing. They just wouldn't ration what little provisions they had left. At first they were too sissified to eat mule meat, but soon they came to likin' it, all right. And they were too poor with their guns to bag much game. I'd go out and shoot something when I could, but as soon as I'd get back into camp, they'd practically kill me for the meat, then fight each other like animals till it was gone. Of course, the strongest ones got all the meat that way, and a few of the weaker ones, women and children and such, began to die off."

Godey shook his head at the memory. "It was awful. If only that fellow'd been able to make them all work together, they might have come out of it a whole lot better."

"How many made it all the way?"

"Ten out of the forty that started. But the worst of it was, half the others got to eating the corpses of the first ones that died."

Fremont looked up from his record book in amazement. "I've heard tell of that," he said. "But I truly can't imagine it."

"People get desperate," Godey shrugged. "Maybe any man would."

"Eat human flesh? I wouldn't, I swear it. You wouldn't either, Godey. I mean, you didn't, did you?"

"No, I didn't. And I think I would starve to death before I did. But then, on that journey, I always knew I could find game of some kind. The others didn't know that. They thought they were staring death right in the eye. 'Course, as it turned out, they were."

Fremont groaned. "No wonder you keep your sense of humor so subdued, Godey."

"But what if you knew there was no way to stay alive unless you ate human meat? What would you do, Colonel?"

Fremont pondered for a moment. "I'd die, because I couldn't stand to live a single day knowing I'd done that. I'd never be able to forget."

"I think I'd die too, Colonel. But I'm not so sure as you are. Seems the older I get, the less I'm sure of."

Next day, the men encountered their first major defeat in their war with the winter weather. Across the broad and treeless plain of the San Luis Valley came a howling snowstorm with winds so cold they cut right through layers of clothing. All morning the men resolutely pushed forward against the storm, heads bowed, working hard just to put one foot in front of the other, but all to no avail. By early afternoon, with no shelter ahead for a campsite, Fremont reluctantly ordered a retreat. Back they went to their campsite of the night before, to the leeward of a shallow rise in the land that at least cut the wind a bit.

A clear, cold day followed, and now the men labored to make up for lost time. Inspired, too, by the prospect of reaching the far end of the windy valley, they marched forward at a hard, fast clip from dawn to sundown. This time, their efforts were rewarded, for they reached the valley's end and the frozen Rio Grande. They camped there in the shelter of a copse of trees, and celebrated when Cathcart and Godey returned from a late afternoon hunt—with an elk to be roasted for dinner.

Afterward, Fremont sat with Old Bill to talk over which way the group might best proceed.

"Different ways," Williams allowed. "Like I told you before, Colonel. And either way I'm tellin' you is better than the way you're thinkin' to go. Say we turn up now from the Rio Grande, meet Saquache Creek, and turn into Cochetopa Pass. That's the northerly route, and a good one. Takes us through the San Juans at a pretty low elevation. Best for that damn railroad, too."

"Not best for the railroad," Fremont said wearily. Old Bill, he thought, would never give up. "What point would there be in starting a line in St. Louis that heads due west to the San Juan Mountains, then detours north around the range just to head south and west again? They might as well run a railroad out of New York or Washington."

"Exactly so," Old Bill grumbled.

"And for the same reason we don't want the southern route, down around the mountains into New Mexico. Then they'd be better off running the rails from New York down to Atlanta, say, and from Atlanta due west across Texas. Fact is, that would leave St. Louis out of the picture altogether."

"Which I'd be more'n happy about, tell you the truth," Old Bill said. "But yes, yes, I know we can't do that. So the middle route is the way we go."

The two men left each other with sour looks.

Perhaps it was the proximity of the river, or perhaps, as Doubleback hinted, it was an omen of sorts, but the next morning brought a dense, rolling fog over the land. Fremont and Old Bill led the men directly along the Rio Grande in a northwesterly direction, away from the rugged hills of New Mexico below them and into the maw of Colorado's San Juan Mountains, the highest and most forbidding range of the Rockies.

By noon the fog had still shown no sign of dissipating. By the sound of running water up ahead, Old Bill guessed that they were approaching Embargo Creek. But not until the men stood on its edge could they see the thin twisting rivulet swollen by melted snow. Only the force of its current had kept the creek from freezing. As the men crossed, up to their knees in frigid water, they shared the feeling of entering some foreign and forbidding country.

Somewhat farther on, they stopped for the night at Aider Creek, which seemed to present yet another omen, for it was, to their surprise, already frozen solid. Creutzfeldt attributed this to the creek's smaller and shallower bed, but nearly frozen feet and the surrounding chilly mist made it difficult not to imagine that every step now would lead into colder territory.

Fortunately, the fog vanished by morning. As he gazed about him at the silent, glistening white valley that fanned out from the creek, Old Bill had an idea. Rather than moving due west and then cutting north along Willow Creek, why not head up in a straight northwest diagonal? It would cut many miles off their trek.

With some reluctance, Fremont agreed. The trudge that morning started out through two feet of powdery, unmarked snow. Up the side of the valley they went, pulling their weary mules behind them. They had hoped for a gentle slope beyond the valley's ridge, but they were soon disappointed. Instead, they reached their first clear view yet of the San Juan Mountains. All the way from where the men now stood to those farthest peaks, snow lay in great rolling drifts. In the distance, too, whole mountainsides of ice glinted brilliantly in the sun. It was a stunning, sweeping vision, so bleak that it seemed like a landscape out of a dream.

To the left stretched three low ridges, leading up to the mountainsides like the splayed fingers of a hoary hand. Toward these the men now marched. It took them an hour to plod up the slope that led to the nearest ridge. After a brief conference, Fremont and Old Bill chose to scale the ridge's south side. That way, they would be traversing both up and west in a direction that would bring them, they hoped, to the route leading north to Williams Pass.

A fresh snow had fallen on the mountains the previous night. As the men arduously wound their way up along the side of the ridge, they encountered deeper and deeper drifts. Harry King, whose feet had nearly frozen only a few days before, again lost all feeling in his toes. Grimly, he resolved not to complain. Besides, he had now grown more afraid of the snow itself than of frostbite. Would the drifts get so deep, he wondered, that the men would have to burrow through them like moles? Surely Fremont would turn back before that happened. Or would he?

Farther back in the long, ragged line of men and mules, Ducatel was having the same doubts. He could barely see through the glare of the snow, and he had to grit his teeth through the pain while he kept moving his toes, else he would surely lose them.

As the way grew steeper, the mules began slipping. First one, then another failed to keep its footing and tumbled off the winding snow-packed trail into high drifts. Each time it happened, the party was forced to pause, and two or three men had to push and pull the quivering beast back up from its haunches. Finally, one of the mules pitched forward and let out a cry of sudden pain. Even before Cathcart rolled the mule on its side to see what had happened, he knew its leg had been broken.

"No chance, eh?" Fremont said as he joined Cathcart.

"Look. You can see the bone sticking out there."

Fremont turned to the mule nearest him and slid the rifle from its pack. At a distance of five feet, only one shot was needed. The report rang out, and the mule's head yanked back. A gush of dark blood ran out from the blackened wound behind its ear. Its leg muscles twitched, then the mule was still. The men pushed on and the mule was left for carrion.

Kern's admiration for Fremont had bordered on reverence from the moment he had joined the expedition. But that confidence was rudely shaken when the men piled out of their pine-bough lean-tos the next morning. Below them lay the sloping ridge, and ahead, almost hidden by a howling curtain of snow that swept like grapeshot into their eyes, rose a rocky, ice-encrusted hillside. There appeared to be no easy route around it, no choice but to go forward or retreat.

Even that choice would dissolve if the men could not find some way to deal with the ever-deepening banks of snow. In many places the drifts rose higher than a man was tall, making the climb clearly impossible for the mules.

Resolutely, Fremont gave the order to chop down pine boughs, which would be used to beat a path. Then, after the strongest mules had been loaded up with some of the baggage the weakest were unable to support, the party prepared to advance against the stinging wind.

It was then that Kern began to feel his first real doubts stirring within himself. The hillside was perhaps only three hundred feet high, but it took the men two hours to climb it. They fought for every step, beating down snowdrifts with their clubs, pulling terrified mules by their tethers, enduring relentless whirls of icy wind that forced them to advance with their eyes squinted closed.

Up ahead, Fremont pushed on tenaciously. One by one, the other men were forced to stop briefly, either to tuck a coat in tighter or to rub warmth back into their faces, but the colonel never stopped. By the time the others reached the top of the hill, he had entirely recovered his strength while waiting for them.

They pitched camp there and settled in, grateful for a dinner of mashed corn and pemmican, and for the feeble warmth of a small fire. Kern discovered that his socks had frozen to his feet. The pain, as the fire thawed them and the blood pulsed back through his veins, was almost unbearable. Had he been alone, he knew he would have cried aloud. Here, surrounded by other men who were equally cold, Kern fought back his tears, gritted his teeth and stared furiously into the fire.

More than two dozen mules died in the next two days. Some fell down steep mountain faces, others simply collapsed from weariness and starvation, for once again the men had been forced to cut the mules' rations. So far, no one had suggested eating the dead mules. Instead, the beasts remained where they had fallen, a mute testimony to the growing desperation of the entire expedition.

Each day the men advanced by only a few miles, despite Fremont's insistence that they march during all but the first and last grey hours between dawn and darkness.

On December 16, the men reached the summit of the Pool Table Mountains. "Six deep canyons, like pockets on a table," Old Bill remarked. So windy was the terrain, and so unprotected, that they were forced

to stagger back down to the camp they had made the
night before.

It was during the next afternoon, as they followed
Fremont back up the slope they had lost the previous
day, that Kern's eyelids froze shut.

For an hour or more, he had kept his eyes closed
except for the briefest instances to squint at the blinding white snow to be sure he was still in line with the
others. Now he could not open them. He panicked and
shouted out to King, who was directly ahead of him.

"Goddamnit, King, I can't see!"

King floundered back to him through the snow,
himself barely able to see.

"Your face is all red," he said, rubbing a gloved
hand against Kern's frozen whiskers.

Kern seized the hand in desperate fear. "Look, I'm
telling you, I can't open my eyes, and they hurt like
hell."

"Okay, okay, I'll go for the colonel."

Kern tried to force himself to walk on. From behind him, Cathcart trotted up and lent him an arm. Together, the men struggled step by painful step.

Cathcart surrendered his charge to Fremont,
whose own face was as raw with windburn as Kern's.

"Can't see at all?" Fremont asked, his arm sup-
porting Kern's shivering form.

"All I see is red. It's like I'm looking right into
the sun, Colonel."

"All right, Henry," Fremont said as easily as if he
were talking from a parlor chair by a crackling hearth.
"Now, first thing, don't try to open your eyes for a
while. Meantime, I'll tie this around your head." Fremont took off his own woollen scarf. "That should cut
the wind and start warming up your eyelids. Pretty
soon your eyelashes will come unstuck, but keep your

eyes closed anyway. Besides, you don't need them. I'll walk you."

Kern nodded numbly. He was bitterly cold, and his eyes ached relentlessly. The wind raged against him as if taunting him, tugging at his clothes and face and hair. It was a burning, sunset red he saw, like the red in a prairie fire. That was odd somehow. Fire red and freezing cold. It was like a preacher describing hell. Kern wished he could paint it. It would be reddest at the center, and surrounded by concentric rings of dark crimson, as if you had tossed a stone into a pool of fire. And it would be scarlet right out to the edges.

The last thing Kern remembered was the grip of a strong hand at his arm, holding tightly to keep him from falling down.

Chapter 11

Jessie Benton Fremont opened her eyes to a bedroom bathed in morning light. Still half asleep, she nestled deeper into the soft feather bed, pulled a fluffy green and white coverlet up to her chin and looked around, wondering dreamily where she was. Westport—it suddenly came to her. John must be down getting breakfast . . .

"Goddamn that Calhoun!" came a thundering voice up the stairs. "Doesn't have a bit of moral fiber left in that white trash southern body of his!"

The gentle murmur of female remonstrance that followed the man's outburst proved ineffective.

"But can't you see, Elizabeth? He doesn't even care. I mean, if he felt owning slaves was truly honorable, why, I might abide by that. Not that I'd agree with it, mind you, but the point is, he doesn't feel at all. He's just a two-bit southern cracker, the kind of politician who tarnishes the reputation of the entire Senate. He would lie to heaven for his own advantage. And furthermore . . ."

His voice was drowned out by a sudden crash of crockery, followed immediately by a piercing, plaintive cry.

Jessie sat up abruptly, now all too aware that she

was once again in her family's home in St. Louis and lying in her old bed. As usual her father was carrying on downstairs in the kitchen. In the eyes of the public, she knew that her father seemed an impressive figure, a powerful senator from Missouri, a fierce fighter for civil rights and a champion of the westward expansion to California. But to Jessie and her family, Thomas Hart Benton was a lovable and undeniably blustery father, given to tirades at breakfast which, of course, often turned out to be the oral rough drafts for impassioned speeches to the nation.

How odd it felt to be back at home. There was, in a sense, nowhere that Jessie felt more comfortable and contented. Here she could sink back into the world she had known as a girl in her first bloom of beauty, a world where she was cared for and cosseted by her father and her sweet, delicate mother.

Yet the place made Jessie feel terribly disjointed. From the moment she had set eyes on John Fremont nearly nine years ago, she had been growing apart from her family. Her soul, she knew, was completely entwined with his own, and to be kept from him, even for only a short while, made even a comfortable place alien and torturous to her.

"What was that noise, Father?" she finally called out.

"Mornin', Jessie! Just some crockery. Hope we didn't wake you, my dear."

Her father spoke to her somewhat sheepishly from the kitchen as he gathered up the last shards off the floor.

"Goodness, no. You'd already awakened me with all that talk of Calhoun."

Jessie, at twenty-four, was the youngest of the three Benton sisters and had always been her father's favorite. At an early age, she had shown a plucky spirit and quick, agile mind, so that everyone who met her called her the very spit and image of her father. "Spunk-and-Gumption," she had been called in school, and at a later age, "Benton-in-petticoats." When she came home with those petticoats torn from climbing trees or racing boys, as she often did, her father had been hard put to show disapproval, for in fact he was delighted to see Jessie grapple with every scrambling, rough-and-tumble challenge she encountered. "You talk to the girl," he would tell his wife gruffly, and then he would walk off somewhere. Of course, he always reappeared in beaming good spirits as soon as he had heard the motherly lecture conclude.

As Jessie grew out of her girlish gawkiness into a striking young woman, she also grew ever closer to her father. Indeed, there were times when Elizabeth McDowell Benton felt that her husband and daughter had a stronger bond between them than she had with either of them. Especially after Eliza and Francesca had been betrothed and married, Jessie and her father would set off on long afternoon walks whenever he was home from Washington. Together they would discuss and argue poiltics so heatedly that they would be utterly oblivious to the many smiles of amusement and affection from passers-by.

And so it had gone until Jessie, with characteristic spirit and passion, fell headlong in love with a dashing young figure who once came visiting her father.

At that point, Jessie and her father had drawn off in fierce confrontation. The senator had railed at her, in stentorian tones, that she was too young for such a strong involvement. Jessie, in turn, had declared herself at sixteen to be quite old enough to make up her own mind about matters of the heart. Besides, her father could scarcely object to the suitor in question. Why, for months and months the name of John Charles

Fremont had been bruited about the household with the greatest respect and affection. Young Fremont, her father had often remarked, was just the sort of fellow the country needed—honest, strong and adventurous.

In the end, of course, Jessie had prevailed, though her father had hurriedly sent Fremont on a far-reaching expedition in the hope that the romance might fade. He had also introduced Jessie to other young women of more conservative tastes who might help to thwart her avowed intention to marry. He had even introduced his daughter to other young men who were closer to Jessie in age and solidly planted in some professional track that would have them in school or apprenticeships for years to come.

All his efforts came to no avail. The women had proved to be simpering bores, and the men had proved fit only for those women. In fact, Benton had grown to disdain these young Fauntleroys so much that he began to wish for Fremont's return. And when Fremont did return, the romance had proved to be undimmed. Jessie and John Fremont had been married with the Bentons' grudging consent, and after an initial period of awkwardness on all sides, Benton came to be so fond of Fremont—and so eager to have him join in the fight for westward expansion—that he even convinced himself he had been the first to suggest the two might get along, had introduced them because of this conviction and had always intended them to marry. "Just not quite so soon as you did, Jess," the senator had explained.

Jessie's relationship with her father had then settled back toward what it had formerly been. The two took walks again when the family was at home and they still discoursed upon contemporary issues. But for all that, they now behaved more as two adults who enjoyed each other's company than as a doting father and his youngest daughter. To Jessie's mother, that change came as a great relief and, in fact, after Jessie's wedding, the Bentons enjoyed a gentle second bloom in their own marriage. They now had only their last child in the house: Randolph, their only son, an earnest, contemplative boy who did little to disrupt the new-found calm that had settled over their modest estate. Only during the older children's visits did the home fill up with the laughter and jocularity it had seen in years past.

"Mrs. Fremont, is my granddaughter up?"

Before Jessie could answer, a bleary-eyed Lilly padded into the kitchen in bathrobe and slippers, yawning so ferociously that she could only wave good morning as she slid into her seat.

"Well!" Mrs. Benton exclaimed. "So this is the lively child who's going to travel through the jungle to California?"

"Sure, Grandma," Lilly managed at last. "Then I can sleep all day in the boat."

"I wouldn't bet on that, young lady," Benton smiled. "You may find the ride a little rougher than the one down from Westport. For one thing, you won't be sailing on a nice, quiet river. You'll be on the ocean. Do you know the exact difference between the two, Lilly?"

"A river is a natural stream of water flowing into a lake or ocean," the eight-year-old replied without batting an eyelash. "An ocean is the body of saltwater that covers most of the earth's surface and can be divided into five sections, Atlantic, Pacific, Indian, Arctic and Antarctic."

The senator cast a wry glance at his wife. "Yes, well—another corn fritter, Lilly?" he asked. "They're quite good, actually."

* * *

"Whoah there, little lady! Careful as you go."

Lilly grudgingly accepted the driver's helping hand and climbed the two high steps into the Silver Stallion Rapid Express Stagecoach that stood awaiting its passengers for its regular run up to New York. Jessie followed, then came a grunting Benton, his younger brother Richard, and the Bentons' maid, Harriet.

The senator had hoped to accompany Jessie and Lilly to California. It would do him good to get a little western air in his lungs again, he had declared. But politics had intervened. President Polk had been swept out of office by Zachary Taylor that autumn, and at last Washington had a man in the White House who felt as Thomas Hart Benton did, that the West must be vigorously charted, settled and kept clean of the British and French. That meant, however, that there was much work to be done in the Senate if California was to be brought into the Union.

So the senator would have to stay East. He would ride with Jessie to New York before heading down to Washington. In his stead, as companion and protector, his brother Richard would make the trip. Privately, Jessie still snorted at the prospect of her sweet, mild-mannered uncle offering her protection from anything. But she knew it would go far toward soothing her mother's concern over Jessie's safety. It would soothe her father, too. Applaud her as he might, Jessie knew that under all his bluster, her father was as concerned over her protection as any father could be.

The other member of the Bentons' party, Harriet, was a slim, stunning young black woman. Harriet, a beneficiary of Benton's kindness, had worked for the family nearly ten years. As a slave girl of fifteen, she had been put up for sale on an Atlanta auction block by her wealthy white master. Benton had happened by, passing through town on a business call, and his compassion had been piqued by the sight of this slim, dark girl being so callously treated. He fiercely outbid a crowd of leering plantation owners, then braved their catcalls as he made off with the girl beside him.

Harriet had at first been terrified of him. Here was this red-thatched, fiery-looking white man who looked for all the world like the master of a hundred slaves and the kind who would beat every one of them regularly. But when she discovered that he intended to take her up to St. Louis to set her free, Harriet fell to her knees, weeping in shock and fright. She was a black girl in a white man's world. How, she cried, would she make her way? He then had agreed to let her come to work for him, at least until she could earn the money to pay him back. Ten years later, Benton had still refused to take a cent from her, and Harriet still refused to leave. Secretly, Benton was pleased, but he did find it embarrassing to explain to friends who came to visit why one of the country's most impassioned critics of slavery kept a black servant in his house.

Now, at last, Harriet had seen a way to both repay her benefactor and strike out for a new life in a new land. When she learned that Jessie and Lilly were setting out for California, she immediately volunteered to go along. She had turned a deaf ear to the Bentons' protests about the rigors of the journey. And when it became clear that nothing would shake the woman's resolve, Jessie embraced her and welcomed her company.

"Mother, there's still something I don't understand," Lilly said as she watched the bare fields and rolling hills of Missouri go by. "If we want to travel to California, why do we go east to New York?"

"It's the only place to get a steamer to Chagres, dear."

"But we could go to Florida and take a boat from there."

"But you can see your cousins in New York," Benton explained. "You'll like that, won't you Lilly?"

"Given the distance of the detour, I'm not sure a visit with relatives is worth it," Lilly prettily informed her grandfather.

"Harrumph," Benton grumbled, sitting back. "Teach this little vixen yourself, do you, Jess?"

When they had ridden for half an hour through the countryside, Jessie brought out a sumptuous basket lunch of home-baked bread, fresh cheese and Madeira. Richard, as usual, succeeded in consuming nearly the entire bottle himself.

Richard was his brother's junior by a dozen years. He was also, unfortunately, his junior in other ways and knew it. Neither as intelligent nor as intrepid as Thomas Hart Benton, Richard had ignored an opportunity to follow his brother into law, and had never considered a political career. Instead, he had let his languor lead him into an appointed government post which was procured for him by his brother.

In the years since, Richard had steered his career slowly and unimpressively. He was now Assistant Purchaser of Municipal Supplies, which gave him access to any sort of booty he fancied. As a result, his home was filled with stationery, quills, cattle yokes, abacuses, rugs, desks, widgets and weaving looms.

There were two other passengers in the coach, both tall and, judging by the elaborate stitching on their jackets and boots, both Texans. They had been silent from the start of the trip, refusing Jessie's offer to share the basket lunch and burying their whiskered faces in their newspapers. Now, from behind the paper, one of the men laughed scornfully.

"Will you listen to this, Edgar," he said, and proceeded to read. " 'It is reported by local residents in the trapping settlement of Pueblo, Colorado, that Colonel John C. Fremont, with a party of thirty-three men and close to one hundred mules, passed through a week ago Monday. He expressed the intention of passing over the entire Rocky Mountain Range by New Year's Day, thereby proving it possible to lay a central railroad line from St. Louis to the Pacific coast.'

"Now can you believe that hogwash, Edgar? That no-good show-off mighta taken a lesson from General Kearny, but no, he's got to go and drag three dozen innocent men into the Rockies, smack-dab in the middle of winter."

"I beg your pardon," said Richard, flushed from both wine and anger. "Do you know with whom you're sharing this coach?"

"Shush up, Richard," Jessie said. "No sense in arguing with strangers."

"This is Colonel Fremont's wife," Richard went on, undeterred. "And this is Senator Benton of Missouri. And who, may I ask, do you presume to be?"

The two men exchanged a quick, conspiratorial look. "It's no matter to you," said the first one.

"Well, what is of concern to us is your insulting the name of Colonel John Charles Fremont," Richard declared.

The first man started to speak, but his partner, a character so tall that his legs were scrunched up halfway to his chest, laid a restraining hand on his arm. "Man's right," he said, then turned to Jessie with an obviously insincere expression of apology. "He was just readin' the paper, ma'am. Didn't mean no harm."

"I did too, Edgar!" the first man exclaimed. "Oh, come on, dag blast it. A little talk don't make a damn bit o' difference to anybody." He turned to Jessie. "Fact is, ma'am, with all due respect, I happen not to think your husband's doin' much good takin' men over the Rockies."

"And what do you know about it?" Jessie shot back. "You know only what you read in the paper, and you draw your own two-bit conclusions out of your jealousy and ignorance."

"That's not true, ma'am," the man protested. "I followed your husband's gadding about in California, and I followed the news of his court-martial. And as you're bein' so forthright here, well, I'll be the same way. Fact is, he refused to take orders from his superiors, and in the army they call that mutiny."

"My husband," hissed Jessie in a tone so cutting it made the two men wince, "had only one superior officer in the territory of California, and that was Commodore R. F. Stockton, to whom, I might add, the Honorable General Stephen Watts Kearny should also have reported. But Kearny worked behind Stockton's back and got Polk's blessing. That's when he said my husband refused to obey his superiors. He got presidential authority to take command, but he didn't show his documents to anyone. He just kept giving out orders, and my husband refused to obey. Now is that mutiny, sir? Well, is it?"

"I'm not sure," said the first man, now looking thoroughly confused.

"Hell," his partner said to him. "You don't know what mutiny is, birdbrain. You never been in the dang army."

"As for his current expedition," Jessie went on, "what objections do you have to finding a route for a central railroad line to California? Why, if we had more trains running across this country, you and I would never have had to share a stagecoach."

"You needn't worry about that again," said the first man.

"Keep your trap shut, you big oaf," his partner growled.

The group lapsed into an uncomfortable silence. Jessie stared angrily out the stagecoach window, and Richard fell quickly into a wine-induced sleep, while Lilly napped with her head resting on his arm. As for the senator, he kept his gaze fixed on the text of a speech he intended to give at the opening legislative session.

Suddenly there came a quick spattering of gunfire ahead. Outside, the driver reined in his horses with an angry oath. Jessie heard him reach around and slide his rifle out of its leather holster.

The senator reached into his vest pocket for the tiny pistol he always kept loaded and handy.

"Hold it right there, Senator."

The voice belonged to one of their fellow passengers. As Benton watched in stupefaction, the first stranger waved a long-barreled pistol in his face. "Oh, this is rich," said the taller one. "I'll be tellin' this one to my grandchildren around the fire."

"What you're going to do folks," said the first man, with a wide, toothy smile, "is to very slowly, very casually, hand over all your money and valuables." He turned to Jessie. "Good thing you're married to a man like Fremont. Fellow like that's always around to protect you." At this he let loose a braying laugh that made Jessie sick with rage.

For a moment no one moved.

"Hey, we're not kiddin', folks," the first man shouted. "Open those bags now and get that money out."

Jessie moved before she had time to consider how foolish her action might be. As the first stranger dropped his jaw in amazement, she reached over with lightning speed, putting her own body between the pistol and her father, then twisted the man's gun hand down, pointing the long barrel at his own leg. The second man, galvanized, pushed a large hand into Jessie's face to force her back. The ensuing explosion rocked the whole coach.

"Yow!" The first Texan screamed in pain and clutched at his leg. Jessie wrested the gun free. Now her father pulled out his own small firearm, and the second man shrank back into the corner of the coach.

"How many men out there?" Jessie demanded.

"Just two, honest."

"There'd better be only two, because if there's more, we'll start whittling the number down with you," Benton threatened in a sharp whisper.

The second man gulped nervously. "Four," he croaked. "Four men."

"All right, stranger," Jessie said, "quiet now." The stagecoach came to a complete stop, and they heard the clatter of hooves fast approaching. "I want you to lean out of this window in a nice, friendly fashion, do you understand? Then I want you to call your friends over to give you a hand with dragging all the money and valuables out of here."

The stranger nodded. His accomplice began to moan through gritted teeth, clutching his leg and rocking in pain.

"Shut up," the second man snarled.

"I'd listen to your partner if I were you," Benton suggested. "Else you might find a bullet in the other leg, too."

The clatter of hooves ceased. The other highwaymen had stopped twenty paces from the coach.

"Now," Jessie hissed at the second stranger.

Nodding fearfully, he leaned out the window. "Got two bags full in here, Mike," he called out. "Need a little help."

One set of hooves clopped toward the coach. A big man slid out of the saddle, his boots hitting the ground hard. Then a craggy, dirt-streaked face appeared in the window.

Jessie pushed the gun tight against the stranger's back. Benton's own gun, which he held down low, was aimed directly at the first man's heart. That man, on Jessie's suggestion, had put a satchel on top of his bleeding leg. His hat was pulled low over his face, and his beard hid any expression of pain.

The second stranger turned the door latch. The door swung open. The man outside set his rifle by the door and climbed in to get a better grip on the bag held out to him. He should have seen the trap, but he was much too nervous. He looked less like a highwayman than a wino in need of a drink.

Before he could reach for the gun at his side, Benton hauled him all the way into the coach, and in one smooth gesture, slid the pistol out of its holster.

"Down on the floor," Benton commanded in a low voice.

The dumbstruck man complied, and when he was on his stomach, Benton pulled his hands behind him. Richard, his face pale with shock, reluctantly accepted the small pistol from his brother and solemnly held it a few inches from the long, matted hair at the back of the prone stranger's head.

"What now?" Jessie asked her father.

"Now it gets a bit tricky," he replied. Despite the danger they now faced, Thomas Hart Benton seemed to be enjoying himself thoroughly.

"Cover me, honey," Benton whispered to Jessie.

With strong, sure movements, he took hold of the door handle, climbed over the stranger and emerged with the highwayman's pistol aimed at the front of the coach. For a moment, the men on horseback failed to see him. Then one gave a shout, and simultaneously, Benton fired once, twice, three times. One of the men fell from his mount. Another clutched his shoulder with an oath and dropped his rifle. The third man got off one shot that caught the horse Benton was standing behind in the rear flank. Now the third man had a bead on the senator.

The wounded horse whinnied, weaved, and fell to its knees in a tangle of reins.

Suddenly a volley of gunfire lifted the third man out of his saddle and hurled him backward to the ground with a thump. In the resounding echo of the shots, the stagecoach driver leapt from his seat, and Benton came out from beside the coach, his gun pointed at the second mounted rider, whose uninjured arm was raised in surrender.

"Nice work, Senator," the driver grinned and spat in satisfaction.

"You know these guys?"

The driver looked at the two bodies lying in the dust. "Yeah, I seen 'em before. Local boys. They used to run with McCluskey before he got took. Guess they're not too great on their own. Are you, Jake?"

Jake also spat into the dust and wiped a speck of spittle from his lips.

"Off the horse, Jake."

"What do we do with them, driver?"

"Personally, Senator, I'd like to line them all up and put them out of their misery, and out of my hair."

"Much as I'm inclined to agree with you, my friend, I'm afraid we'd best restrain ourselves. What's the nearest town?"

"Richmond. Got a good, strong jail there, don't they, Jake?"

Jake did not answer.

"All right," the driver said. "Let's tie 'em to their

horses, hands to the horn, feet to the stirrups. Two of 'em are going to have to ride double, 'cause we need one of their horses to replace the one they shot."

The wounded horse was lying in the dust sweating profusely and drooling. The driver stepped over to the suffering animal.

"Had this horse for three years. Never once let me down." Calmly the driver took aim at the horse's panicked eyes and fired. The animal kicked and struggled to rise. Another shot followed. The horse lay still.

"Best not to let Jess and Lilly see this," Benton told the driver. "Jess can abide a gun pointed at her heart, but she cries to see any animal die."

From inside the coach, Jessie stuck her head out in consternation. "You all right, Father?"

"All fine, all fine," Benton answered, rejoining his daughter at the window. He peered inside solicitously. "Everybody safe in there?"

"I think so. Lilly?"

"I'm okay, I think," Lilly said.

"Richard?" Jessie asked.

Still guarding his quarry with a limp and shaky hand, Richard managed, "Is it all over now?" Laughter rocked the coach.

"And where, pray tell, is Harriet?" Benton asked.

From under the seat came a tiny voice. "Is it safe yet, Miz Benton?"

"Oh, Harriet, you can come out now. It's all right," responded Jessie.

Harriet emerged sheepishly, her eyes darting distrustfully from one face to another. "Well, I didn't have no gun," Harriet declared, trying to rescue her dignity.

Benton and Jessie broke into peals of laughter again.

"Harriet, how are you going to make it to California when you get the wits scared out of you by a few third-rate highwaymen?" Benton asked.

"Travelin' on water, that's different," Harriet said confidently. "They's no robbers in the ocean."

"No, I suppose there aren't," the senator mumbled.

Chapter 12

Lilly's first glimpse of New York hardly provided the stirring spectacle she had thought it would. In her mind, she had pictured a fairyland of winding, red-bricked streets lined with the neat facades of elegant town-houses and rows of stately gaslights flickering at dusk. There would be black lacquer carriages trimmed with lacy fringe, conveying beautiful, porcelain-skinned society ladies in white, ruffled hoop skirts. Escorting the ladies would be slick-haired rich young men dressed in riding tails and ascots.

Instead, as the stagecoach drew within five miles of the city, Lilly began to see the rudest little homesteads imaginable, wooden shanties with sagging roofs, set on ragged patches of farmland.

Closer to the city, the farms became more sizable and the houses better constructed. Here and there Lilly saw a horse-drawn plow, followed by the tiny, stooped figure of a farmer. Not until they were almost to the Hudson River, however, did she lay her eyes on the rough, colorless assemblage of smoking houses and buildings that cluttered Manhattan Island.

"Mother, is that all it is?" she cried out.

"Hush now, Lilly, it just looks bad from a distance. Close up, you'll find nice parts to it, don't you worry."

The stagecoach discharged the Bentons at the far banks of the Hudson River. They then boarded a steam engine ferry, but not before the driver had fervently shaken the senator's hand in gratitude for his help with the highwaymen.

Because of the strong current of the Hudson, the steamer ferry debarked from upstream, then half chugged, half drifted across and down the river to reach its gunnysack-lined slip in the midst of New York harbor.

As she jumped off the ferry, Lilly's eyes widened. She could barely take it all in, the bustling crowds, the shouting, the motley red-brick buildings that stood against each other like dominoes askew. Out across the harbor was a sprinkling of tiny islands, showing almost no signs of life except for a lighthouse or a moored boat. In the harbor itself, long, sleek clipper ships and schooners lay rocking at anchor, their wooden masts bare of rigging.

All around her, as she stood on the quay, was the greatest assemblage of people and carpetbags, horses and carriages—and filth, not just fruit rinds and paper, but the unmistakable stench of human refuse.

"Stay close now, Lilly," Jessie commanded. "And you too, Harriet."

Harriet looked almost as stunned as Lilly, and considerably more frightened.

"Grab us a carriage, Father, while I watch the bags."

Off went the august senator, also a bit flustered by the city, familiar as it was to him after a half dozen visits. He quickly procured a carriage, and the Bentons piled in, picking their way gingerly through the piles of horse manure that lay about in the street.

"Fifteen Charles Street," announced Benton to the driver.

"Any particular route, guv'nor?"

"He's not a governor, he's a senator," piped in Lilly.

"Oh quiet now, honey," Benton shushed her. "Whatever way offers the most pleasant scenery, sir, would be amenable to us."

"Scenery? Well, I don't know," the driver returned, swinging the horse around. "We'll do what we can on that one, sir."

The Bentons settled back to take in the unfolding panorama of colors and sights. A few blocks away from the harbor, the cobbled streets became quieter. They drove up a tree-lined avenue just a block in from the riverside. At every crossing, Lilly could look out and see the Hudson glimmering, dark blue in the afternoon sun, and beyond, the imposing cliffs of the outlying farms in New Jersey.

At last the carriage turned into Charles Street, which wound through two quaint rows of brownstones almost as well-kept as those in Lilly's imagination. As the Bentons alighted, the senator offered the driver fifteen cents, and Lilly ran up the stone front steps to bang the heavy brass door knocker.

"Lilly! My gracious! How you've grown, child!" the merry voice boomed as the door opened and a portly, fashionably dressed woman of perhaps forty bent down and lightly kissed young Lilly on the forehead. It was Anna Prescott.

"Welcome Bentons! Welcome all of you! I am surprised you made it so soon!"

"We're surprised we made it at all," Jessie laughed.

As other curious faces gathered behind the parlor windows next to the door, Jessie hastened to make introductions all around. She was bubbling with good spirits. It was good to be on solid ground, at last.

Originally a banker from Norfolk, Virginia, Samuel Livingston Prescott had accepted a transfer to New York six years before with frank hopes of seeing his daughters become society debutantes. This had come to pass, as did nearly everything that Sam Prescott put his mind to. The move had proven just as felicitous for Samuel's cheery wife, Anna, who soon became ingratiated with a proper set of bankers' wives, who were always involved in organizing, as Anna put it, "the most marvelous dinners and doodahs y'all ever did see."

Privately, to her father, Jessie admitted that Anna Prescott had learned a few ill-favored airs. She seemed to find it most difficult to talk with any woman outside her circle of friends. In addition, her daughters now pointed their noses so high that it was a wonder they could keep them attached to their faces. The two of them, Anna Lee Titian and Elizabeth Botticelli, had been named after painters in the hope that each would mystically inherit an artistic genius of her own.

This small vanity had proven fruitless. The girls had, however, acquired some manners, and this was of far greater consequence than the flights and fancies of any of the fine arts, as their father liked to say to anyone who would listen. Now the girls were eighteen and twenty years of age, and concerned above all with the challenge of acquiring the richest and most dashing husband their looks and social standing could secure. In this pursuit, their father was their closest confidant. To their mother, it seemed simply a matter of meeting the right young bankers. Their father, however, was a man of vision, who could admit that not only were there better suitors to be had than young bankers, but that there were some who might not even work for a living, preferring to tend the properties and businesses their own fathers and grandfathers had handed down to them.

To this end, the daughters were forever soliciting escorts to charity balls, at which the ostensible pastimes of eating and dancing were not nearly as important as being seen by the proper men.

Yet, for all the vigor and tenacity with which the young girls struggled to be seen, they were not, as it happened very pretty. Indeed, one was more dowdy than the other. Both were blondes, with fair complexions and clean, regular features, but Jessie observed that they were imbued with soft, fleshy looks that would collapse like a sugary pastry in ten years' time. Still, Jessie's own modesty made it difficult for her to imagine her cousins as anything but elegant at any age.

When the guests and luggage had all passed inside the high, arched portal of the Prescotts' gracious home, Anna clapped her hands for the servants to take the bags, and then led the Bentons on a grand tour of the place. Jessie, who had seen it only once before, was still impressed by the towering, ornamented ceilings in the foyer and living room, the marble fireplace and huge mantel mirror, the formal English furniture and the flickering gas lamps protruding from the walls.

Upstairs, Anna led Jessie and Lilly to a cavernous, sunlit bedroom facing Charles Street. The senator and Richard found that their own room, on the same top floor, faced a lovely rear garden with a willow tree and symmetrical paths around flower beds now made bare by the crisp December air. Benton was exhausted from the day's traveling, and Richard was cotton-headed, as usual, from too much wine. While the two of them adjourned to take a late afternoon nap, the women, including Lilly, convened in the drawing room for tea and gossip.

"Now Jessie, you must tell us all about your trip from St. Louis."

She started reluctantly at first. Then, as she beheld

the shocked expressions on her listeners' faces, Jessie enthusiastically launched into the news of their nearly calamitous stagecoach journey.

"Oh, I can't believe it, I just can't believe it," Anna sputtered. "The nerve of your father, subjecting you to such dangerous antics. Why, you might well have been killed, Jessie!"

"Never a chance. I could see from the start that neither of those fellows would have ever pulled a trigger on a woman. They looked much too nervous for that."

"Nervous!" cried Elizabeth Botticelli. "Well, they seem no better than common thieves, fit only to be hanged."

"Oh, you know, you can't judge so harshly," Jessie smiled. "After all, I wasn't harmed. None of us were."

"You might find it difficult to be so understanding if you one day find yourself on a back street in this city with a gun pointing in your ribs," said Anna Lee. "And don't think it doesn't happen here. It does! In every sort of neighborhood. I tell you, it just isn't safe to walk these streets anymore. Nowadays, if we go out during the evening, Elizabeth and I have to take a carriage. Isn't that right, Mama?"

"It really is, Jess. This isn't the sort of city it was even six years ago. Crime, murder . . . it's simply incredible. Why, you might think it was London." Anna sighed and shook her head. "And the police say they can't do a thing about it."

"Well, then, at least I ought to be grateful I'm leaving for California," Jessie grinned. "Right, Lil?"

"Wrong!" piped Anna and her daughters virtually in unison. From the vehemence in their voices, it was all to obvious that they had thought through this subject long before Jessie's arrival.

"What do you mean by that?" Jessie asked, somewhat taken aback.

"Exactly what we said," Anna replied, her features drawing into a dark frown. "Now Jess, we've thought this over, and we've all three of us decided that we must dissuade you from this foolishness."

"And what," said Jessie, now more amused than concerned, "is so foolish about going to join my husband?"

"That's not the point," Elizabeth broke in. "The point is that you, and probably your husband and father, have no idea how dangerous it is now for civilized people in California."

"We assume you know," said Anna Lee, "that they've found gold out there?"

Jessie sat up in surprise. "Why no, not exactly."

"Yes," said Anna. "Lots and lots of gold. Why, reports are coming out in the newspapers every day. The westbound ships are teeming with gold diggers, most of whom are nothing but shiftless, out-of-work drifters who couldn't make good any other way. That's the sort of person you'll find yourself surrounded by if you go."

Jessie sat still for a moment, collecting her thoughts. "Is it the same on all the boats?"

"All of the ones you can find," said Elizabeth. "We hear that now hardly any boats are bound that way. Those that have already dropped anchor in San Francisco Bay never seem to return. No one wants to join a crew going east—they all want to go digging for gold. So the boats just stay there and rot."

"Jessie Benton, listen to me," Anna implored. "Your father just doesn't know about this situation. When he learns of it, I'm sure he'll argue against your going. And if he doesn't, why, he's an empty-headed fool who doesn't care about his own daughter's safety."

At this, the double doors of the parlor swung open, and a collective gasp went up from the Prescott ladies. There stood Thomas Hart Benton, fiery-eyed and fuming.

"A fool, am I?" he exclaimed. "To let my daughter join her husband?"

"Oh, Thomas, calm down," said Anna. "We all love you, and we love Jessie, too. That's just the point. Neither of you seems to realize how dangerous it is to make the journey to California just now."

The senator nodded slowly and pushed the door farther open. For a moment there was silence. All eyes were on him as he paced to the tall windows overlooking Charles Street. Then he turned and paced the other way.

"Jessie," he said at last, "I have a confession to make. I've been fully aware of the gold rush through these last weeks, and I know exactly what your cousins are talking about. But I haven't bothered to tell you about it until now, because frankly, I didn't think you'd listen."

"Do you believe I'd be risking my life, Father? Or my daughter's?"

Benton shrugged. "You just might be. On the other hand, as I couldn't help overhearing out there, you'd obviously be risking your life on the dangerous streets here as well. Or in Washington. Or even back home. The point is, there's danger everywhere you look in this world, and the way I see it, what you have to do is look beyond the danger to what you really want. And if I don't misunderstand you, Jess, you want to meet your husband in California."

"Well," Jessie sighed, turning back to face the other women, "that about sums it up, I guess. I appreciate your concern, but the fact is, I'm going to California and so is Lilly. Aren't you, darling?"

"I've been in dangerous situations before," Lilly replied smugly.

Chapter 13

Harriet was absolutely enraptured. First, she was back in a kitchen, where she enjoyed passing the time more than in any upstairs parlor, for she loved to cook. The Bentons had always allowed her to choose the family meals and prepare them as she pleased. In her ten years at the household, Harriet had become a gourmet chef.

As much as she respected the Bentons, Harriet always preferred passing time with other colored folk. In St. Louis, that meant lingering at the market, where all the servants shopped for their white households. Here in New York, it meant spending her time downstairs in the servant's quarters.

What made this especially fascinating was that one of the two servants in the Prescotts' kitchen was the most handsome, dreamy-eyed black man she had ever seen. And apparently, he thought well of her, too.

"So how come a sweet thing like you isn't married off and got herself four screaming kids," smiled the attractive gentleman. "Don't they recognize beautiful women in St. Louis?"

"Oh, now you shush up, Fairfax," groused the other servant, an older woman named Elsa Kay. "He's one black devil, that's what he is," she confided to

Harriet. "You best keep your distance, chile. He be the type to charm, disarm, and bring harm to every sweet young thing he see. Ain't you, Fairfax?"

The three of them burst out laughing, and then Harriet caught Fairfax's eye with an amused, inquisitive glance. His gentle gaze reassured her.

"So tell me, how these northern white folk be to work for?" Harriet asked. "Bad as they look?"

"Oh, worse," Fairfax laughed. Unlike Elsa Kay, he spoke in polished tones without a trace of southern inflection. "They're so bad, they set me to dreaming about cotton."

"Now, come on, that ain't the truth by a damn sight," Elsa Kay said. "I been a lot worse off in my time, a lot worse off."

"Oh, they're all right, I guess," Fairfax conceded. "At least they don't try to take the whip to the help. And they do pay a wage, even if it's only enough to keep us here for the rest of our lives. Only problem with the Prescotts is they think they're high society." Fairfax leaned forward in a conspiratorial whisper. "Fact is, high society folks laugh at them behind their backs. I know, 'cause I know every butler in this town, from the Astors' man on down. And the airs these Prescotts put on—whew! It's a wonder there's enough air left to breathe."

Had Jessie heard this, she might have been tempted to agree. Lord! How her cousins had changed. At supper, during which Lilly had committed the *faux pas* of using the wrong spoon, Sam Prescott engaged the senator in a vigorous discussion about the new president. Taylor, said Prescott with cold authority, seemed all too likely to jeopardize the treasury by expanding the country's westward frontiers too far and too fast. To which Benton replied heatedly that the sooner the country looked west, the better.

"And I suppose, Senator, that you would advocate California's entry into the Union, with all the attendant expenses and financial obligations that would involve?"

"Certainly I would!" the senator boomed. "We can't expect to reap the benefits of the territory without assuming some responsibility for its protection. We cannot go on taking its gold and its land, all the while hoping that the Europeans and Mexicans will stand aside politely and watch."

"But the Union doesn't need the land!" Prescott returned. "Our cities, our culture, and our society, dirty a word as it might seem to you, are all here in the East. It's here that we should be spending the government's money, to see that our cities are not overrun by crime and pestilence."

Jessie quickly and adroitly broke in and began to steer the conversation away from politics as Fairfax and Elsa Kay, assisted by Harriet, brought out a platter of roast turkey stuffed with chestnuts and decorated around the edges with cranberry sauce and trimmings.

"Anna, you simply must tell me all the latest news," she urged. "And Father, I'll hear no more of politics at this table. We ladies wish to enjoy our meal."

There ensued a lively exchange of gossip that continued on into the evening, was picked right up at breakfast and crackled along with no sign of flagging as the younger women wended their way down the city's cramped and crowded streets for their morning constitutional.

First they passed along narrow, crooked cobblestone avenues where smart-looking townhouses were interspersed with clusters of carriage houses.

Soon they came out onto a much wider and more crowded thoroughfare called Broadway. Lilly, tagging along after Jessie, was for once rendered speechless by the spectacle, and particularly by the big, horse-drawn trolleys that careened up a set of gleaming rails with a great clashing of gears and deafening whistle blasts. All around them, hungry-looking vendors hawked their goods from sidewalk stands.

"Penny apples, penny apples!" cried a girl no older than Lilly. They exchanged a look of mutual curiosity, and then the crowd swept them apart.

Around one hawker a large group had gathered. Curious, Jessie stopped to look. Past the bobbing heads in front of her, she beheld a young black man talking very fast and shifting three downturned playing cards on a wooden crate top.

"Okay people, we got a bidder, we got a bidder. Two dollars down, sir, two dollars down. Now I move the cards like this, you see, just like this, no tricks here, no tricks. You just tell me where the queen went, queen of hearts."

"It's a trick," Anna Lee whispered in Jessie's ear. "It's a game they call three-card monte. The dealer keeps shifting the cards, and you think you know which card is yours because a corner was nicked or folded. But then he folds another card exactly the same way, and if you haven't played before, you get fooled."

Jessie was fascinated. "What about the man who's playing now? He doesn't look like any country bumpkin to me."

"You're right, he's not. He's in with the dealer. He's a shill, don't you see? And when he starts to win, someone else will try to win too."

Now a third man brusquely elbowed his way through the crowd. "Close it up, close it up," he shouted to the dealer.

"That's the lookout man," said Anna Lee. "There must be a constable coming."

Sure enough, a moment later, the crowd parted

again as two uniformed officers appeared with their nightsticks ready. By now, though, the dealer, his shill and his lookout man had vanished. With a derisive string of oaths, the constables pushed on.

Farther down Broadway, the sidewalk stalls were better kept, and past there were proper storefronts with multipaned windows. Fine notions and fabrics, perfumes and toiletries sat snugly inside, awaiting New York's most affluent buyers. The Prescotts steered Jessie and Lilly in and out of a few of their favorite shops, then brought them up before the colonnade of a magnificent hotel, which bore its title in carved marble letters above the portal.

"The Astor House wasn't here when you came before, Jess," said Elizabeth. "It has seven stores inside and the most genteel tea room."

"It's the best place for meeting men, too," Anna Lee giggled. "We'll end up there later. First we have to get your picture taken."

"Oh my word!" Jesse exclaimed. "But that must be so expensive!"

"It is," Anna Lee laughed. "But it's worth the price. After all, how soon are we going to see you again? Not another peep out of you about the expense. It's our treat."

Just around the corner from the Astor House, an elegant, imposing storefront sported a sign which read, "Mathew Brady's Photographic Gallery." Inside, the women found a rather dour young man adjusting the lens on a large, boxlike contraption that stood on four legs. Behind it, near the wall, three armchairs were arranged in a semicircle against a simple backdrop of white bedsheet.

"Pardon, but where is Mr. Brady today?" Elizabeth inquired.

"He's mixing chemicals and can't be disturbed,

ma'am. If you'd like your picture taken, I'd be happy to oblige you. Same camera, same daguerreotype, same price."

"I suppose you must be a new assistant," Elizabeth rejoined. "You see, we'd like to have *Mr. Brady* take our picture."

"I guess you don't understand, ma'am. He's busy, and he takes very few pictures himself nowadays."

"Only celebrities, is that it?"

"If you choose to call them that, yes."

"Perhaps you could tell him that the Prescott girls are here. Would you do that?" Elizabeth requested icily.

"Prescott . . . Prescott," the man repeated, turning the name over in his mind. "That wouldn't be the same Prescott who's Mr. Brady's banker, now, would it?"

"Quite."

"Ah." The man's manner changed abruptly. With an ingratiating smile, he excused himself to call the photographer from a back room.

"Insolent creature," Anna Lee hissed after him.

In a moment, he returned. At his heels followed a portly, bearded man, his hands plunged into the pockets of his long, black smock.

"Good day, ladies. What may I do for you?"

Jessie was startled to see Anna Lee's own manner change as quickly as that of Brady's assistant.

"Why, Mr. Brady, how kind of you to take the time to see us today," she gushed. "We've brought along our cousin Jessie Benton Fremont, the wife of Colonel John Fremont, the famous explorer."

Now it was Brady's turn to show respect. "Why, Mrs. Fremont, it's an honor. I'm a great admirer of your husband."

Brady bade his guests to be seated in the armchairs by the wall, then proceeded to adjust the lenses of the big box camera. His assistant brought him a clean photographic plate.

"Now the important thing," Brady said, ducking under a drop cloth, "is to keep perfectly still for two full minutes if you can. You, especially, little lady," he told Lilly. 'Scratch any itch you've got now."

Holding what appeared to be a perfume atomizer on a long, black cord, Brady pressed a button on it and Jessie heard a click from within the box. She found it excruciatingly difficult to hold a smile for the entire exposure time, and Lilly abandoned the attempt altogether, letting her features slip into glassy-eyed solemnity. The Prescott sisters, of course, held their own smiles radiantly.

When at last the camera clicked a second time, Brady pronounced himself satisfied. He pulled out the daguerreotype plate, on which the Prescotts and the Bentons could now see their own taut expressions and stiffly held forms.

"Now one for us to keep!" Elizabeth cried.

"And if I may be so bold," added Brady, with a nod in Jessie's direction, "I should like to make one for myself."

The Prescotts could not disguise the stabs of envy they felt upon hearing his request, but they managed to recover, and the two daguerreotypes were promptly produced.

"Now how about a shopping spree?" suggested Elizabeth as they left the studio. Over Jessie's amused protestations, the group headed off first to Barnum's famous shop to see the exotic treasures and photographs of curious creatures, and then they proceeded to a new emporium called Lord and Taylor's.

By midafternoon, the exhausted women were overloaded with packages. With a last gasp of energy, they made their way into the Astor House lobby for tea and crumpets. Jessie and Lilly, straggling behind the Prescotts, gawked at the mirrored walls, lush oriental carpets and gaslight chandeliers that hung from every room and hall.

The lobby, where tea was served every weekday at three, was now filled with the pleasant hubbub of sophisticated voices. Nearly every couch and chair was taken, but the Prescotts succeeded in locating one available circle from which they could watch everyone.

"Oh, there's the Buckley boy," Elizabeth exclaimed. "And look who he's with—Margaret Hennessey! She'll marry him quick as you please. Anna Lee, we haven't got a chance."

They burst into giggles, and Jessie suddenly felt very old, though she was only four years older than Elizabeth. With her young daughter beside her, and her heart already given to one man, she had difficulty understanding her cousins' lives now. She would never have thought of marrying for money and position.

The silent arrival of a porter across the carpeted floor, bearing a small envelope on a silver tray, interrupted her thoughts. The Prescott daughters, holding their breaths, looked for all the world as if the envelope would surely contain their own verdict and sentence.

"Oh my God," gasped Elizabeth as the porter bowed and extended the tray.

"Lucky little twit," her sister sulked. "It's probably from some tomfool like Hieronymous Wattles."

"How wrong you are, sister dear," said Elizabeth through lips frozen coquettishly. "Try Worthington Mather."

Now it was Anna Lee's turn to mutter, "Oh my God."

Half-amused, Jessie let her eyes rove discreetly across the crowded room. The sender of the message was not hard to locate. A portly young man with pasty features and a bulbous nose sat on the edge of his chair. He craned his neck as he looked toward Elizabeth with forced bravado.

"All right, Elizabeth, come on. What's he say?" demanded Anna Lee, her eyes set demurely on her cup of tea.

"He says he wants to take me for a carriage ride, if you must know, dear sister."

"I don't believe it."

"And I'm going to accept." Upon which Elizabeth looked coyly across at Worthington Mather, smiled her coquettish smile, and nodded ever so slightly.

As if cut loose from a cactus seat, young Worthington Mather shot up to his feet, sauntered over to the Prescotts and took Elizabeth's proffered hand in his own with a flourish, a bow and a kiss.

"Shall we?" he asked with a flash of uneven teeth. "My carriage is just outside."

"Always nice to see you, Worthington," said Anna Lee, fluttering her eyelashes flirtatiously as her sister rose to go.

"Tell me," said Jessie to Anna Lee when the couple had walked away, "why is that young man considered such a catch?"

"That young man, Jess, will one day be worth enough money to paper this town from the east side to the west. His father owns a great deal of land. And you should see the Mathers' townhouse—circular driveway, big iron gates—I tell you, it's more like a castle."

"Ah," Jessie said sadly, "I understand perfectly."

"Of course, that little snoot left us with all the packages," Anna Lee added, though her anger seemed to be fading.

"I guess we'll have to hire a horse and carriage to take us home."

"Yes," Anna Lee agreed, somewhat distracted. "The Astor House has its own cabs now."

Jessie turned to follow her gaze. Coming toward them, once again, was the porter with the silver tray. This time he bowed toward Anna Lee.

"Thank God," sighed Anna Lee, her lips curved in a smile identical to her sister's.

She opened the envelope with barely disguised eagerness, though she had no idea who had sent the message.

"Oh my God, oh my God," she muttered, as if in prayer. "Jessie, I don't believe it. All season I've hoped for this! You must be good luck for me."

"Thaddeus Mercantile the Fourth," Anna Lee gasped. "Why, he's just about the richest young man in New York. In fact, next to Christopher James Astor, I guess he is. But then Chris Astor never sends notes to *anyone*. He's such a prig. Oh, Jess! I can't stand it, I'm so happy!"

Jessie scanned the room, again quite discreetly. Ah, there he was. Or could it be he? True, he was looking their way, but he was hardly a young beau. Tall, frail, with dirty blond locks combed unsuccessfully over a receding hairline, Thaddeus Mercantile the Fourth was certainly no younger than thirty-five. Moreover, he had a pretentiousness about him, an affected way of sitting that struck Jessie as decidedly effeminate.

Blushing, Anna Lee nodded self-consciously in his direction, then thanked the porter. She reluctantly tore her gaze away to face Jessie.

"I feel just awful leaving you here, Jessie," she said, trying to hold in her excitement. "Would you mind terribly, just this time, bringing all the packages back home? Actually, you can get a porter to bring them out to a carriage, and when you arrive at the house, you can ring for Fairfax and Elsa Kay to unload them for you. Jess, I feel awful about it, but you understand, don't you?"

Jessie shook her head with a winsome smile. "Don't you worry, Anna Lee," she said as Thaddeus Mercantile arrived at their table.

"Why Thaddeus! I'm so flattered. Thaddeus, this is my cousin, Jessie Benton Fremont."

Thaddeus bowed and took Jessie's slender hand in his own clammy one. "Divinely pleased, I'm sure," he said.

"Bye, Jess," said Anna Lee hurriedly, rising from her chair with another quick smile at Thaddeus. "And bye to you too, Lilly. Be good, now. I'll see you both at the house for supper."

"Mother," Lilly said when Anna Lee and Thaddeus had departed, "was there something funny about that man?"

"He seemed like a pleasant gentleman," her mother replied. "Anna Lee was the one behaving strangely, I think."

"People are awfully odd in New York," Lilly remarked.

"That may be true, dear," Jessie said. "But we don't have to behave the way these folks do, now do we?"

Lilly paused, taking a sip of tea, then asked, "Mother, tell me what California's going to be like. Am I going to like it?"

"Oh yes, honey, you will," Jessie laughed. "It'll be much different than New York. Not so settled, not so many streets and houses, but many, many people. Of course, they won't be so very grand. Most of them will have beards, too."

"Even the women?"

"No, silly! But I don't know how many women there'll be, to tell you the truth."

Jessie went on for a while, mixing her own thoughts with answers to Lilly's interrogations. This was something she did often, and it soothed her when her husband was gone. For hours, she could sit and talk with Lilly, almost as if she were talking to herself.

She was interrupted by the startling reappearance of the porter, carrying another envelope on his silver tray.

"Oh," Jessie exclaimed, as if awakened from a bad dream. "There must be some mistake. I'm just a visitor in town."

"No ma'am," the porter shook his head soberly. "It's quite definitely addressed to you."

More annoyed than amused, Jessie tore open the envelope and read out loud to Lilly. "Mr. Christopher James Astor requests the pleasure of your company for cocktails at five o'clock."

Almost as an afterthought, the writer had scrawled at the bottom, "Please come."

Jessie gazed in consternation around the room. There did appear to be one dashing young man, of perhaps Jessie's own age, propping his strong chin pensively on one hand while gazing her way with a look of wry amusement.

"But he doesn't understand," Jessie told the waiting porter. "Tell him I'm married."

"Very good, madam," the porter bowed and made his way directly back to the young man.

A brief exchange ensued. Then, to her amazement, Jessie watched as the porter returned to her bearing yet another envelope.

"I don't care who you are," the writer had scrawled. "And I don't care if you are married."

Jessie smiled wistfully. "Tell the gentleman," she said, "that I *do* care. And thank him for me, please."

Chapter 14

The day of the departure dawned clear, cold and blue over the New York skyline. The steamer was scheduled to leave at nine o'clock. Jessie had packed the night before, and now, standing at the top of the stone steps, she directed the servants who labored with her baggage.

Harriet had decided to remain in New York. She and Fairfax had approached Jessie the night before to inform her, Fairfax having done most of the talking. He had explained that Harriet did not want to leave New York and that he wanted to make her his bride. Harriet just wept and nodded her head in agreement. Finally, she managed a few words. "But I don't want to desert you, Miz Fremont. I know how much you need me and all, and I don't want to let you down."

Harriet had looked so forlorn and was so obviously contrite at deserting her mistress that Jessie didn't have the heart to scold her. She had given Harriet her blessings.

Now remembering that parting, Jessie smiled to herself. But she still felt a twinge of regret. She would miss Harriet.

Trying to distract herself from her thoughts, she looked over at the Prescott daughters. They were standing beside their mother, both bleary-eyed from lack of sleep. They were sipping strong coffee and shivering against the cold.

Jessie was about to remark how quickly the week had passed, but in truth it had dragged on interminably. She was all too grateful to resume her journey. So, too, she could see, was Lilly. Only Richard showed any regret about departing. For him, the week had been restful.

The harbor was even more crowded than it had been the previous week, and most of the people centered around the farthest dock, from which Jessie's steamer was scheduled to depart. A half dozen leaky old vessels, draped in soggy bunting and festooned with hand-painted signs that read: "Immediate Departure to San Francisco!" and "Fastest Route to Riches!", lulled in the gentle waves. Around them bustled a pandemonium of shouting men, weeping women and howling babies. From every side, as Jessie alighted with her father's help, they could hear the magic word "gold"—whispered, shouted, confided, derided, and spoken like an incantation.

"Oh, don't you see, Jess, it's horrible!" the Prescott daughters chorused from their carriage.

Not nearly so horrible, Jessie mused, as another week at 15 Charles Street.

While the others waited with the baggage, Jessie and her father went off in search of the ship's captain. This, it happened, was an old acquaintance of Colonel Fremont who had fought with the California Battalion in 1846, parlayed a few modest real estate holdings into a private steamer line and was merrily getting set to make a fortune from the gold rush without ever lifting a pan to do it.

Admiral Curtis O'Lunney, as he now dubbed himself, was never one to forget his benefactors, and when he had established his steamer line from New York to

Chagres, he had made a generous offer of free passage to any member of the Benton family. This the senator refused to countenance, but it did offer another pinch of reassurance that Jessie would be well cared for.

"What a pleasure and a privilege to have you both aboard!" the admiral's voice boomed from his cabin even before he appeared. He emerged, pork-bellied and rosy-cheeked, with a fleshy hand extended to greet them.

It was hard for Jessie to avoid the mean-spirited thought that Admiral O'Lunney looked more like a short-order cook than an admiral, and that his vessel looked more like a platform and pump than a sea-faring steamer ship. But if the boat had made the journey before, she presumed it could certainly do the same again.

With the Prescotts, their servants and the admiral himself all helping, the baggage was aboard in no time, and the two families found themselves down on the quay making their good-byes. The Prescotts wanted to make an elaborate parting, with many tearful embraces and prayers for Godspeed.

Jessie had quite the opposite intention. In her family, partings always took place in the least amount of time and with the least amount of sentiment.

Jessie was spared too long an agony with the Prescotts by the sudden clanging of the ship's bell. Hurrying up the gangplank, she pulled Lilly by the hand with Richard right behind, and turned just long enough to give her father a quick bear hug.

"Good-bye, my brave Jessie. Be of good spirit," he said, his brown eyes brimming with love.

"Good-bye, Father. Fight hard," Jessie smiled.

The senator bustled down to the dock. The gang-plank was pulled up onto the deck, and the ship, with a billowing burst of steam, began chugging out of its

slip, away from New York, away from all that Jessie
Benton Fremont had known, and bound for the Central
American port of Chagres.

For Richard, the next few days proved grueling
and ghastly. He had never sought passage on a steamer
before, and his constitution, already weakened by his al-
coholic excesses, now rebelled completely as the ship
headed into stormy weather off the coast of Virginia.
Confined to his tiny cabin and unable even to sit up in
bed, Richard became the mystery passenger on board,
whose place at the table always sat vacant.

This left Jessie and Lilly to roam freely around
the small, single deck of the steamer. They loved to
shout over the ferocity of the waves, and they remained
outside in all but the most forbidding gusts of wind and
rain.

Then, as violently as the storm had raged, so it
peacefully receded, ushering the steamer into the
balmy, blue waters of the Gulf Stream. Jessie sat out
on deck with her skirts pulled modestly over her ankles.
Lilly followed her example, though she complained
that she wasn't allowed to pull her skirt up over her
knees, for the warm sun made her uncomfortable.

Richard emerged finally, shaken, but ready to recuperate.

This calm was shattered once again as the steamer
came within sight of Chagres, not by a storm this time,
but by a ground swell. The steamer had eased past a
sandbar a half mile from shore, and Jessie had begun
to pack. Suddenly the ship pitched and swayed violently. Through the starboard porthole, the sea came
sweeping up. Water sloshed down the hallway and
under the cabin door. Then the entire process repeated
itself.

Back and forth the frail steamer dipped, its deck

railings nearly touching the waves. Jessie heard the admiral shouting angrily to his crew.

"Well, I'm going to see what this is all about," Jessie told Lilly. "You stay here, honey. It's too dangerous up there."

Gritting her teeth, Jessie threw open the cabin door, half expecting a torrent to slam through. Instead, only a sloshing residue of salty water spilled over her feet.

Up on deck, only the admiral and his crew rushed about, bailing water in large wooden barrels.

"Good Lord, woman, what are you doing up here?" the admiral shouted at Jessie. "You get back to your cabin where you'll be safe."

"But Admiral," smiled Jessie as she waded through the ankle-deep brine, "we seem to have weathered the worst of it already. Please, as long as I'm up here, I might as well be of some help."

The admiral muttered, "Well, if you insist," and handed Jessie a barrel.

So it was that Jessie got her first look at the colorful trading port of Chagres. By the time the crew had cast anchor and the engine had ceased its comforting rumble, Lilly had creeped up on deck, beaming from all of the excitement. Jessie just barely had the strength to continue, her arms aching from the labor.

"Jessie, what have they made you do?" a shocked voice cried out behind her.

She turned to see Richard, bags in hand, looking pale and weak from the ground swell.

"This is one determined little lady," the admiral said, putting a hand on Richard's shoulder. "But I'm telling you, mate, she doesn't know what she's getting into now."

"What do you mean?" Richard asked.

"Well, my friends, first of all, there's this place

to contend with," the admiral said, yanking a thumb toward Chagres. "Every kind of nationality in the world is here. Every kind of disease and pestilence, too. And if the diseases don't get you, the critters surely will."

"What kind of critters? Big ones?" Richard demanded.

"Why sure, mate! Spiders as big as your hand. And snakes twice as long as you are tall. Poison stingers, bloodsuckers, fever bugs and paralyzers."

"Jessie, I've been telling you all along this is madness," Richard now claimed. "From what this man says, it all sounds worse than I ever imagined."

"From Chagres, you'll take another steamer up the river, but pretty soon the water'll get too shallow," the admiral explained. "Then you'll have to go by canoe."

"Oh my God," breathed Richard.

"Thank you for your warning, Admiral," Jessie said cheerfully. "We'll be going ahead anyway, but I do appreciate your kindness. Come on, Richard, let's get the other bags."

Looking more like a prisoner than a protector, Richard shrugged in resignation and padded after Jessie and Lilly.

"I'll tell you, Mrs. Fremont, you're making a mistake," the admiral sighed. "But if you insist, then God be with you. Just one parting bit of advice—don't you go drinking any water that isn't boiled first. And try not to eat any local food."

Jessie laughed. "What shall we eat, if not the food?"

"Look for a boat from Jamaica. If you're lucky, you can get some yams and plantains, maybe even some lamb meat."

Thanking the admiral again for his kindness, Jessie made her way to the railing. Bobbing a few feet below were a dozen wooden dinghies, each manned by a grinning native in loincloth and sandals.

"This way, ma'am. Easy does it."

Jessie went first, pulling her skirts in with as much modesty as the circumstances allowed, then climbing down the rope ladder cautiously into the waiting hands of the native boatman. Richard now guided Lilly over the railing and held the ladder steady as she descended into Jessie's arms. Richard came last, serving at least one useful function by clinging to the ladder midway down and relaying the baggage, piece by piece, to the smaller boat. The admiral waved good-bye as the native boatman pushed off and rowed toward shore.

Jessie's first impression of Chagres was olfactory. Even before she stepped ashore, she was struck by a battery of nauseating smells: putrefying fish, tar, garbage. Above them all hovered one unmistakable aroma: cinnamon.

As the admiral had warned, the port town was crowded with natives from all over the Caribbean, as well as men from Spain, France and America.

The boatman, apprised of their destination, steered his passengers through the murky, garbage-strewn water to a steamship that made their previous vessel look every bit the yacht that Admiral O'Lunney held it to be. This boat was half that size and more like a metal gunboat, with cramped quarters below deck that appeared, by the portholes, to contain room enough only for baggage.

A small man with a boatswain's cap sat up on deck, making notes in a log. Taking furious pulls on his pipe as he worked, he sent up plumes of smoke with such regularity that Jessie half-wondered if he, himself, was not part of the engine.

"Pardon me, sir," said Jessie, holding on to the gunwales of her dinghy. "Would this be the boat to Gorgona?"

"It might be. Then again, it mightn't be." The man on deck spoke with an accent that seemed incongruous in the Caribbean. Jessie realized it had a strong New England flavor to it, and New Englanders sometimes required special treatment. She tried a different tack with the fellow.

"Does it matter which boat we take to Gorgona?"

The man took a long pull off his pipe, sent up a plume of smoke and said, "Not to me it doesn't."

"What," said Jessie with barely contained fury, "are you doing so far from New Hampshire, and why don't you go back there, where people won't trouble you for help?"

Incredibly, a big, toothy grin came over the man's face. "Why, what do you know," he exclaimed. "You from New England, for Gawd's sake!"

"Missouri, thank you all the same. St. Louis, Missouri." Jessie set her jaw. "And I'm an American, plain as you are, so you might give me the decency of a proper reply."

"Yes, yes. Well, all right," the man said, shoving his pipe in his pocket and slamming his book shut. "There's just so many fool-headed gold diggers about, a man can't be too friendly. To most folks, I just say I'm full up every day, which, in fact, I am today. But I can fit you on, I reckon."

At the man's direction, Richard stowed the baggage below deck, and Jessie prepared to climb on board.

"Hold it, hold your horses," the man admonished. "We don't leave for three hours, and I like my privacy. 'Sides, that way you can walk around the port and do some shoppin' the way women like to do. Be back two o'clock sharp."

"How do we know we can trust you with our bags?" Jessie asked.

"Oh, now, don't you worry none about that. If you can't trust one of your own, you can't trust nobody in this world."

Jessie grimaced, but the man did seem honest enough, if a bit eccentric. "What's your name, then, sir, and the name of your boat?"

"Name? Eleazor Wheeler, if it pleases Your Majesty. And my boat's the *Rumbarrel*. Just ask anyone where I am if you get lost."

Jessie nodded wearily and ordered the boatman to take them ashore to the splintery, tar-smeared wooden dock. She wondered briefly whether he would accept American currenoy, but in the end she had to stop him from repeatedly kissing her hand when she handed him a shiny new silver dime.

"I guess goods are cheap in this town," she said drily to Richard.

Indeed, as they strolled up the waterfront past an unbroken row of crude, thatched stalls, it seemed that everything from tropical fruit to native shell necklaces could be bought for a penny or two. And few passers-by appeared to be actually shopping, so that Jessie, Lilly and Richard soon became objects of curious attention. All down the street native vendors, calling loudly in pigdin English, invited the Americans over to their stalls.

The beleaguered trio, moving slowly toward the center of town, followed the flow of the crowd into a huge open market. Here the townspeople shopped, selecting from colorful stands stacked with tropical fruit and long racks of freshly killed meat. At the far end of

the largest meat stall, native women cooked the stripped
and pounded meat in boiling cauldrons for customers
waiting at a makeshift counter. As Jessie watched in
fascination, a steer was led up to a group of jabbering
native butchers, who waited with heavy, blood-stained
machetes. The terrified steer fought to escape its fate,
but in another moment the animal's head had been
hacked apart from its body, and the butchers set about
drawing and quartering its bleeding carcass.

Perhaps it was the meat market that finally did
Richard in. Pale and shaking, he demanded of Jessie
that they abandon the scene of all this carnage, as he
called it, and sit down somewhere cool, where he might
also find a pleasant native drink.

So Jessie and Lilly, remembering the admiral's
edict, sat at a small, streetside table and sipped hot tea.
Richard, however, recklessly guzzled down a cherry-
colored concoction full of native rum.

In an hour, he was sweating uncontrollably.

"Doctor . . . medicine . . . help!" Jessie spouted
out a myriad of words at the native official, a tall,
Spanish-looking fellow, whom she finally located on the
waterfront. But he understood none of it. In desperation, she took the man by the arm and pulled him
back to the bar.

Now the official understood.

Chapter 15

"No time," Jessie said, pointing to the sun. "We must catch the boat in one hour."

With the official and Jessie holding Richard by the arms, they supported him as they made their way through the narrow streets leading away from the waterfront. The farther they walked from the harbor, the more nervous Jessie became. At last, the official stopped in front of a mud-and-wattle house with a thatched roof. Incredibly, the sign on the door was in English. It read: "General Medicine and Corrective Surgery, J.T. Blithering, M.D."

"Welcome, welcome," resounded a friendly voice with a British accent. Jessie felt almost ready to fall at his feet in gratitude, but Richard saved her the trouble. He simply collapsed.

"Trouble? Trouble?" Dr. Blithering, a bushy-haired, jolly-looking fellow with extraordinarily large hands and feet, helped Richard up onto an examining table.

Jessie described Richard's sudden attack of what appeared to be a fever.

"Hmm," the doctor said, knitting his brows. "Sounds like our local specialty, yes, indeed, our local specialty. But what confuses me, if I may say so, yes, what absolutely confounds me is his flushed face and profuse sweating. You see, the local specialty, Chagres fever, as we call it, manifests itself in a markedly green complexion with no sweating at all. Do you understand? You see, his flushed face and profuse sweating . . ."

"Yes, yes, I do, I do," attested Jessie impatiently. "But you must understand, Doctor, that we have a boat to catch in less than an hour's time. What can you give him to put him on his feet in short order?"

The doctor knitted his bushy brows again, clucked in consternation, and covered Richard's forehead with one of his hands. "I think the problem, ma'am, is that he's got two fevers at once. One he picked up from wherever he came from, and one he picked up here. No, I really don't know how I can get him into fine fettle at all today. Two fevers, you see, two fevers at the same time."

"Oh no, Doctor, it can't be. Perhaps we should stay here overnight."

"Wouldn't recommend it, wouldn't recommend it at all. Horrid accommodations, if you see what I mean."

Now Richard raised his head weakly and held up a restraining hand. "Jessie, I'm afraid the situation is all too clear. Much as I'd like to continue with you, I'll not be able to. Perhaps we should all head back . . ."

"No!" Jessie retorted. "I'm not heading back, and neither is Lilly. But I think you're right, Richard. I think you ought to head back yourself. I'd love to have you on the rest of the trip, but who's to say how long you'll be ill?"

"My sentiments exactly," Richard agreed. "But I feel I'm letting your father down, and your husband, too."

"Don't worry, Richard," Jessie smiled. "My father knows I can take care of myself. As for my husband, the only way you'd be letting him down is if you dragged me back to St. Louis. No, don't you worry. This is all for the best, I'm sure of it."

"For the best, for the best, yes, exactly, exactly," Dr. Blithering cut in. "I can put him up here for a bit. As soon as his fevers break, I'll put him directly out on a steamer back to New York."

"Why, Richard, you might even be able to catch the admiral's steamer going back," Jessie brightened. "Didn't he say he's to be here for three days?"

"Right. I shall. Absolutely," Richard promised.

With a quick embrace, the two parted. Jessie was certain that he was as relieved at the unexpected turn of events as she was. They had proven to be a drain on each other for most of the trip thus far.

In another hour, Jessie and Lilly were safely aboard Captain Eleazor Wheeler's *Rumbarrel,* albeit crammed together on deck with a full score of other passengers, mostly Americans. With what seemed a Herculean effort, the steamer chugged its way past the thatched huts along the muddy shore of the town and headed up the Chagres River. Before long, the town, lost to sight around the river's langorous curves, seemed little more than a dream.

"Do you think Uncle Richard will be all right?" Lilly asked.

Jessie laughed. "That poor man has been ill from homesickness all along," she said. "He was never a tonic for my courage, dear Lilly. Let us hope he finds a tonic for his own."

Soon the meandering river began to grow shallower and narrower at every curve. Its banks finally hemmed in so close that the overhanging vines, stippled with white and scarlet blossoms, touched the sides of the steamer.

Jessie and Lilly had barely enough room to stretch

their arms about them, so closely packed in were they with the ship's other passengers. But when Jessie beheld what awaited them up ahead, her sturdy spirits plummeted. Perhaps only Lilly's panic prevented Jessie from falling into utter despair.

"*Riteiswa! Riteiswa!*"

Jumping, shouting and waving their arms wildly were at least two dozen loinclothed Indians in dugout canoes. These, Jessie realized with cold dread, would be her escorts the rest of the way up the river.

"Captain Wheeler, are we really going to travel by canoe with those savages?" Jessie asked plaintively.

"Savages! Hell! I seen worse in New Hampshire! Nah, don't you worry, little lady. They're good boys, and anyways, there's a Yankee in charge of 'em."

"*Riteiswa! Riteiswa!*"

Through the ranks of chanting savages, a single white man wended his way toward the steamer from dugout to dugout.

"That there's Mr. Curtis, least that's what they call him. The natives just love him to death."

As the steamer's passengers began to jump gingerly ashore with their bags in hand, Mr. Curtis exchanged a hearty greeting with Captain Wheeler. He was, Jessie could hardly help but notice, a stunningly handsome man, a head taller than anyone present, with dark blond hair, sun-bronzed skin and piercing, green eyes. But what made the strongest impression on Jessie was his air of strength and confidence as he bade the other passengers good day. And there was a dark, brooding magnetism to him. It was to this that the natives clearly responded. As Jessie observed them awaiting his command, she felt an inexplicable, foreboding chill.

"And you are, madam. . . ?"

"Jessie Benton Fremont, and my daughter, Lilly. Good day."

"Fremont . . . Fremont," Mr. Curtis repeated.

"Wife of Colonel John Fremont, thank you," Jessie said primly. Lilly looked up at her in surprise. Such formality in her mother was unusual.

Jessie kept her eyes locked with Mr. Curtis'. Was he mocking her, she wondered, waiting for her to drop her gaze?

Finally he dropped his own and turned abruptly to indicate the shouting natives. "They won't harm you, Mrs. Fremont."

"I didn't imagine they would. But what are they shouting, if I may ask, Mr. Curtis?"

"They're saying, 'Right this way,' " Mr. Curtis intoned with a broad grin of flawless white teeth. "Just a little civility I taught them."

The daylight was fading rapidly when the passengers and baggage were finally loaded into the dugouts. Mr. Curtis took his place in the lead canoe, and the party moved slowly up the river. The passengers had poised themselves nervously in the front and middle of the rocking canoes, while the natives in back poled them along like gondoliers.

At dusk, they reached a clearing on the shore where a small but comfortable camp of tents had been erected. A handful of natives hurried about, tending to a large cauldron over a crackling fire. Apparently, they were preparing for their guests' arrival.

"This is my base camp," Mr. Curtis explained when the dugouts had been moored to the bank and the passengers had assembled. "It's quite comfortable, really. We've been running people up and down the river for half a dozen years now, so the natives are quite accustomed to the needs of us strange white folk. Actually, they've been kept rather busy these last few months with all the gold diggers bound for California."

Dinner was nearly ready. The passengers gathered

around the campfire and took the wood-carved bowls offered to them. In the flickering flames, Jessie had her first chance to evaluate the people at some length. Such an odd and motley group they were. All ages, sizes and accents, and all bearing a few traits in common, too. With the exception of Jessie and Lilly, no two of them appeared to know each other. Also, they all were men, and bearded men at that. Jessie could not remember the last time she had been subjected to similar circumstances and, despite her customary vigor and strength, she was taken aback.

The last trait that all bore in common, including Jessie and Lilly, was their destination. Stories were traded of fortunes won and lost in a matter of days, descriptions made of how gold looked when you first came upon it in a mountain stream.

Soon the stars appeared, twinkling like beacons from a more familiar world. The bearded faces were sleepily content, their emptied bowls being cleaned in the river by obliging natives.

"So tell us, Mr. Curtis," one voice was heard, "What in the hell was that tasty dinner we ate just now?"

With a smile, Mr. Curtis leaned forward out of the shadows around the campfire. "Baked monkey stew with a little snakeskin flavoring."

"What a dirty trick," Jessie told him later, after the moaning and groaning had subsided.

"Why do you say that, Mrs. Fremont?" asked Mr. Curtis with a look of wide-eyed innocence.

"You know very well why. You didn't have to serve such exotic fare, did you?"

Mr. Curtis' eyes narrowed now. "You're an intelligent woman, Mrs. Fremont, and you're also a very attractive one."

"Well, you are absolutely loathsome, Mr. Curtis."

"I'm not at all sure of that, Mrs. Fremont. But I do know who holds the upper hand in this affair." Mr. Curtis flashed his broad, white smile. "Camped alone with a company of natives and a crowd of gold-hungry, lonesome men, you could do worse than to have an ally like me, Mrs. Fremont."

Two more days on the river brought the party close to Gorgona. They also brought Jessie close to a nervous breakdown. At every opportunity, Mr. Curtis made some veiled suggestion to her. While he always stopped short of demanding that she sleep with him, he also made it clear that she eventually would. The awful part was that she had no one to turn to. Lilly was much too young to even understand the dilemma, much less offer advice or consolation. And of all the men present, there was not one who seemed even aware of her cir-cumstances. Indeed, of all of them, the most intelligent and sophisticated and handsome was by far Mr. Curtis himself. But he was also, Jessie knew, the most malev-olent.

By the fourth afternoon, Jessie began to fear for her life. Who would help her if Mr. Curtis stopped making suggestions and simply attacked her in her tent at night? From all these sex-starved brutes she could expect only gleeful applause, if not the unthinkable nightmare of others then attempting to rape her as well.

That night it happened. Jessie had been feeling a terrible forewarning, due in part to her constant pre-tending that she was safe, and in part to her suppressing of all the revulsion she felt at Mr. Curtis' advances. But, oddly enough, on this day, Mr. Curtis had made no passes at all. Instead, he had utterly ignored her.

Jessie was hardly fooled. Way back in the line of

canoes, as surely as if he had sent out a magnetic force, Jessie felt the brutal touch of his dark passion.

Dinner was a quiet affair, for by now, the men had exhausted their stories. They had also exhausted themselves from helping the natives chop away the jungle creepers in the heat of the long, tropical day. As soon as they had finished eating, they adjourned to their tents.

Jessie and Lilly, in turn, went off to their tent. Lilly fell asleep almost immediately, but Jessie remained awake, staring up at the dark-green shadows on the canvas.

An hour passed, then another. And then, the inevitable happened. The flap of the tent went up, and Mr. Curtis crept in silently, believing Jessie to be asleep. He was startled to see her lift her head suddenly.

"What are you doing here, Mr. Curtis?" she demanded in the chilliest tone she could muster.

"You know," he said savagely. "And if you wake the girl, I'll kill her. Now come with me."

Numbly, as if in a dream, Jessie allowed her limp fingers to be taken into his strong hand. He pulled her out of her tent and led her over to his.

"You know what to do."

Jessie nodded. She wanted to fight him, but knew she could not. Her daughter's life was at stake.

She shivered as the cool night air touched her bare skin. Mr. Curtis took her clothes and threw them to one side. Then, slowly, he began to take off his own.

Chapter 16

From the start of the expedition, Kern had kept a careful diary of events, through the party's first exuberant days out of Westport and into the colder reaches of winter as the men tackled mountain range after mountain range and braved the snowswept plains between. Kern had faithfully recorded every change in weather and circumstances. Many of his early writings ran to considerable length, but as time wore on, the entries grew shorter.

Now, for the last week, Kern had made the same, terse entry each day in his diary: "Camped in the same damn place."

They had dubbed the site Camp Desolation. It was no more than a pit dug in the six-foot-deep snow. Inside, a dim, flickering fire was kept alive by whatever deadwood branches the men could find on their painful ventures into the mountain wilderness.

Three days ago, when they had failed to turn up any game, Fremont had given the order to carve and roast the mules that had died most recently. This was an easy task, for there was no shortage of dead and dying mules from which to choose. Kern counted fifty-nine remaining on December 20, 1848. Those still alive were frantic with hunger, and gnawed constantly at their tethers, at the leather of the packs, and even at each other's manes and tails. With deep, bestial intuition, the mules seemed to understand that not only were the regular provisions gone, but they themselves had become the only available food.

There was simply no way to advance. Nevertheless, Fremont and a half dozen other men would trudge off every day from the campfire pit, coats wrapped tightly and hats pulled low, to struggle up the icy incline that banked the camp on three sides. And every day the men would stagger back, their hands and feet nearly frozen, shivering violently, defeated as much by the wind as by the mountainside.

On December 22, Fremont gave the order many of the men had been expecting a week earlier.

"We have no choice," he said. "We're heading back down. But I want you all to understand that this is not the end of the expedition. We've already come halfway across the Rockies, and we've shown that any strong group of men can do it in the roughest weather. We've hit an impasse, that's all. It could happen to any group. There's nothing we could have done to avoid what's happened here."

Fremont paused, searching for the right words. "The important thing is not to panic. We could leave all the baggage here, take only what we need to go down the Rio Grande, and be in Taos within a week. But we're not going to do that. Now I know that all of us have thought powerfully about how good it would feel to get down to Taos, to have a hot bath, sit by a fire, have a home-cooked meal. We'll get to those things by and by, believe me. But not in Taos. In San Francisco!"

If his last words had been stated with the intention of rallying spirits, they failed miserably. The haggard faces around the campfire continued to stare at their leader without expression, like hollow-cheeked corpses in a cold purgatory.

"I know it's cold, and I know you're hungry. So am I!" Fremont said. "But we can find food and warmth by the Rio Grande, and we can send for supplies if we have to. I promise you, when you've got good food in your bellies and warmth in your feet, you won't want to give up all we've gained so far.

"So what we'll do is get ourselves down the mountain, and all the baggage, too. We'll take clubs to the snow if we have to. We'll pass the baggage piece by piece if we have to do that. And if we work fast, we ought to be able to cook a Christmas dinner by the river."

This prediction proved unsound. At Fremont's instruction, the men ranged out in single file, the strongest up in front. The men in front began the torturous effort of beating a trench through chin-high snowdrifts. For clubs they used saplings chopped from the few weathered pines they could find at such a high altitude. For food they relied on the mules.

Christmas Day found the men halfway down the San Juan Mountains and still out of sight of the Rio Grande. Squinting back upward, they could see their own long, undulating trench in the snow, running like a scar up the mountain. Many of the men were now bruised and bleeding, for the descent had proven more perilous than the way up. The trek had been fraught with steep, slippery stretches down which the baggage had to be thrown, the men sliding haplessly behind.

Using pots and plates, the men dug out another pit. This one they called Camp Hope, at Captain Cathcart's solemn suggestion. Here they nestled around a fire for a Christmas dinner, cooked by Godey. They ate frozen elk meat, slightly spoiled, but tolerable when cooked in a simmering stew and seasoned with the last of Doubleback's spices. Rice doughnuts, flour biscuits and mule meat pie, all washed down with hot tea, rounded out the sorry banquet.

Afterward, Fremont again addressed the men formally, thanking them, praising their courage, and blessing whatever families they might have waiting at home. It was a somber speech, and it seemed to bother the men more than console them. Kern, mulling it over, suddenly realized why the words ate at him. For the first time on the expedition, Colonel Fremont was showing real feelings—sadness and even a touch of self-pity. The man was as homesick as the rest of them! The realization stirred a concealed fondness in Kern for his leader.

Out here in this frigid landscape, with nothing more than a tiny flame between him and a painful death, Kern felt a sudden glow of sleepy contentment and warmth—a feeling he had not experienced since childhood. It reminded him of a game he had played as a child. While his parents read or knitted by the hearth, he would drape a blanket over the oak table and play underneath it, as if he were hidden inside his own private house. Right now, wrapped in his single, thin army blanket by the fire, he felt that same private contentment.

Yet, he felt troubled, too. For Fremont to show his feelings reminded Kern of the time his father, having floundered in business and finally landed in bankruptcy, had come home to tell his family they would all have to work to survive. Kern had been older then, and he had felt angry and shameful—not because his father had failed in business, nor because he would have to work himself, but because his father had spoken in a trembling voice, eyes full of tears and anguish.

"I've made a decision," Fremont announced to the men. "I thought we could get all the way down the mountain before we sent a relief party out. But now I'm not sure we can, and I don't want to take the chance. We'll all feel better knowing help is on the way, so tomorrow, I want King, Doubleback, Williams, Creutzfeldt . . . and Breckenridge to go on ahead. And King, I'm putting you in charge."

His words were met by silence, but it was a comfortable silence. The men were full, the fire was warm and the promise of supplies went down like fine Tennessee whiskey. As they drifted off to sleep on that Christmas night, there was not a man among them who imagined his own life might soon end.

By noon the next day, the relief party, taking only three loaded mules, left the rest of the men far behind. For a while, the column behind looked like a long, sinewy snake slithering through the brilliant whiteness. Then, as if dismembered, the snake broke into parts, the rearmost part lagging farther and farther above the rest. Finally, the entire snake was swallowed up, obscured by a turn in the mountain pass.

"Well, I've half a mind to say to hell with 'em. What do you say, King?"

The others looked in disbelief at Old Bill Williams.

"You ain't serious, are you, Williams?" King replied uncertainly.

"Serious? Whoa, you bet I am," Old Bill cackled. "Now, I'm not sayin' we will or we won't, understand, and the fact is, we likely won't, but what I'm feelin' with half my mind is just to keep goin', if you catch my drift."

"But why, Bill? Could be someone else here and you back there," said Creutzfeldt, the bespectacled botanist.

"I know it," Old Bill quickly agreed, "but I'd

understand if they did the same thing to me. It's every man for himself out here. I don't mean to sound heartless, but that's the way it is. And if we truly get hungry, or one of us can't go on, or breaks his leg or whatever, you're goin' to feel the same way, Creutzfeldt."

It was too cold to keep talking. The men's breaths came in labored gasps as they continued their descent. King wanted to stop when the sun got low, but Old Bill guessed that they could make the river by dark. He was right.

"Gawd, it's good to get down to some level ground," Doubleback gasped. "I think I'd kiss it if it wouldn't freeze my lips."

While the others stamped down snow for their bedrolls and tended to the mules, Doubleback built a small fire. Besides a hunk of frozen mule meat and the mules still on the hoof, all the men had to eat was a paltry ration of macaroni, a small bag of sugar and a half dozen tallow candles. Unless they could scare up some game—they did, at least, have rifles, ammunition and powder—they would soon be reduced to a steady diet of mule meat pie.

Their circumstances had grown worse by the next morning. They awoke to discover that the sugar bag, having been left loosely stuffed into a pack, had been blown by the wind out over the snow, where it was eaten by the mules. Resolutely, they now went down-river, driven as much by the need for self-preservation as by thoughts of aiding the party. By the next day they were completely out of food, for overnight the three mules had frozen to death.

"I say we cut across the way there," Old Bill declared, trying to rub the cold of a long night's sleep from his freezing hands. "Makes no sense to follow this damn river down, it curves too much. We follow every damn oxtail and we'll travel twice the distance to get there."

King was skeptical. "Maybe so," he allowed, "but if we follow the river, at least we'll know we're going in the right direction. We look for short cuts, we might just find ourself taking a long cut to nowhere."

"Oh, come on, King," Doubleback grumbled. "How hard is it to cut across a river bend? I'm with Williams."

"Creutzfeldt, what do you say?" King asked.

"Hell, don't ask him," Old Bill exclaimed. "He'll say he wants to look at the flowers by the riverbank. Won't you, Creutz?"

"Can't say as I think it's such a good idea to leave the Rio Grande when we know it goes right down into Red River and Taos."

"Jesus everlovin' Christ," Old Bill raged. "All right, Breckenridge, it's up to you, farmer."

"I say go with Williams," Breckenridge declared abruptly. He seemed more relieved just to have made a decision than to have made one he thought was right. "He's the most experienced of any of us, so he oughta know, I figure."

It turned markedly colder as soon as the men left the river's protective tree line and trudged into the snowswept plain that fanned out in three directions. Old Bill walked up ahead, loping in his strange, distinctive gait, aiming for a distant copse of trees that appeared to signal the next sweeping bend in the river.

As if a harbinger of ill fate, the sun vanished behind a towering mass of cumulus clouds, and the wind, tearing at the men's clothes, chilled their ears painfully beneath their thin scarves.

Distance took on new dimensions. The trees appeared to recede somehow, and the plain expanded in a pulsating way. The snow seemed blindingly white one moment, grey and dirty the next.

Now, too, time seemed to lose its edges. Had they not been walking many hours? Was this not the afternoon? But wait—this was another day. That was why the sky seemed brighter—it was morning.

Creutzfeldt lost all feeling in his feet. He began to think that if he could only reach that copse of trees, his feet would be warm again. The trees would help. But how? He was confused. He didn't want to think about it.

"Creutzfeldt!"

He had fallen. He looked up, his face red and stinging with snow. Williams was standing over him.

"We'll stop here."

Creutzfeldt nodded, but stayed where he was. In a while he saw a little fire flickering up above the snow. Were the trees on fire? he wondered.

"Here. Take this. It's dinner, Creutzfeldt."

Gratefully, he took the steaming hot portion he was offered. Meat: Why, yes, it seemed to be, but from where? He had heard no shots, seen no mules go down.

He chewed thoughtfully for a moment. It was certainly tough, and it had a taste unlike any other game he had ever chewed. Rough, but revivifying. Creutzfeldt swallowed, feeling the meat go down to fill the gaping chasm in his gut.

Halfway through, he felt good enough to focus on the gaunt, chewing faces around him. "What'd you find, Bill?" he asked.

"Take a look at your feet."

Creutzfeldt looked down. His boot soles were gone. With a crashing shock of reality, he realized he was eating them.

*   *   *

"Listen, I'm tired. I'm going to rest," King called up when they had been walking an hour or so the next morning. "You all go on ahead. I'll catch up with you."

They turned back to face him.

"How are you going to catch up?" Breckenridge called back across the snow. "It'll be harder if you stop to rest."

"No, I . . . I don't know, I'm just tired. I'll be all right in an hour or so. I'll follow your tracks. Go on."

Creutzfeldt was feeling much better today. He seemed to have tapped some well of reserve energy. He was cold, still, and his muscles hurt, but he kept pace easily with Old Bill and Doubleback. The remnants of his boots were wrapped onto his feet with thick strips of blanket.

"You ought to eat shoe leather more often, Creutz," Doubleback teased. "Looks like it's your kind of vittles."

Creutzfeldt laughed and nodded. "Yes, yes—I do feel a whole lot better today. Good, good . . ."

Old Bill looked quickly over at him, then traded a meaningful glance with Doubleback. Sounded like Creutz was cracking up. Old Bill had seen it happen before, just like this. Things got bad, and a weak man started to panic. Things stayed bad, and a fellow might suddenly come out all smiles and full of hope. You could tell the difference. Making the best of a bad time was one thing, but getting all silly like a kid was something else. And when the smile began to quiver and the panic came back—well, it was best to be somewhere else when that happened.

They made the copse of trees an hour or so after leaving King. Doubleback and Breckenridge began cursing violently a quarter of a mile from it, when they saw they had lost the river. Old Bill turned stone-faced, the way he always did when confronted by an error in judgment. Creutzfeldt, though, started crying.

"It's not that goddamn bad, Creutz," Doubleback said when his own string of curses was spent. "I mean, look, it's still headed south, right? It just means this here mottlehead put us through a lot of pain and misery we didn't need to go through."

"You would have done the same thing, cracker," Old Bill shot back. "Fact you did. You voted to go this way."

"Look, it doesn't matter now anyway," Breckenridge said. "We're here, and we're freezing our asses off. That's all that counts, right? Now, what the hell are we going to do about King?"

Way off in the distance, King's tiny, dark form remained where they had left him. It appeared that he had not moved at all.

"Tell you what, Creutz, since you're so full of zip, why don't you go back and give him a hand?" Old Bill said.

Creutzfeldt now started to cry in earnest. "Me? Why me?" he moaned, taking off his glasses to wipe the tears from his eyes. "We could at least have pulled straws or something."

If Doubleback and Breckenridge had had any sympathy for Creutzfeldt before, it was lost now. Old Bill might have been a heartless son of a bitch, and he did not have any right giving orders when Fremont had put King in charge, but tears were intolerable.

Creutzfeldt glanced from face to face. He could feel them all against him. Well, all right then, he would get King. At least King would understand.

"Where will you be?" he asked his voice still wavering.

"Right here, Creutz, right here," Old Bill answered. "We wouldn't want to leave you behind."

Creutzfeldt nodded numbly and cast his blurry eyes to the ground. He didn't want to look at the others. He would go find King. King would understand.

He began walking, picking his way back along his own footsteps. Soon, his feet fell into a rhythm, up and down, one hole to the next. "Daisies and lilac . . . and daffodils . . . and lace . . . See all . . . the flowers in . . . this magical place."

It was a rhyme he had learned as a child, and it came back to him now as he walked. It seemed to take his mind off his cold feet. After a while, his feet hardly felt cold at all.

He hardly dared to look and see how much farther he had to go. "Daisies and . . . lilac . . . and daffodils . . . and lace . . . None match . . . the prettiness . . . of Katherine's . . . face."

Then he stopped short, startled. He was looking down at a pair of boots.

King's eyes stared blankly into his own. His mouth was slightly ajar, and his beard was white with frost.

Creutzfeldt screamed. His legs gave way under him. He fell into the snow and took hold of King's knees. They felt brittle and cold. He butted King backward with his right shoulder, King fell over stiffly with a dull crunch into the crusty snow.

He was dead. But he couldn't be. Creutzfeldt shook King by the shoulders, then screamed at him. He put his slavering, whiskered cheek against King's cold, dead lips. He could feel no air.

All around now, as the white world closed in, the line between snow and sky vanished. Creutzfeldt was the axis of a gyre that began to turn around him, slowly at first, then faster and faster until he could hear it whirling, like a rush of the ocean in a conch shell, growing more insistent, louder, and finally deafeningly loud.

Sometime later, Creutzfeldt opened his eyes to find himself sprawled face down in the snow. The part of his face that lay wedged in the snow was red and raw with cold, beyond feeling. He pushed himself up and blinked at the snow. Something was wrong. The spinning had left him dizzy, and it seemed to have blurred his vision. He reached for his spectacles. They were gone.

Frantically, Creutzfeldt searched in the snow where his face had been. He took his gloves off and plunged his bare hands into the soft, surrounding drift. He reached out and touched King's boot. It was a dark blur, nothing more, but he could feel the stiff, cold leather, the frozen laces.

A dread as deep as any feeling he had ever known racked Creutzfeldt's body. His arms and legs shook. His stomach fluttered violently, and abruptly he retched. For a long time he stayed on all fours, vomiting into the snow but bringing almost nothing up because his stomach was so empty. His heart pounded and his arms and legs shook.

He finally stood up. The world was a blur. So what? It was all white anyway, focused or not. He stood over King. Creutzfeldt took hold of King's arms. They felt incredibly heavy.

Digging into the snow for a more secure stance, Creutzfeldt put one of the dead man's arms over one shoulder, took a deep breath, then pulled the body onto his back.

The weight of it plunged him down into the snow.

King lay on top of him, pinning him to the ground. King's whiskers bore down on the back of his neck.

Just a game, Creutzfeldt thought. Play it as a game. He elbowed his way free of the corpse, got up, and again tried hauling it onto his back. This time, braced for the awesome weight of it, Creutzfeldt managed to shoulder the body. With heavy, aching steps, he slowly began to walk back toward the trees. He couldn't see them at all, but he knew he was headed in the right direction by following the deep footsteps in the snow.

"Daisies and . . . lilac . . . and daffodils . . . and lace . . . See all . . . the flowers in . . . this magical place . . ."

"All right, Creutz, it's all right."

Creutzfeldt had the sensation of awakening from a long, drugged sleep. It had seemed such a pleasant sleep that he wanted to slip right back into it.

But there were interesting shapes, too. There were three of them, clustered like petals on a flower. And there in the middle was another blur, round as a daisy's pistil.

The others were doing something to the blur in the middle. They were playing a game!

"What are you playing?" Creutzfeldt asked as he rubbed his eyes, trying to clear them. His hand grew wet with tears. That was strange. He wasn't sad at all. He was happy.

"Just playing a game, like you wanted, Creutz." The voice was Old Bill's.

"Can I play, too?"

There was some laughter from the blurs, but it was strange laughter, harsh and guttural, like animals clearing their throats.

"Sure, Creutz, you can play," came the voice again.

Someone thrust something into his hands.

"Well, don't just sit there, Creutz. Take some and pass it back."

Someone forced him to raise the thing to his lips.

It was certainly a strange thing! It was long . . . and round . . . and rough and wet at the top.

Creutzfeldt let his hands explore down the far end of the strange, wet thing. It got narrower . . . and narrower . . . and what were these?

The scream came uncontrollably. For a brief moment he was jolted into sanity. His eyes opened wide and struggled to focus on the thing he was holding.

It was Harry King's arm.

Chapter 17

It was a bitter blow.

For the better part of the day, Fremont had led the men down a mountainous ravine that seemed a promising detour around an especially steep escarpment. The men had separated into three groups, not by choice or command, but simply by the restrictions of their own different paces. Up with Fremont walked Godey, Charles Preuss, Brattle and the half-Indian, Gregorio. Farther back was the largest contingent, including the petty moralist Vincenthaler, Ducatel, Ferguson, Wise and the Illinois recruit, Carver. And considerably behind both these groups plodded Kern and Cathcart.

Fremont was the first to recognize his mistake. The ravine led circuitously around one last mountainside, then plunged into a sheer, ice-walled canyon. They would have to turn back.

This they did, briefly meeting up with Vincenthaler's group, then pulling ahead again down the steeper but more reliable escarpment they had scaled only ten days before.

Kern and Cathcart were at least granted the blessing of avoiding the detour altogether. They were not much weaker or more fatigued than the others, but they

were more cautious. Rather than burn up precious re-
serves of strength, both had agreed to move slowly.

"Another thing," Cathcart said. "I don't like what
I'm feeling about that main bunch. I don't like it at all.
I wouldn't put it past them to try something stupid."

"Are you serious?"

"You're damn right, I'm serious. I've listened to
their grumbling."

Indeed, in Vincenthaler's group, a few muttered
oaths among the men had made their attitudes clear.
To see Fremont trudging back toward them up from
the ravine was more than most were willing to stand.

"But it would be mutiny," Carver hissed at Ferguson's suggestion.

"You're not in the goddamn army, Carver,"
Ferguson spat back. He was a big man, one of the biggest in the party, and had been a logger before he joined
up. He was also one of the youngest, which was why
he had gravitated to the baby-faced Carver.

"Doesn't matter," Carver retorted. "I know mutiny
when I see it."

"Might do us better than following that mule's ass
Fremont around in circles," Ferguson offered. "And I'll
tell you this, Carver, I'm not the only one saying it. So
you'd best keep your trap shut or you might end up on
the losing side."

The same desperation that pushed them closer to
challenging Fremont also restrained them at present.
There was nothing to be gained from rebellion at three
thousand feet above sea level, and maybe Williams and
King and the others would be waiting for them, mirac-
ulously, with supplies when they reached the river.

Three more days of slippery descent ensued. Under
cold, clear skies, with a brilliant view of the Colorado
horizon to the east, the men felt almost exultant at
times. There was no lack of water. Gurgling streams ran

down on every side. Nor was there any shortage of wood. The lower they descended, the more thickly arrayed were the pines, cedars and trembling aspen trees.

They came to a good many precarious drops, where a carelessly placed boot might plunge the wearer into a brutal fall, but for all the bruises that were sustained daily, not a bone was broken, and not a life lost. Some of the drops, in fact, were exhilarating. The men would reach a hillside twenty or thirty feet steep and go sliding down seated on their packs, with great whoops and hollers.

The mules were less inspired by the hills. They would balk as they looked down and take a wobbling stance of defiance, but now they were too weak to resist. One false step, and they would go tumbling in terror to the bottom. The animals' injuries were more severe, so whenever one incurred a broken leg or rib, the men would shoot it for food.

By now the men were killing mules as a matter of course. Felled by one shot at close range, the chosen creature would be skinned and carved, the pieces boiled for several hours and the resulting mule steaks seasoned with a coating of cornmeal and a sprinkling of salt. It was a rough fare, but going without was rougher still, and the men had grimly gotten accustomed to it.

Still, a cloud of brooding discontent hung over the group. It darkened palpably on New Year's Day. Though no one spoke of it, the realization that the new year had begun in such dire circumstances went down hard. And there was no one who failed to remember Colonel Fremont's proud boast on the day they had ridden out of Westport that they would reach San Francisco by New Year's Day.

The second morning of 1849 brought no better tidings. Fremont's advance party reached the Rio

Grande amid fresh-falling snow. As the temperature dropped, Vincenthaler and the main contingent remained along the stretch of the Embargo Creek where it joined the river, looking for a more protected spot to camp. Behind them were Kern and Cathcart, now joined by the two Indians, Gregorio and Joaquin, who had perceived the volatility among Vincenthaler's men and discreetly fallen behind.

King's relief party was nowhere in sight.

"I guess he knows which side his bread is buttered on." Vincenthaler was emerging as the spokesman for his group, partly because his constant homilies were now directed toward inflaming the anger and despair that every man was feeling. It was more than that, though. It was as if the men knew, deep down, that no matter how badly the expedition had turned out so far, Colonel Fremont had done his best to make it go well. They could not, in truth, justify a revolt—not in their own hearts, and not to each other. And yet they were angry and bitter, and they were tormented by the prospect of having to forge on by some other route into the same, icy impasse from which they had just descended. All they wanted now was a warm, comfortable winter around the hearth. So they let Vincenthaler voice their dissatisfaction, while they marched dutifully on.

The showdown came after Proue died.

Charles Proue, a Frenchman from Missouri, had been with Fremont on all three of his other expeditions. He was a good, strong, quiet man. But he had one shortcoming—he smoked too much. He had long since run out of his supply of tobacco and papers, and had borne his deprivation stoically. His circulation, though, was still sharply affected. And his feet, as a result, were more susceptible to painful chilling and frostbite. Now, as the weather turned colder again, Proue's feet, already purple, became excruciatingly painful.

Vincenthaler's men set Proue by the fire when he first spoke of his discomfort, but it was too late. The arteries in his feet had frozen and ruptured, and the fire seemed only to encourage internal bleeding.

"Just sit there till it gets better," advised Ferguson. "Or till them bastards get here with the supplies."

Proue shook his head sharply, his eyes shut tight with pain. "No," he managed, "I can't wait. I know I can't. I got to get going on my own."

No amount of reasoning could coax him out of it. Four days after they had been bivouacked on the creek, Proue pulled on his boots, stood up, and started out in the direction of Fremont's campsite seven miles downriver.

Halfway between the two camps, he collapsed and died.

Ferguson was the one to find him.

"I've had enough of this madness!" Vincenthaler cried, when Ferguson brought back the news. "Goddamnit, one bird in the hand is worth two in the bush, and I don't aim to stay in the bush!"

The others quickly agreed. They would head south. Leaving most of the baggage stashed by the creek, they set out and reached Fremont in two hours' time.

They found him bundled around a small campfire with the others, writing in his notebook. He stood up as they approached. Fremont seemed to realize, even before he saw their faces clearly, that something had gone awry.

"Proue's dead."

"How?"

"Frozen. He was halfway here when it happened."

Vincenthaler was trying hard to put an edge on his words, but there was something about Fremont's stern impassiveness that dampened his resolve. Somehow, after all he had endured, the colonel still appeared to be unfazed. He stood tall and leveled his clear blue eyes on Vincenthaler.

"You bury him?"

"No. We didn't bury him. For God's sake, Colonel, we've got little enough grit left in us as it is, without spending it all on a dead man."

Fremont's gaze never flickered. He might have been about to issue a few choice words about respect for one's commander, but he said nothing.

"Colonel, we're here for a reason," Vincenthaler finally continued. He looked around behind him at the others and felt a sudden queasiness. No one would meet his eyes. "We're here because we're going south to Taos, Colonel. We've had enough of this freezing and starving."

Fremont still said nothing. Vincenthaler was a nervous man. He could bluster about like a human steam engine and argue vociferously when a man contradicted him, but he couldn't endure this silence.

"Don't you see, Colonel? We've had enough. You've had this bee in your bonnet from the start about the railroad, and it's led you out of the frying pan and into the fire."

Was it Vincenthaler's imagination, or had Fremont's lips turned up ever so slightly, just for a second, in a mocking smile? Behind him, Vincenthaler heard a low snicker.

"Now you can't say we haven't kept pace with you, Colonel, because we have. But this whole notion of a central railroad is like pounding a square peg through a round hole, and frankly, we don't aim to get hammered any longer."

"If I understand you," scoffed Fremont, "you are intending to mutiny, Mr. Vincenthaler."

For the first time, the gravity of Vincenthaler's intentions seemed to weigh upon his own brow. Once again he turned to face his cohorts, and once again their eyes shifted to the ground.

"No, not exactly mutiny, Colonel," Vincenthaler said. "We've been with you all the way. It's just that we want the way to end here."

Fremont nodded reflectively. Then he walked past Vincenthaler to Carver. "Are you also intending to mutiny, Carver?"

"No sir, not really. That is, I don't think so, sir."

Fremont moved on to Hubbard and asked him the same. Then he went to Ferguson, Ducatel and Wise. Each one stammered a similar reply and lapsed into embarrassed silence.

"Vincenthaler, I believe you've been deceived," said Fremont as he turned back to the ashen-faced man. "But I'm glad you've come, because I have an announcement."

He looked over the tired, shivering men, and the disdain seemed to leave his voice as he spoke. "I know you're hungry and tired, and you've been hoping desperately, as I have, that King would come back any time now. But we may as well admit to ourselves that he's not coming back. My guess is that he never made it to Red River. He might have been cut off by the Indians, or he might have run out of food. But he's probably out there somewhere needing help even more than we do.

"So tomorrow morning we'll split up again. I'll head down to Red River with Godey, Preuss, Brattle and Gregorio. I figure we've got as good a chance as any of making it."

Vincenthaler's rage and bluster had now evaporated, and like a chastised student raising his hand, he said, "Colonel, why don't we all go? Why should any of us stay?"

"Because we've got to get down with all the bags and equipment. And because if we do get enough mules and supplies back up here, we stand a damn good chance of pushing on farther south, around the mountains.

"The rest of you men," Fremont snapped, "will stay here under Vincenthaler's command."

At that, Vincenthaler straightened up. His jaw tightened and the pride returned to his eyes.

"In a week or less, I'll either be back myself, or I'll send up Mexicans with supplies and directions. In fact, that's probably what I'll do. And if so, you'd all better hurry on down to meet me. Because if you don't, you'll find me off and gone to California."

They had been following the river for two days when Gregorio saw tracks. A New Mexico Indian, he had spent all of his twenty-five winters out West, learning to hunt and find game in the snow, to live on berries and bugs if he had to, and simply to go without if there was nothing at all to eat. He and Fremont had always kept a formal distance between each other, and each respected the other more for it. Next to Godey, Gregorio was the member of the expedition Fremont respected most as an outdoorsman, a hunter and a surveyor.

There were four sets of horse tracks. They came from the southeast, stopped right at the edge of the river and continued westward from the opposite bank. In rapt concentration Godey and Gregorio bent over them.

"One Indian," Gregorio said at last.

Godey nodded. It was easy to tell by the unshod

hooves that an Indian's horse had made the tracks. As for the number riding, that was just as easy. One set of tracks was wider around than the others. That horse had been bearing a man's weight, and had been struggling more to move through the snow.

"Can you tell what tribe?" Fremont asked Gregorio.

"Pueblo, maybe. Maybe Pawnee."

Friendly enough either way. The more important question was whether to keep heading down the river in the hope of finding the source of the tracks. Fremont decided they would follow the river. He was confident they would at least find game of some sort, and they had no shortage of powder. Besides, he insisted, it was better to keep their noses pointed toward the settlement. Even now, they could hardly have more than eighty miles to go.

"If he's loaded down," Godey asserted, "he's probably come from Red River himself. He can't be going much farther. Otherwise he'd have gone to some other post for supplies."

"Or he's a hunter," Gregorio put in. "And he's loaded down with game on his way back home."

They left the river to scale the western bank and to follow the tracks. They had only their rifles, powder and bedrolls to carry on their backs. Since the night before, none had eaten, and though they were all strong men, they knew they could not go without food for too long.

Again, it was Gregorio who boosted their spirits. Toward the end of the cold, bleak afternoon, he spied a curl of smoke against the horizon. It was only a hair-thin line of grey, almost imperceptible. But it was, on close inspection, unmistakable.

With renewed energy, the hungry group pushed on. By darkness, they were crouched on a hilltop, barely daring to breathe as they looked down at a crude collection of adobe huts, with split-wood roofs, nestled in the snowbound valley.

In silence, each man made the rough calculations: a dozen huts meant two dozen Indians, all male and all hunters. This was clearly a winter hunting post for a tribe based farther west, in the mountains perhaps, or northwest near Saquache Creek. Here the best hunters would come to kill deer, elk and bear. They would send one of their number back routinely, with fresh game for the tribe.

They were obviously not hostile. Yet who could guess how they might react to the sight of Fremont and his men, straggling down the hillside? Fremont was no stranger to Indians. He had encountered about fifty tribes in his travels, but rarely had he met one from such a position of weakness—a position, indeed, of supplication. Indians, for the most part, were neither as noble nor as savage as easterners were given to believe. They were just as proud and passionate, selfish and narrow-minded as white men. And like white men, many of them were shrewdly aware of power—what constituted it, who had it, how to trade for it or how to take it away.

He traded glances with Godey and the others. From all eyes came the same understanding, and the same conclusion. They would risk it.

Fremont smiled. There was a very good reason why they all felt willing to take this risk, and he was mightily affected by it, too. Wafting up the hillside, from the cauldrons over the campfire, was the most delectable aroma of boiling elk stew.

Fremont stood up and shook his bedroll into place. The others stood up with him. Slowly, holding their weapons in plain sight with barrels pointed to the stars, they began to walk down the snowy hill. For a while they remained unseen. Then one of the Indians gave a shout, and those around the campfire scattered to grab for their bows.

"We come in peace," Fremont called out. He wasn't sure they would understand his words, but they would understand his tone of voice—friendly, guarded and calm.

The Indians made no immediate response. As Fremont and the others approached, their guns still held out in a gesture of peace, a few braves gathered around the campfires with knives and hatchets drawn. The rest remained in the shadows waiting.

"We come in peace," Fremont repeated. "We are hungry. Who is your chief?"

One of the Indians, older, but still stronger than most, stepped forward.

To Fremont's amazement, he spoke nearly perfect English.

"Where have you come from?" the Indian asked.

"From the North. From up the river. We were traveling in the mountains, and we had to come down. Our men were weak and hungry. Most are still up the river, waiting for us to bring help."

The Indian chief digested all this information slowly, as if inspecting a piece of turquoise that might not be genuine.

"You were up in the mountains? In the snows?"

"Yes, we were trying to cross, to the West. We are explorers. We are scientists."

This made no impression on the Indians.

"We are searchers," Fremont tried. "We were searching for a way over the mountains in winter. We wanted to find a path."

"A path." the chief said, gazing at Fremont incredulously. "Why this path? For trading?"

Fremont could see he would have no luck explaining his mission. These Indians had never seen a railroad, and had they known what it was, they would only have been further alienated to learn of Fremont's purpose. The last thing the Indians needed was a belching, iron horse roaring through their mountains.

"To trade, yes," Fremont said in exasperation.

"And now you are hungry, and you need food?"

"We need more than food," Fremont said, locking his clear blue eyes with the chief's mocking gaze. "We need help. We need four horses and a guide to help us get to Red River—to the white man's trading post down the river."

"Four horses and a guide!" The chief could not keep from turning to explain this joke to the others. They laughed when they heard.

"Do you think, perhaps, that the Indian lives to help the white man?" the chief asked, turning back to Fremont. "Do you think the Indian learns to hunt and stay warm in winter so that he may teach these things to the white man, who is so hungry and so cold?"

"I think," said Fremont, "that one man should help another."

"One man should help another!" the chief repeated sarcastically. "You must have been a child in Santa Fe."

Fremont shook his head.

"Well, that is a surprise. Because I was a child in Santa Fe. And I went to the Spanish mission school to learn Spanish and English. And this is what I heard from every teacher: one man should help another. The white man should help the white man. And the Indian should help the white man, too! But you know what? They never taught that the white man should help the Indian! Why is that?"

Fremont shrugged. "I don't know."

"Maybe the white man is not supposed to help

the Indian. Maybe that's what it is. And you know, that is exactly what has come to pass. Here comes the white man, into our hills, into our mountains, hunting and fishing and shooting any Indian who tries to stop him. But when the white man gets hungry in the Indian's house, what does he do? He asks for food!"

"I cannot speak for other white men, as you cannot speak for other tribes," Fremont said quietly. "I know that if you were hungry, and you came to my camp, I would give you food to eat."

The Indian chief stared at him intently for a moment. "Perhaps you would. But I would never need your food, so what does it matter?"

Now Gregorio stepped forward. For some time, the other Indians had been eyeing him with suspicion and disdain. The chief had noticed him, too, but had purposely spoken only to Fremont.

"I, too, come from Santa Fe, Branded Pony," Gregorio said.

The chief stared at him in disapproval. "Who are you?"

"Gregorio, son of Three Fingers."

A murmur of recognition swept through the assembled braves.

"You have come a long way over a very short distance," the chief said wryly. "Why are you with this white man?"

"I am with this white man because he is an honorable leader," Gregorio said. "He has crossed the mountains many times, and he has never harmed an Indian, or destroyed Indian land. He is a strong man, and a good man. Now he needs help, not just for himself or for us, but for his men. If they do not soon eat, they will die."

The Indian chief mulled this for awhile, then turned to relay Gregorio's words to the other braves.

"You say you are a trader," he addressed Fremont again. "What have you got to trade for horses and food?"

"Our guns and powder."

The chief laughed. "We have guns."

Fremont had seen no guns in evidence. He guessed the chief was bluffing. "We have nothing else."

The chief's eyes dropped to Fremont's neck. There, gleaming softly in the firelight, was the gold necklace Jessie had given him when he asked her to marry him nearly nine years ago. It was a finely wrought piece, the work of a renowned master craftsman in Boston, and Fremont had vowed never to part with it.

"You have gold," the chief said.

"I must keep it," Fremont replied. "It is a gift of betrothal."

"But your men are starving, and I like your little gift. Give it to me."

The chief held out a large hand, palm up. Fremont stiffened. Then with a grimace, he set his gun on the ground, reached up with both hands behind his neck and unclasped the necklace. In the chief's palm, it looked like a shimmering band of molten ore.

Now the chief ordered his men to confiscate the guns. In a moment, the rifles and side arms had vanished into one of the adobe huts, and the necklace had found a new owner's neck to adorn.

"Very well, white man," he said when this was done. "You will have horses, and he," indicating one of the younger braves, "will be your guide. There will be food with the horses, and there is food now. Come."

Fremont thanked him quietly. "Perhaps someday," he added, "we will meet again, Branded Pony, and I will trade you something for my necklace."

* * *

The next day Fremont had ridden nearly twenty miles south of the Indian hunting camp when he reached up instinctively to touch the necklace and found it around his neck. The chief was a proud, arrogant man, he thought, but an honorable one. Fremont would not forget to send his thanks back with the young scout.

Revivified by the stew and a night's warm lodging, the small party rode steadily through the day. Their guide, who went by the name of Double Edge, was known to Gregorio from the mission in Santa Fe, and they were two of a kind: silent until spoken to, strong without swaggering, and steadfastly loyal.

So it may have shocked them even more than it shocked the white men when toward the end of the afternoon, they came upon the morbid, gut-churning spectacle of King's relief party.

The riders spied them a long way off. From a distance, they looked like dark specks huddled downriver against the snowy bank. Grimly, Fremont noted their number. One was missing.

"A lot of help they would have been," Godey muttered.

The dark specks appeared not to notice the approaching riders. They were grouped around a cold campfire, and they appeared to be sleeping. Their coats were pulled up over their heads. Only their uncontrollable shaking gave them away as living men.

"Hey, there," Fremont called out sharply as they rode up. "King! Williams!"

Startled, they raised their heads. Then they began to cry. If the riders had felt proud at the thought of saving these men, their pride was vanquished by a wave of revulsion and pity.

Doubleback, who had been thin when he had set

out two weeks before, was so emaciated that Fremont
had trouble recognizing him. His hair fell to either side
of his face like black seaweed from a skull. Williams'
flesh was stretched so tight that the cross-hatched lines
in his face had smoothed out. His nose, always gaunt
and beaklike, now stood on his face like a leaky pump
spigot. Breckenridge looked less ravaged only because
his eyes were clear and he wasn't whimpering. Fremont
turned to him first.

"What happened to him?" he asked, indicating
Creutzfeldt.

"He's crazy, Colonel. He's gone plumb out of his
mind." As Breckenridge spoke, his voice cracked.
Then he began to sob. "I can't believe you're here,
Colonel. I was sure we was all dead men."

Pity washed over Fremont. He knelt to lift Breckenridge up by the armpits. The man's tears fell uncontrollably now. And like a small child turning to his
father for refuge, Breckenridge buried his head in the
colonel's lap.

Meanwhile Gregorio had opened one of the packs
of provisions and come forward with a loaf of corn
bread and a piece of cooked elk meat. "Just a little,
now," he cautioned the starving men. "Too much and
your stomach will break."

Fremont had to hold some food to Breckenridge's
mouth, for the man was too weak to lift his arms.

"How about you, Creutz," he said gently to the
fourth figure in the snow.

Unlike the others, Creutzfeldt was sitting up, and
his arms were locked around his legs as he hugged them
to his chest. Rocking slightly, he hummed a snatch of
some song over and over again. His eyes were glassy.
He didn't understand that help had arrived. Then, as
Fremont began to speak, Creutzfeldt smiled and began
to sing: "Daisies . . . and lilac . . . and daffodils . . .

and lace . . . See all . . . the flowers in . . . this magical . . . place!"

"He's been goin' on like that for a while," Breckenridge managed. "He's just gone plain crazy. That and his games."

Creutzfeldt took a piece of elk meat from Fremont's hand and put it to his own lips. Suddenly his smile froze, he stopped singing, and with a feeble cry of terror, he threw the meat into the snow.

"Why doesn't he eat?" Fremont asked.

"Havin' it rough, it twisted his mind," said Williams. "We shot a coyote and had to eat it raw, and ol' Creutz got pretty upset about that. Ain't ate nothin' ever since. Plus he lost his spectacles and he ain't been the same since."

Even now, Old Bill Williams grated sharply on Fremont's nerves. He had never come to like the man. It was impossible to say whether Williams was to blame for leading the men to the impasse they had reached. Any other guide might have done the same, and no one had ever tried to cross the San Juan Mountains in winter. But Fremont could not escape the conviction that Williams, out of ignorance or senility or maybe even malice, had led the entire expedition astray when it could have succeeded in crossing the first time. For that, he would never forgive him.

"Where's King?"

Old Bill looked down at his meat. "Dead, Colonel. King's dead."

"Where is he?"

"Back there. 'Bout five miles. He just sat down and died, Colonel. And then the coyote came and ate him, the one we shot."

"How exactly did King die?" Fremont addressed the question to Doubleback. Suddenly there was a tension among the men around the cold campfire.

"Well, Colonel, just like Williams says, he sat down and died." Doubleback's voice was scratchy, as though he were half asleep. "We'd cut off away from the river, thinkin' it would be a shortcut. But it weren't, after all. It was a lot of hard goin' through a wide stretch with no trees or nothin' and the wind was blowin' somethin' fierce. We got nearly to a bunch of trees, 'bout seven miles northwest of here, and just afore we made them, King sits down and says he wants to rest a bit. So he did, and when Creutz went for him later, he was sitting dead in the snow. Ain't that right, Creutz?"

"Did you find King, Creutzfeldt?" Fremont asked. "In the snow?"

Creutzfeldt made an effort to focus. His eyes narrowed and became a bit clearer.

"In the snow," he said. Then he smiled again. "I was playing a game in the snow! I came all the way to the trees with him. And he was on my back, too. I carried him."

"Then what happened, Creutz?" asked Godey. He too, was beginning to feel suspicious.

"Then they played another game," Creutzfeldt said. His smile turned into a frown, and he knit his eyebrows. "A nasty game."

"Ah, for Christ's sakes don't listen to him. He's gone out of his mind," cried Williams. "Let's just get goin'."

Fremont looked at him hard. "We'll get going, Bill. Soon as we find the body."

Taking Godey with him, Fremont set out on horseback to follow the tracks going westward. One set of tracks curved off and back to cross the others. There was a large, rough impression in the snow beyond. Around it, the other sets of footprints had gathered.

They found King's body by the copse of trees. It looked less like a human corpse than a barrel-shaped, dismembered carcass of a pig. A wide, dark stain of blood colored the snow beside each of King's limbless sockets.

"No animal did that," Godey said softly.

King's arms had been cleanly amputated, with no sign of teeth marks, and the limbs were nowhere to be seen. A strong stench permeated the area. To Fremont, this was a crime, an outrage. But it was also the most pathetic reduction of human dignity and grace he had ever seen. How quickly a man might tumble from the lofty perch of his pride to this sorry place!

Fremont took his bedroll and knelt to wrap King's mutilated body tightly within it. Godey cleared a deep space in the snow, and without a word to each other, the men silently buried the body.

As they rode back, Fremont stared straight ahead. The anger had gone out of his face. What he felt was a strong and unexpected twist of guilt. It was easy to tell himself that he would never have done this grisly thing, that he would have died first. Maybe so. But these were his men. He had brought them here, and was he not to blame, at least in part, for their miserable fate?

"We buried him," Fremont said simply when they reached the others.

Creutzfeldt smiled blissfully. The scarecrows around the campfire looked up at Fremont with guarded expressions.

"You found him, then," Old Bill said finally.

"Just followed your tracks."

"And you seen how the coyote and such got to him?" Breckenridge asked nervously.

"We saw that, yes."

Fremont kept his gaze on the cold, black ashes of

the campfire, ignoring Godey's questioning look. He seemed to be struggling with some painful thought. The others waited, hardly breathing. Only Creutzfeldt remained unaware of the extraordinary tension that hung in the air.

"I'm sorry he had to come to that end," Fremont said at last. "It's a terrible thing when a man's remains are set upon by any kind of beast."

Chapter 18

No one had alerted the village to the arrival of the ghostly pack of riders, yet even from a great distance, Fremont's party drew the entire village, some fifty Mexican faces, out from their mud-and-wattle huts. They waited in curious silence as the men rode toward them.

Fremont saw the tiny figures assembling against the snow line, and he felt a spasm of panic that made him rein up short. Why would they do that? After all this anguish and effort, would he be cut down and kept from getting supplies to the others?

"Not much choice, is there?" Godey remarked.

They rode on. When they drew to within one hundred yards of the phalanx of Mexicans, Fremont relaxed. Not one was armed. Many were women and children. But they had a strange look, as if they were watching a funeral.

They could hardly be blamed, Fremont realized. He had been apart from vigorous, well-fed people for so long that the wraithlike figures he traveled with had come to seem normal. Even he and Godey had come to look emaciated. Their hands were bony as talons, and their hair lay matted and twisted.

Williams, Doubleback and Breckenridge looked much worse. Their faces were greasy and blackened by the soot of greasewood fires. Their eyes looked like bulbous orbs set in deep, dark pits.

But it was at Creutzfeldt that the awed and terrified Mexican children pointed their fingers. He was as gaunt and blackened as the others, but he wore a wide, fixed, cherubic smile, and his eyes darted askew, as if his mind had split right down the middle, each half going off in the opposite direction with one eye to guide the way.

"You know me, Alfonso. I am John Fremont, from Missouri."

The wizened old Mexican looked up quickly at the man on horseback. "You are not. You cannot be." Then the surge of recognition hit him, and he clapped his hands sharply at the boys standing near him. "Felix! Hernando! Bring food!"

Three of the women were quickly dispatched to prepare two huts for the men and to boil bathing water. In a moment, the silent town exploded into a hubbub of activity. Children, darting among their elders, searched for any article they might present to the riders and thereby approach them for a closer look. Their suspicions dispelled, the elders also went bustling off to seek out some gifts of food or comfort.

"You look older than I do," the old Mexican said reprovingly. "What have you done to yourself?"

"It's been a long trip, Alfonso," Fremont said to his old friend.

Briefly, Fremont related his story. Alfonso Salazar was a man he respected even as much as Kit Carson. In his day, Alfonso had ridden hard and skillfully. He could still do astounding feats with a lariat, and with a knife he had no equal. At thirty yards, he could pierce the heart of a tree knot. But now he walked rather than rode, and except to show young boys, he preferred to do little with his knife but whittle figures out of pine. Still, he remained the unspoken leader of the village, and whatever he decreed was done.

"We need mules, Alfonso," Fremont said when he had finished telling Alfonso about the expedition. "Fifteen mules, with grain and pemmican." He saw the old man shaking his head sadly.

"I have no money now, but I will pay you soon."

"Colonel, don't talk about money. I would take no money from you, even if you had it. But I have no mules. This has been a hard winter, and many have died. We have only four left now. They are too weak, and would not help you."

"So we go to Taos?"

"I'm afraid you must. But not today. Stay and rest one night."

Fremont looked over at Godey. "I don't know. We should be going, I think." Godey's face faded out in a screen of grey and white spots. Fremont felt himself slipping from his mount. Then a strong hand steadied him. His vision cleared, and he managed a smile. "Tired, I guess."

"Come, Colonel, this is no time to be pushing on. It's already late in the day. You'll be too tired to get a mule team together." Alfonso laughed. "Besides, anyone who doesn't know you and sees your scary face will shoot you on sight."

Embarrassed, Fremont tried to fend off the hands that came up to help him from the saddle. To his surprise, he found he lacked the strength even to lift his arms. The screen of grey and white pulsated more intensely now, blocking Alfonso from his sight.

The next thing he felt was another hand against his skin, but this one was smoother, more delicate. Fremont opened his eyes. Wrapped in Indian blankets, he realized he was lying in an extraordinarily comfortable bed. And he was, he realized with a start, naked.

A slender, sloe-eyed Mexican woman sat over him, her hand cool against his forehead. She could not have been older than twenty, with soft, bronze skin, long dark hair and pendulous breasts that rose and fell gently as she breathed.

"Is it morning yet?" Fremont asked.

She shook her head. "It is only just after dinner. The rest have eaten. Are you hungry?"

"God, yes."

Hungry and also in pain, Fremont realized. Every muscle in his body seemed to have rebelled during his brief sleep. His right leg in particular throbbed with a painful insistence. It had been close to frozen in the last days down the river. Now, he guessed, his blood was pushing back into it. The pain was excruciating, but at least that meant his leg was still functioning, and not completely frozen.

The young Mexican woman went rustling off, then reappeared almost immediately with a steaming bowl of stew and a hunk of buttered bread. Fremont ate as though he had never encountered food before. When he was done, he sank back on his pillows and took a look around him. He was in a hut. A fire blazed in the hearth across the room, and a thick, woven rug covered most of the dirt floor. Other weavings hung from the walls, interspersed with the mounted heads of bear, moose and elk.

"Where am I?"

"This is Alfonso's hut. He wanted you to stay here." The girl had a gentle, spontaneous smile.

"Where will he stay then?"

"That is not a problem," the girl replied. "He has many relatives in the village."

"Are you his wife?"

The woman nodded. "My name is Soccoro."

As she spoke, he watched her full, red lips move. To his utter dismay, Fremont realized that this woman was exciting him. Desperately, he tried to divert his attention. It was no use. Despite his pain and his fatigue, the sight of this full-breasted, beautiful woman, after all his weeks in the wilderness, stirred in Fremont an uncontrollable desire. The worst of it was that he lay wrapped so tightly in Indian blankets that the bulge in the covers was all too apparent.

"How do you—get along? I mean, you are young and beautiful, and well, Alfonso, he must be at least seventy."

"I get along fine," she smiled. "We have an understanding. I do as I please. Alfonso, too, has others to fulfill his needs."

A small groan escaped Fremont's lips, more of despair than desire.

"You are in pain?"

Soccoro now looked down at the covers. "Oh, I see. A different kind of pain."

"Please, I'm sorry. I don't know why. I have been in the mountains a long time. I mean, you are an attractive woman, Soccoro, but I must tell you, I am married to someone I love very much."

"So am I," she replied.

Before he could answer, Soccoro ran a hand down the blanket. She pressed gently once, then again.

Soccoro smiled. "Your wife is very lucky."

His thoughts raced. How to explain that marriage meant more than that? Not the time to try. She might get angry. Or laugh. Oh, Jessie, I miss you . . .

For a while neither of them spoke. Fremont became aware of the fire crackling in the hearth, a wonderfully soothing sound—different, somehow, from the sound of wood in a campfire. And as it burned, it emitted a delicate scent. She lay down with him.

All too soon their lovemaking was over, and Fremont felt himself racked by guilt, almost paralyzed by it.

"You are upset," Soccoro said. "But why?"

"I can't say exactly. I don't know." Fremont swallowed with difficulty and raised his eyes to look at the ceiling. "I've let everyone down."

"Why do you say that?"

"Oh God, it's not your fault, Soccoro, you've just given me the most beautiful gift I've had in . . . a long time. But I'm here, in a warm bed, by a warm fire with a warm, beautiful woman——and the men I led into the mountains are still up in the mountains, freezing and probably starving. Don't you see? It's my fault they're up there. It's my fault they don't have help yet. It's all my fault, and I tell you, I always thought I was a good man. I thought I was an honorable man, strong enough to get through any kind of country in any kind of weather. Now I don't know. It seems like I deceived everyone, that underneath I was doing whatever I could to command undeserved respect and recognition."

Fremont propped himself up on one elbow, flinching at the pain that shot through his leg. "Take the railroad. This whole expedition was to prove that a goddamned railroad could run across the Rockies. I believed in that! At least I thought I did. But you know what I believed in, really? Being a hero to my father-in-law and his business cronies. You see, he fought for me hard, and he had always been good to me. He was so powerful, you know? A senator. And when the court-martial ended so badly, no one talked about it much except to say how wrong the decision was. But deep down, I knew I'd let them all down. I couldn't be looked up to anymore! And the senator, bless his poor soul, felt just as bad. It was like a light had gone out of his life. So when the chance came along to make an expedition at the expense of his business cronies, and to regain my lost fame and respect, I took it. Oh, God, did I take it! I think if they'd wanted me to prove they could put a railroad across the North Pole, I'd have taken it."

"Every man wants his comrades to love him," Soccoro said quietly. "Everyone needs respect."

"But not everyone has to drag three dozen men into danger and death to get it."

"They came because they wanted to, yes? And they knew where they were going?"

"Yes, of course they did, but they also knew I'd managed expeditions before, and so they trusted me. I let them down, and I let them die."

"You are so hard on yourself," Soccoro soothed him. "Your friends will get down safely, I know they will. And when they do, it will be a fine story to tell to their children and to their grandchildren."

"Three of them won't come down," Fremont said grimly. "And a fourth one's probably going to be crazy as a loon for the rest of his life. And, Soccoro, I just don't know how many of the others will make it."

He broke down and wept, his shoulders trembling, his thin hands covering his face. He did not notice Soccoro reach up behind her neck and unclasp her necklace. Nor did he observe her unfasten her dress and let it fall.

She got into the bed and sat up against the wall beside him. Then she cradled his head against her full, warm breasts. The fire was burning lower now. A log fell into the cinders against the clay hearth. The flames hesitated and settled lower, darkening the room.

She knew, somehow, that what he had told her tonight would never be heard by another soul, and if it had been necessary for him to confess to someone, she was glad he had chosen her.

At Alfonso's urging, the rescue party split up the following morning, with Fremont and Godey leaving the others behind to recuperate. Of the two, Godey was in much better shape. His powerful build, the result of years spent trapping and traveling in the northwest country, had served him well during the recent weeks. He was thinner, and his face was gaunt and hollow-cheeked, but the loss of weight seemed only to highlight his sinewy musculature.

Fremont, on the other hand, had plainly suffered more than one night's rest could heal. He shivered too much in the cold, and he began to cough uncontrollably. Worst of all was the nearly frozen leg that continued to pain him as he rode toward Taos. And in the back of his mind was always the nagging thought that the leg might still become infected and require amputation.

They made Taos by midafternoon. Fremont knew they were approaching the bustling Indian town even before it came into view, as the landscape began to contrast from mesa and mountain to rolling hills, studded with nut pines, that would slope down into central New Mexico.

Taos was a curious place. More than the nearby settlements of Santa Fe and Albuquerque, it offered little evidence of change after the U.S. Army's occupation of New Mexico under Kearny's command. Many who lived in Taos were Indians. The rest were Spanish descendants of sixteenth-century conquistadors who had swept north from Central America. Nearly all the houses, as a result, were squat adobe dwellings built with wooden roof beams. The Spanish influence showed itself in the open square, which defined the center of the town.

There were, however, a few American settlers in Taos, trappers and pioneers mostly, who had found Indian and Spanish ways more to their liking than the tumult of California. One of these was Kit Carson.

Godey and Fremont found Carson's place easily enough. It lay along a road that led from the town's mountainous perch down into a wide, snow-covered plain. There, neatly divided by wooden fences, were a dozen small farms.

Carson's spread was the largest and the farthest south from town. The terra-cotta main house was surrounded by lovely flower gardens, and in the distance, horses milled about playfully in their corrals.

"Looks like old Kit's done all right by family livin'," Godey observed as the riders headed through Carson's gateposts.

It seemed that way. Fremont was amused and touched, but also a bit saddened. Carson was nearing forty now; he had been with Fremont on two expeditions, as well as through much of the Kearny nightmare in California. Before that, he had been a trapper, and a great one. He knew the West better than most men knew their own hometowns. He rode as well as he shot, and most important of all, Carson was a man of honor—quiet, unassuming, unafraid. There were those who thought him a man so modest as to be ordinary, but Fremont knew that nothing could be further from the truth. Time and again, Fremont had seen him shoulder another man's troubles. Time and again he had seen Carson solve difficult problems—which trail to take, how to fight off an Indian attack, how to make it through snow or drought—and never had a foolish decision been made. Although some men were merely capable at trapping and shooting and surviving, Carson was supremely gifted at it. And it was a pity he had given it up to start farming.

Chapter 19

"Is it here we be findin' Kit Carson?" Godey hailed the slim, young Indian woman silhouetted in the doorway as they reined up.

"This is his home, yes. And who are you, please?"

The two men identified themselves, and the woman's searing dark eyes lit up at the mention of Fremont.

She curtsied, turned and disappeared, leaving the door slightly ajar. From the depths of the house came a bellowing cry of delight. In another moment, the husky frame of Kit Carson charged through the doorway. He took Fremont and Godey in a sweeping bear hug, clapping his strong hands against their backs. "Heaven help you both," he said at last, standing back for a good look at them. "What'd you do to yourselves? Marina! Bring us some coffee and hot tortillas!"

Fremont recounted the arduous last weeks. Godey sat across from him at Carson's varnished oak table, feeling very much apart from his comrades. Carson and Fremont shared an understanding and friendship that seemed to shield them from everyone else. It didn't bother Godey, but he was curious at the woman's reaction. She took offense immediately.

"More coffee, Marina," Carson said, pointing to Fremont's nearly empty clay mug.

Marina, who had still not been introduced, turned brusquely toward the kitchen, though her ire was lost on the two old friends so absorbed in conversation. She returned with a large, glazed pottery jug and poured the mugs full all around. As she poured Godey's, she met his gaze fleetingly and the corners of her lips turned up in a wry smile.

"But you can't go back so soon with that leg!"

Carson's voice broke into Godey's thoughts. With a start, he realized he had been steadily watching Marina in the kitchen, shaping tortillas and fixing dinner. He liked the way her dark Indian hair, hanging nearly down to her waist, moved gracefully, sensually, as she worked.

"I have to, Kit," Fremont returned. "My men are all up there. The leg'll be all right. Won't it, Godey?"

Godey shrugged. "No reason you have to go back, Colonel. I can take the supplies up to Red River myself. Then I'll head up the mountain with one or two of Alfonso's Indians. Only thing I'm wondering about is what kind of provisions we can get."

"That's not a problem," Carson assured him.

"How do you mean, Kit?" Fremont asked. "I've got hardly any money left at all."

"Friend of yours in town, who might just help," Carson grinned. "Old Ed Baily."

"Baily! My Lord, what's he doing in these parts? I thought by now he'd be out in California for sure."

"They made him a major. Major, U.S. Army, stationed up here with a hundred men."

Fremont whistled softly in surprise. "Good for Baily. Though I still say if you and he'd let Kearny fight the Mexicans alone, I'd be the governor of California today."

Carson laughed. "Well, I reckon so, Colonel, I reckon so. But at least we can make up for it now.

Baily can do pretty much what he likes with the commissary. Order up a turkey dinner any time he wants—or thirty of 'em. And mules, packs, coats and boots. We can get right over and see him, Colonel. Only lives down the road a piece."

Carson turned back toward the kitchen for the first time. "Marina? We got time to take a quick trip to Baily's."

Marina seemed torn between anger and chagrin, but she quickly composed herself. "Dinner can keep. How long will you be?"

"Barely 'fore you notice we're gone, hon."

Carson kissed her quickly as he pulled on his buckskin jacket. "Comin', Godey?"

"No. I guess I'll just sit a spell, maybe help set the table and whatnot."

"I tell you, Kit, he's gettin' soft," grinned Fremont. "Next thing you know, he'll be wantin' to set up a farm across the road."

The men clumped out in their heavy snowboots, and Marina closed the door behind them. She was wearing moccasins, so her footsteps were barely audible as she padded toward the kitchen.

"Really got you runnin'," Godey said.

She flashed him a quick, tight smile. "It is all right. He is my husband, after all."

Godey nodded slowly. "How long you been married?"

"One year almost."

She had been debating whether to go back to the kitchen or to sit at the table. Now she sat across from Godey, her back to the fire.

"What'd you do before that?"

"Before that? Nothing. What does any woman do before marriage?"

"Heck, I don't know. Go to school, learn to make pottery or somethin'."

"Oh, that. Yes, I learned pottery. In my pueblo, everyone makes pottery."

Godey indicated the jug and coffee mugs. "You make those?"

She nodded, suddenly embarrassed.

"They're beautiful."

"That was before, at the pueblo. I don't do it now."

"But why not?" Godey asked, taken aback. "Don't you fire plates and cups for the house?"

"A wife has no time for that here," Marina said. "There is so much cooking and cleaning. Every day cooking and cleaning!"

"Least you got no kids yet."

At the very thought, Marina seemed to stiffen. "That will come soon, I'm sure."

"You don't seem so happy about it," Godey said. "Fact is, you don't seem too happy 'bout any part of it."

Marina looked up at him, and her luminous dark eyes filled with tears. "Happy? What right has a wife to be happy?" She spoke with deep bitterness, almost spitting out the words. In a strange way, it made her look even more attractive to Godey.

Godey mulled this over for a moment, staring into the fire. "Do you love your husband?" he asked finally.

Marina had dried her eyes and was smiling at him now. "Of course. He is a very good man. But he is like all men. He thinks he loves a woman, and so he marries her. Then he behaves like he really loves her for a while because he is married to her. But soon he is back to what he was, and the friends he has among other men become more important again."

"Like Colonel Fremont?"

"Yes," Marina admitted. "I know it is wrong to be so jealous, but my husband talks all the time of Colonel Fremont, how brave, how good, all of this. I think he likes that man more than he likes me."

"Oh, come on, now," Godey laughed.

"No. He doesn't have the understanding of women that you have, I think."

"What makes you think I understand women any better than they do?"

"I can feel it in you," Marina said.

Their eyes met, and suddenly her hands were on top of his, taking hold.

Major Edward F. Baily of the U.S. Army was in his long johns when they rode up and hammered on the door. A slight, wiry man, he looked too small for the cigar he was smoking.

"The Colonel needs food and mules," Carson said when Fremont had finished relating his story. "And you're the only one who can help him."

"Of course," Baily said simply, his barrel chest puffing up with pride. "It's an honor. But Colonel, how is it you have no money left? Have these backers of yours treated you so badly?"

Fremont smiled ruefully. "No, Ed, they're fine men. It just took more cash than I thought it would. Now I've got two dozen men freezing up there and hardly a penny to bail them out."

Baily shook his head sympathetically. "I guess not every expedition can be a smash-bang success, eh? Got to be a tough one somewhere."

Fremont turned somber. "It is a success in that we've held to our course. Maybe not all the way, maybe not clear across, but we've gone far enough to know that a railroad could be laid down."

After a quick glass of port, the men bade Baily

good night, promised to meet him next morning at the commissary, and then rode back hard to Carson's place. They found Marina stirring a stew in the kitchen. She greeted them with a disinterested nod. Godey, too, seemed quiet. He sat cross-legged in front of the fire, a rolled cigarette between two fingers.

"Long time since I had one of these," he smiled. "Where'd you get the tobacco, Kit?"

"Come up through Santa Fe," Carson explained as he poured a glass of whiskey for his guests. "That's Georgia grown, that there. Best you can buy. And this whiskey—it's from Georgia, too. Trader I know brings a stash for me every time he gets up this way."

Dinner was a strange affair. Carson, who had always been so quiet on the trail, that days might pass without his speaking, talked now as if he would never have the chance to talk again. Farming, building houses, cutting wood, the joys of settling down—he needed only a nod of encouragement to race from one story to the next. The whiskey had loosened his tongue, but also, as both Fremont and Godey began to realize, Carson began to feel a need to justify his settling down. Perhaps he wasn't so sure of his choice. Perhaps, after all the right decisions he had made in his life, he had finally made his first mistake.

Talkative as he was, Carson failed to notice something else. Marina was seething. And now her anger was directed not just at her husband but at Godey as well. When he passed her the salt, she nearly snatched it from him. Whenever he glanced at her, she turned away.

The eruption came as the meal ended.

Carson had just finished telling them of all the spring chores still to be done. He would have to find good Indian laborers, fix the rusty farm tools, invest in a bit of livestock. Finally, he turned to Fremont, his handsome, rugged face flushed with landowner's pride. "Come out and look at the barn," he commanded with a grin. "Come on, Alex, you too." To Marina he said only, "Let's have some coffee."

"No!"

With an anguished cry, Marina picked up her plate in both hands and crashed it down again. It broke with a terrific clatter, the clay pieces flying in all directions. As the men sat in stupefied silence, she let out a string of Indian oaths, picked up the two plates nearest her and threw them against the wall.

They shattered instantly. Red sauce splattered on the adobe and trickled down to the floor.

"You want the coffee? You get the coffee! You want the dishes cleaned? You clean the dishes! And you want little babies? You go make little babies with someone else!"

Before her, three of the frontier's toughest explorers sat speechless.

Marina ran into her bedroom and slammed the door behind her. In the silence that followed, the men could hear her sobbing.

Ashen-faced, Carson stood up awkwardly, and with shaking hands, carried the serving bowl of stew into the kitchen. Godey and Fremont glanced uncomfortably at each other.

It was Carson who spoke first. Returning with whiskey and three washed glasses, he poured a small round for his guests. "I don't know," he said in a hushed voice. "She didn't used to be like that. She does it more and more now."

He gave a sad little shrug and met their eyes at last. All his exuberant confidence was gone. He sat down heavily. "I keep thinking that she must want a child and . . ." he paused, acutely embarrassed. "We don't seem to be having much luck there yet."

"If you'll pardon my saying so, it doesn't seem to me as if that's the problem," Fremont suggested gently.

"Well, I know! And that's what has me all confused," Carson exclaimed. "I mean, what else does a woman want from a fellow? I give her everything! Food, clothes, a home. And I work as hard as any man. Sweet Jesus, I work all day for her."

Godey cleared his throat nervously. "Course you do, Kit. And she got all she could want, in the way of comfort and whatnot. But maybe—aw hell, I feel like a fool givin' a man advice on his own wife."

"No," Carson said. "I know what you mean, but I want you to. Can't hurt none, at any rate."

"Well, Kit, you ever talk to her much? Just about little things and such?"

"Talk?" Carson looked at him in astonishment. "Why, sure we talk. Hell, we talk all the time."

"About what, though?" Fremont asked.

"About all kinds of things, I guess. I mean there's lots to runnin' a farm, you know. What to fix for breakfast and dinner, what to do in town . . . talk about how the crops is comin' along . . ."

"Okay," Godey nodded. "But you ever just talk about what you're feelin' from one day to the next? Or what she's feelin'?"

"Feelin'?" Carson rolled the word over in his mind as if it came from a foreign language. "Now what the hell kind of bushwhack is that? If it's a sunny day you feel good. If it's cold and rainy you feel bad. If the crops are goin' good, you feel satisfied. If there's a drought, you feel ired. What the hell does that have to do with anything?"

"That ain't enough Kit, if you want to know the truth of it," Godey explained. "It's enough when you're out on the trail, maybe. I don't know. Men don't seem to need to talk things out. But hell, Kit, women ain't like that. And bein' married ain't like muckin' about in the mountains. You got a problem, that's obvious. You don't talk to your woman. A wife is supposed to work around the house, maybe, but she isn't just a servant. She's supposed to be your best friend, too. And if you don't talk things out and learn what's on her mind, you ain't never goin' to keep her happy. I mean, I'm sorry to say so, but I know it, 'cause I seen it, and cause she told me, too."

Godey lapsed into silence as the others looked on at him in open surprise. Finally, Carson said, "How do you mean she told you?"

"Just what I said, Kit. You all went off to Baily's, and we sat here, and she told me. All it took was askin'."

"But . . . what did you say to make her talk?"

Now it was Godey's turn to look up in surprise. He shook his head and laughed. "Well now, Kit, it ain't so hard to make a woman talk! I just asked her why she seemed kinda low, and she took it from there."

Carson digested this carefully, as if Godey's words contained some kind of trickery. "But how did you know she was feelin' low? She must have told you, right?"

"No she didn't, Kit. Never said a thing. I just watched her and saw it, that's all. Not so hard, if you're watchin', that is."

Carson looked at him suspiciously. "Watchin'. You mean you was givin' her the eye?"

"No I wasn't, Kit. I was just lookin' at her like I would you or anybody, which frankly you weren't doin', 'cause you were goin' on so much about the farm."

"Hmph," Carson grunted. He seemed to be weighing the words as he stared somberly into the fire. What impression they made on him was impossible to tell.

After a long, contemplative silence, he turned and spoke to Fremont about plans for the coming day. Then Fremont rose, announcing that he was tired, and the three men drank the last of their whiskey. Carson showed his guests to a small, comfortable bedroom near the kitchen.

"Help you clean up them dishes?" Godey offered.

"Nah, go on to bed, the both of you," Carson said, waving off the question. "They can sit till mornin' I reckon."

Fremont eased himself into bed with some pain, then waited until Godey was settled before snuffing the small gas lamp that lit the room.

"Didn't know you felt so strongly about marriage and women," he said to Godey in the dark.

"Didn't know I did either," Godey whispered back.

They shared a low laugh, and then Godey turned over. Within seconds, his breathing assumed the measured rise and fall of deep slumber.

Fremont was just as tired, but his leg nagged him. He lay on his back, eyes open in the pitch black, wondering if Kit Carson would ever learn to love a woman as well as he had learned to shoot a gun, or ride a horse.

From his bedroom, Fremont could hear a weary Carson out by the fire, shifting his weight as he brooded. Then there came the sound of broken crockery being gathered up. Footsteps came into the kitchen, receded, came in another time. The crockery was all picked up. Now the footsteps receded, hesitantly it seemed, into the master bedroom. Boots fell clunking to the floor and were shoved against the wall

A long, low murmur followed. The last thing Fremont heard as he drifted off to sleep was the unmistakable rhythm of two people making love.

* * *

My very dear wife,

I write to you from the house of our good friend
Carson. This morning, while I was yet in bed, a
cup of chocolate was brought to me. To an over-
worn, overworked, much fatigued and starving
traveler, these little luxuries of the world offer a
satisfaction that is not possible for you to conceive.
While in the enjoyment of this luxury, then, I
pleased myself in imagining how gratified you
would be to picture me here in the care of Kit,
who is constantly endeavoring to make me comfortable. Do you remember how he enjoyed the
pleasant hospitality of your father's house? The
farthest thing then from my mind was that he
would ever repay it to me here. . .

He paused, his quill poised above the paper. It was
a brilliantly clear, cold day, the sun streaming through
the windows, bright against the dirt-packed floor of the
bedroom. Marina, who had brought him a cup of hot
chocolate, was humming out in the kitchen. The mouth-
watering aroma of baking bread left no doubt about her
morning's work. Though it seemed a considerable effort for her to pound down the dough, one loaf after
another, she did not mind. In fact, she was cheerful—
a different person from the night before. Could her
husband have made a first attempt to really talk with
her?

Fremont smiled and returned to his letter. The
events of the recent weeks poured onto the page as
he wrote. He spared no detail of the expedition, save
that of the night with Soccoro.

As I told you, I shall break up my party here.
I have engaged a Spaniard to take us down the Del
Norte to Albuquerque. From there, my road will

take me about one hundred and sixty miles south, to the passes between the heads of the Gila, and to a little Mexican town called Tucson. Thence to the mouth of the Gila and across the Colorado, direct to Agua Caliente and into California. I intend to make the journey rapidly, arriving in the middle of March, with the hope of hearing from home. I look for a large supply of newspapers and documents, though having them reminds me of home more than their actual content does. When I think of you, I feel a warmth in my heart, which strengthens me like good medicine, and I forget painful feelings. We shall yet, dearest wife, enjoy quiet and happiness together. Frequently, I think of the happy home we are to have, with a library lit by a bright fire on the rainy, stormy days, and its large windows looking out upon the sea in the bright weather. I have it all planned. There are two gods which have become very dear to me—Hope and Sleep. My homage will be deeply divided between them; both will make the time pass quickly until I see you. So I go now to pay a willing tribute to one with my heart full of the other.

Love,
John

Chapter 20

A bird with orange feathers and a green crest alighted on a jungle vine across the stream. It tucked in its beak and began to clean its plumage. A breeze came up. The bird flicked its wings out and adjusted its footing on the vine perch. Then, as if by previous arrangement, the bird looked up to see its mate sweeping down to perch alongside it. In a moment, they flew up through the dark canopy of tropical leaves and disappeared.

Jessie had held strong through this awful night and into the morning, refusing to cry or to show any emotion, lest it should scare poor Lilly. But now, seated at the stream's verdant bank, her knees pulled up to her chin, her hands locked around them, she felt her stern resolve give way. The two birds had stirred deep, sharp pangs of longing for her husband. Life could be such a simple, lovely affair. A bird flying off with its mate, for example. So why was she so miserable, all the while shaking with hatred and fear, far from her sweet husband?

Jessie began to cry. Behind her, they carried out Mr. Curtis.

He was bound and gagged. Only his eyes conveyed the manic rage within him.

Four natives, like pallbearers, supported him. Two men lifted his shoulders and two supported his upper legs. He made a token struggle to wrestle free of their grasp, but they twisted his arms behind him until his elbows nearly touched.

Jessie turned away as they put Mr. Curtis into one of the dugouts. Only when he had been laid on his back did the other natives and passengers venture down, baggage in hand, to board the other boats for the day's travel. They were silent, all of them. A few cast sympathetic and curious glances toward Jessie. She looked at no one except Lilly, who came over to sit beside her.

"Are you all right, Mama?" she asked in a hushed voice. All vestiges of her childish ways seemed to have been dashed by this strange experience.

Jessie nodded and reached out to pull her daughter close. "I'm fine now, honey. Soon we'll be through with this wretched trip, and we'll see your daddy again. Won't you like that?"

"Yes, Mama." Lilly could sense the uncertainty in her mother's voice, and it bothered her. "Mama?"

"Yes, dear."

"What happened last night? I heard you shouting, but they wouldn't let me come to you."

Jessie dabbed at the tears on her cheeks. "Well, honey, nothing that matters now. That man just tried to . . . kiss me, and I didn't want him to."

"To kiss you? But that wouldn't be so bad. I mean, you wouldn't have started crying and screaming just for that, would you?" Lilly wrinkled her brow.

"He's just a nasty man, honey. And the natives don't like him either. That's why they came to help me when I started screaming. And that's why they tied him up and put him in the boat by himself. He's been bad, and they're punishing him. But you've been very, very good, Lilly, and as soon as we get to Gorgona, I'm going to get you a present."

"What, Mama, what?"

Jessie stood up and gratefully took her rolled bedding from one of the bearded passengers. "We'll see, honey," she sighed. "We'll just have to see."

They made Gorgona by early afternoon. As before, the natives were forced to stop often and to hack at the vines that had grown across the stream overnight. They seemed to enjoy this task, however. Calling instructions to each other, they would stand up adroitly in the dugouts, and their machetes would glint in the tropical sun as they cut their way through. The passengers would sit quietly by, resting up against their packs, their hats pulled low over their bearded visages.

Gorgona, looming ahead, seemed a miserable prospect. The village was a hodgepodge of thatched huts running along either side of the stream and even on stilts over the water. The stream itself had been widened into a harbor for dugouts. Mangrove, coconut and palm trees crowded all around the town's clearing. Having seen how quickly the jungle creepers grew across the banks, Jessie realized that the natives here had to hack away at the tropical undergrowth daily to keep their town from being overrun.

Nothing, however, could keep Jessie's spirits from soaring. To set eyes on any form of civilization, to see an end to these nightmarish days of poling upstream with Mr. Curtis, was enough to set her weeping for joy.

As the dugouts slid through the shallow, murky water toward the oval strip of shore, natives gathered to greet them. From the largest hut appeared a wizened old man dressed not in a loincloth, as the others were, but in a long, colorful silk robe and sandals. This one entered into a rapid exchange with the boatman in his native tongue when he perceived the bound and gagged Mr. Curtis.

At his stern reaction, Jessie's heart jumped in fear. What if the native Indian boatmen who had come to her rescue were now to be punished as mutineers? Surely Jessie would be branded the instigator. Visions of imprisonment in some sunless, thatched hut raced through her mind. And what would they do to Lilly?

All eyes were now on the native chief as the dugouts drifted alongside each other up against the shore. To the gold diggers, Jessie's near-rape at the hands of Mr. Curtis had quickly become a rousing good yarn, with much laughter at the hapless perpetrator, and already much embellishing of details. But their own good humor palled as they beheld this chief, his minions around him, and realized that their fate could well hang in the balance of his decree.

The chief clapped his hands twice, and the native polemen jumped out into the murk. They drew their boats up onto the sloping shore, with the passengers still inside. At another clap of the chief's hands, they stood in a phalanx before him, hands clasped behind their backs. Nothing in their faces indicated the tenor of what the chief said, until suddenly the natives sprang into action.

Two hustled off toward the chief's thatched hut. Another two picked up Mr. Curtis by the arms and dragged him toward another hut. A third pair grabbed Jessie's baggage from her dugout and also made off toward the chief's hut. And two more natives, still expressionless, stood on either side of Jessie herself. Frozen with fear, she waited for them to pin her arms behind her. Instead, each reached out a hand to take her own. With grace and dignity, they escorted her up to the chief.

How to greet a chief? Jessie chose simply to bow her head toward him.

As she did, she nearly let out a scream, for his wizened hand touched the top of her head. But the touch was gentle and lasted only a moment.

"You have been through a terrible experience. I feel it is my responsibility. Please accept my deep regret."

Jessie looked up, speechless. The chief spoke perfect English. What was more, he was smiling now. The many lines etched in his face crinkled and crossed each other, lending him great character. Jessie warmed to him immediately.

"I am the one to apologize," she said, as Lilly came up and took hold of her skirts. "I have caused a confrontation with your Mr. Curtis, and led your boatmen to rise up against him."

"Nonsense, madam! I have never trusted him. And I am delighted now to have him exposed for the scoundrel he is. He has taught my natives to work the boats. Who needs him now?"

Jessie could hardly help but laugh. "What will you do with him?"

"We will hang him by his thumbs in a bamboo cage and feed him to the piranhas."

Jessie paled. "Oh, but—"

"No, no," the chief laughed. "We shall not do that. We must maintain our friendship with the police at Chagres. We will send Mr. Curtis back with the boats when the next passengers come. We will give him to the police, and tell them what happened. They will be more than happy to help, I assure you. Mr. Curtis is not well liked in Chagres."

To Jessie's embarrassment, Lilly now pulled at her dress. She chose to ignore the child's entreaty for attention, but the chief took notice.

"What do you need, my child?"

Lilly looked up at him, saucer-eyed.

"She's hungry, I think," Jessie said. "We have not yet had a proper meal, and Lilly, I'm afraid, has a ravenous appetite."

"Quite right! The way a young maiden should!" The chief clapped his hands three times, and the natives who had been dispatched to his hut reappeared instantly. A rapid exchange determined that a meal had already been prepared. The gold diggers would eat at a long table which had been carved from a tree trunk and propped above the ground with poles. Jessie and Lilly, however, would be the chief's personal guests.

The chief's hut proved a far more commodious and comfortable dwelling than it had appeared from outside. Woven straw mats covered the dirt floor, and sunlight slanted through the shaved poles that held up the roof. A low, round table served the chief for business and banquet alike, and it was here that he bade his guests to be seated to partake of the steaming delicacies in front of them.

None of the courses, Jessie observed with some consternation, looked in the slightest bit familiar. Into individual wooden bowls was poured a greenish broth with pieces of some boiled creature, chopped up but not divested of its scaly skin. A bowl of coconut milk sat beside this.

Jessie sipped the milk first, discreetly eyeing her broth as she did so. Lilly, to her mother's amusement and surprise, took up the bowl of soup without hesitation. In barely the time it took Jessie to sit cross-legged on the straw mat, Lilly had already disposed of the soup and was reaching for a plate of fried plantains.

"It looks absolutely delicious," Jessie said of the soup. "What is it?"

"I think that everything at this meal should be a surprise," the chief smiled at Jessie, with a sidelong glance toward Lilly.

"Ah, yes, of course," Jessie replied with a pasty smile.

But nothing discouraged the child. Down went the plantains, and down went a plate of what looked like boiled monkey tails, and down went a grilled steak of some ochre-colored creature.

"Slow down, honey," Jessie chided Lilly.

But the chief was elated. Again and again he clapped his hands for the attending natives to bring more food. And again and again Lilly dove into it. Embarrassed by her daughter's gluttony, Jessie helped herself to dainty portions and cautiously sampled each strange new dish.

The meal lasted nearly the entire afternoon and left Lilly looking a bit sallow. Over a strong herb tea that made everyone drowsy, Jessie at last said brightly to the chief, "Well! Now that our feast is over, you must tell us what we ate!"

"Of course," the chief nodded approvingly. "You should remember these dishes, too, because your daughter is so fond of them. In fact, I think maybe she is an Indian daughter in disguise. Are you, Lilly?"

Lilly shook her head shyly. She felt very full and sleepy with the tea, but also very happy, as she always was after she ate.

"The soup? Boiled iguana in broth. Then a paste made from boa constrictors, sliced up the middle like this . . ." the chief made a quick chop through the air. "And baby piranhas and black-eyed sole and, finally baked ringtail monkey!"

If the chief had expected a round of applause at the recitation, he must have been sorely disappointed. Before he even finished, Jessie had staggered to her feet, yanked Lilly by the hand and bolted out of the hut.

They set off the next day after a fond parting with the chief, who insisted on giving Jessie and Lilly a leather pack full of local delicacies. In return, Jessie bestowed upon her host the only possession she thought could be of use to him: a cookbook.

"It has American dishes in it," she explained. "Though they might seem strange to your taste."

A guide led the way through the jungle. Gorgona vanished around the first bend, and soon the trail grew narrow and steep. Mangrove and alder trees leaned in from either side, their huge leaves brushing against the sweaty faces of the marchers. Flushed out of the surrounding verdure, birds cawed and burst into the air. Now and then a lizard cut across, startling the pack mules. In a way, thought Jessie, this must be what her husband was going through, crossing the Rockies. Here the foliage was different, as was the temperature. But the hypnotic rhythm of riding, the camaraderie that grew among fellow travelers on the trail and the exhilaration of being so far away from civilization, so much a part of nature,—all of this, she knew, was the same.

For four days they rode on in this fashion, camping in tents, eating any game the guides happened to shoot, and nursing their saddle-sore muscles with the anticipation of reaching Panama. Riding her own mule, Lilly soon gave out, so the guide propped her side-saddle in front of him. Jessie, too, became painfully tired but made light of it. She was certainly not going to make a spectacle of herself on this journey a second time.

Panama appeared first on the horizon as a dark smudge between the green of the tropical forest and the robin's-egg blue of the vast Pacific Ocean beyond.

"No boats!" cried a man in response to the query from a bearded gold digger. "No boats 'cause they can't get a hand to work 'em. Every Christian soul that can is up workin' the fields."

Jessie and Lilly rode with the rest of their group to the sagging, two-story stable where the mules would stay. The stable keeper told them the same story.

"Bad news boys, and I don't know when it's going to get any better. We got so many teed-off panhandlers in town, there's fights every night in the bars, and sometimes right on the streets. They can't get a steamer up to Frisco for any price, 'cause none showed up to take 'em. Only boat in the whole blamed harbor is the army mail boat, and that's got 'em madder'n hell. Damned army won't give out any mail that's addressed to Frisco, even when the fellow it's addressed to is still here. And anyway, they're runnin' out of money sittin' idle here. You all might just have had a better time in the jungle."

Grumbling bitterly amongst themselves, the men barely noticed Jessie and Lilly walking wearily off, bags in hand, toward the nearest hotel.

"Could you tell me where I might find Madame Arce?" Jessie asked the registrar.

"Arce, Arce. Yes, well let me see," the fellow mumbled. "Down Digger Street aways, 'cross Goldust Street, and there's a pink building."

They found the place without much difficulty. Madame Arce had been a proper St. Louis lady some years back, and had married a much older man, who was French by nationality and a furrier by trade. There had been much cruel gossip and innuendo about the marriage, with starchy matrons sniffing that she had married him for his money. Jessie remembered how John had been especially annoyed by the gossip. His own mother had married under similar circumstances, and a young John Fremont had had to endure the ridicule of his classmates until the day his family moved south.

Madame Arce had also moved, though not until her husband died of gout. Then, with her considerable inheritance, she had taken her baby daughter to Panama, opened a lodging house and started a new life. The Fremonts' many kindnesses to her in St. Louis had induced her to write of her changed circumstances, and Jessie had been delighted to plan a stay at her hotel.

They found Madame Arce, knee-deep in laundry, folding a pile of spanking-white towels. She looked up querulously at this grimy mother and daughter, both stinking of mule, who stood before her. Then squinting, she took a closer look and threw her towels into the air in amazement.

There followed a joyful reunion, with Madame Arce asking question after wondering question about the journey, the colonel and the people back home. Jessie at first obliged her affectionately, but soon betrayed her bone-deep fatigue.

"Goodness! How can I have been so inconsiderate!" Madame Arce cried. "I haven't even let you sit down."

Gratefully, the Fremonts trailed her up the outside stone steps of her lodging house to a delightful room with a red-tiled balcony that overlooked the garden and an ancient cathedral across the street.

Of all her deprivations during the recent weeks, Jessie had found the lack of a bath, with clear water and strong soap, the most intolerable. When Madame Arce tactfully suggested that she might bathe at the spring, Jessie laughed weakly and let herself be led down to an outside rock bed, surrounded by curtains. There a servant girl, summoned by Madame Arce, filled a variety of ceramic jars with water from an underground spring. Jessie disrobed and stood on the rock bed. The girl poured the smallest jar of water over her head. The second jar was larger, and every succeeding jar larger still, until finally Jessie was soaped, shampooed and rinsed clean, shivering but refreshed.

That evening the two women, with Lilly between them, took a tour of the town, down through the ancient streets to the crowded waterfront. All around, bearded gold seekers roamed the quay, mumbled angrily about their circumstances and boasted of how much gold they would find.

The word that recurred most often on everyone's lips was "constitution." Soon Jessie found out why. The *U.S. Constitution* was the name of the mail ship that had been anchored in the harbor now for nearly a week without dispensing its California-bound letters. Jessie could feel the tension among the men, and she chanced to mention that they seemed ready to explode. The next day, they did.

It happened at noon. Jessie, bearing a glass of guava juice and a stack of St. Louis *Courier Dispatches*, had just stretched out on a hammock slung between two garden palms. Suddenly, in the distance, there arose a tumult of cries. The words were not clear, but the voices were angry.

Slipping on her shoes, Jessie padded out of the garden and onto the dusty street, where no one walked in the midday hours. The voices grew louder as she hurried toward the waterfront. They became clearer, too. "Mail or jail, and blood for bail," ran the insistent chorus.

Some five hundred men had collected. As Jessie came around the corner and saw them, she realized that she was the only woman in sight. Not that anyone took notice of her. All the men were chanting and raising clenched fists at the small boat that sat bobbing at anchor only fifty feet from them.

At the front of the rabble, a tall, dark-haired man was leading the chant from a wooden crate. Beside him, looking very miserable, were two men in blue uniforms, whom Jessie correctly assumed to be agents of the U.S. Mail Service.

"We have a right to this mail," the rabble-rouser shouted. "And no windy-assed officer of the U.S. government has a right to keep it from us!"

Fists were raised and shaken, and fingers pointed at the two hapless agents who stood before the mob. Then voices began to shout in unison that the agents themselves should speak. These voices became a vociferous chorus, until the rabble-rouser moved aside to oblige the will of his crowd.

Up on the wooden crate podium stepped one of the two government agents.

"Friends, friends, friends, please!"

"Please your ass, O'Malley! Just give us our mail!"

Agitated, the dark-suited man tried to wave the crowd quiet. "Now listen! You don't want to hear it nice, we'll give it to you hard and straight. I can't give you your mail. And you can't get it yourselves. There ain't no use in shouting about it. The only one who can give it to you is the consul, and he's sitting on that boat with his guns ready to blow apart any damn fool who tries to come aboard. Now you can get mad as hell at me and shoot me right down from this box. But it won't get you your mail any faster. Fact is, you ain't gonna get that mail at all until you set foot in San Francisco. That's the law."

The leader of the crowd now spoke up again. "You ain't tellin' us nothing new, you damned government hack, and you ain't offerin' any kind of compromise."

"How you gonna compromise with a crew full of gun-toting soldiers on that boat, eh?"

"We send a representative," the leader shouted with a flash of inspiration. He turned to face the crowd behind him. "I say we send out these two fellows here in a boat with one of our men. Have him talk to the consul in person."

A rousing cheer went up at this suggestion.

"Oh, that's a fine idea," shouted O'Malley. "But I can tell you right now, it ain't worth even trying. Jackson here'd get on board and start speechifying, and they'd have him in leg irons before he could get his shoes off to oblige them. Consul told me personally that anyone who tried to board the mail boat would be thrown in the brig, and kept there in the San Francisco harbor while everyone else goes out for gold. Now you tell me, who would like to find himself headed back to New York in the brig after all the travelin' you done to get here? Eh?"

There was a low grumbling of anger among the men, but it was plain that the uniformed government official had made his point. Even the mob spokesman appeared subdued. At the fringes of the crowd, some of the men turned away in disgust.

"I'll go, Mr. O'Malley."

Those nearest Jessie spun around, startled, and gave way as she pushed to the front.

"Well? You need a representative? I'll do it."

The man craned to catch a glimpse of this strange character. The agent who had been standing on the wooden box stepped down, somewhat embarrassed, and shoved his hands into his coat pockets.

"Maybe you didn't hear right where you were standin', ma'am. Consul says he'll lock up anyone that tries to come aboard. Ain't no use in trying. Besides, you're a lady. This is no business for a lady to be meddlin' in."

"Mr. O'Malley," said Jessie, drawing up to her full height with a cold-eyed dignity. "I heard you quite clearly from where I was standing. I understand the consul's threat as well. And I don't think this is a man's business any more than it is a woman's. As it happens, I believe I have a letter sitting on that boat, too, and I should like to have it."

The men burst into cheering applause, and the spokesman for the crowd raised up Jessie's arm with a defiant look at the government agents. "Here's our emissary!" he shouted. "She's got the best chance of any of us, I reckon. I say we let her go."

The spokesman was no fool. He had no influence at this point over whether Jessie would go or not. With a few words, she had determined the will of the crowd. But by shouting his approval, he had retained at least the appearance of control.

Swept on now by the crowd's expectations, Jessie followed the two government men to the mailboat's dinghy. O'Malley got in first, took Jessie's hand to help her in and bade her to sit at the stern. With the other man at the oars, they pushed off from the dock, amidst loud hoots and cheers.

Not until they touched up against the gunboat's barnacled bow did Jessie feel a tremor of fear. Above her, jutting out directly overhead, the boat's gunwales looked dark and foreboding, with cannon barrels protruding out like a long, unbroken line of gargoyles.

Over the unseen railing above came a rope ladder down to meet them, its wooden rungs banging against the metal prow.

"You first," O'Malley said to Jessie with a thin-lipped smile.

Jessie took hold of the rope without a word.

"It ain't too ladylike," O'Malley added. "But then, this whole thing ain't too ladylike either."

"I'll be the judge of that," Jessie shot back.

Resolutely, she climbed upward and took hold of the strong hand that reached out to pull her on deck.

"Well, well, what's this? A little entertainment from the local house? My God, we could use a bit of that!"

The sailor who addressed her was a tall, strong, sun-bronzed fellow, stripped to the waist. Even in her anger, Jessie could not help but be aware of the power in his bulging chest and forearms.

"I am not your entertainment."

"But madam, you're wrong. You're entertaining us already."

The other sailors who had gathered round broke into laughter. Behind them came the two blue-suited government agents, struggling over the railing onto the deck.

"Thanks for the helping hand," O'Malley said to no one in particular.

"Ah, stick it in your ear," remarked one of the sailors. "Begging your pardon, ma'am."

"I've come to see your consul," Jessie announced. With no love lost between the government agents and the sailors, she could see it might be worth allying herself with the latter.

"And that you shall, madam!" the big sailor declared.

Into the ship's dark, narrow quarters Jessie followed him, past metal cabin doors barely high and wide enough to let his broad shoulders through. They stopped in front of a door that stood no larger than the others, made of highly polished walnut with a polished brass handle.

"Yes!" came a harsh voice when the sailor knocked.

The door opened to reveal a cramped but rather elegantly appointed study, with stained mahogany paneling, white porthole curtains and a thick, plum-colored oriental rug. A small, ornately carved desk faced the door from the far end of the room. Behind the desk, illuminated by a shiny brass gas lamp with a green glass shade, sat Nicolas Mikovich Mihaesco, Consul of the United States.

Consul Mihaesco was not a large man. Even before he rose to greet Jessie with a stiff military bow, she knew he would stand no taller than five feet in his high-heeled boots.

As if to redress this embarrassment, Consul Mihaesco sported the longest waxed moustache Jessie had ever seen. Had it been extended directly out from his face, it would have spanned nearly two feet from tip to tip, but the consul had curled the ends elaborately, and had also waxed to a sharp point his triangular goatee. This dandyism carried to his French-cut, double-breasted suit. His brass buttons had obviously just been polished, for they shined brightly.

Trouble, thought Jessie as she introduced herself. A man so groomed and garbed was likely to be as prim in his comportment. The deep frown that now knit his eyebrows was hardly a good omen.

Curtly, the consult waved the sailor out. The door closed behind Jessie with the heavy thud of thick wood on oiled hinges. Jessie felt strange, as if she had just been shown into the schoolmaster's chamber for committing some prank.

"My name is Jessie Fremont. I've come about the mail," she said. Silently, she cursed herself for speaking in such a weak voice.

"What about the mail, madam?" The consul's own voice was cold and cutting. There was not, as far as Jessie could discern, any sympathy in his eyes.

"Sir, you know exactly what I mean. There are a thousand men on shore that want their letters."

"And you, madam, must know why I cannot distribute those letters."

"Yes, but . . ."

"And do you also know, madam, of the punishment I have sworn to impose upon anyone who should come aboard this vessel?"

Jessie's heart dropped. "Yes, I do."

"Then I assume this conversation is finished."

The consul reached over to pick up a brass bell that lay on his desk.

"Now just one minute," Jessie snapped, her fear giving way to anger. "How dare you hide behind your position like that and not talk straight to me! Who do you think you are—Napoleon? I didn't come all the way out here to talk to some cardboard character with a ridiculous moustache just to have him behave in a surly manner with me! Do you understand?"

The consul stood frozen in his boots. His hand remained above the bell, his eyes locked with Jessie's. It was impossible to tell if he would tolerate another word out of her, or if in another second he would ring for help and have her locked in irons.

Recklessly, Jessie plunged on. "Now, sir, you tell me why you can't give out the mail, even if it's against some orders that make no sense in this situation."

There was a long pause. Then the consul's hand

fell back to his side. With a weary sigh, he slumped back and waved her into one of the two chairs across the desk.

"Madam . . . may I call you Mrs. Fremont?"

Jessie nodded as she sat down.

"You are, I have heard from my informants, John Fremont's wife."

Jessie nodded again.

"Mrs. Fremont, those silly orders, as you put it, are not so easy to break as you might imagine, even though the situation has changed, even though they now seem absurd. We are a long way from home, Mrs. Fremont. But in Washington, all that matters is obeying one's orders—to the letter. If I go back to my superiors and try to explain why I handed out San Francisco mail in Panama, they won't listen to my reasons. They won't listen at all. They are not paid to listen, as they are so fond of putting it. They are paid to give orders. And even if they did listen, just a bit, do you know exactly what they would say? They'd say I committed a breach of military orders and compromised the United States government. And that, Mrs. Fremont, would be the short, sweet end of my military career."

"But why would they have to find out?" Jessie asked.

"For one thing, Mrs. Fremont, the world is smaller than you think it is. I guarantee you that word would get back, somehow, in less time than it takes to cross by covered wagon. For another thing, all mail must be stamped with the seal of its point of arrival. So all this mail, bound for San Francisco, would have to be stamped with a Panama seal. And that, my lady, would put the seal on my own career."

"It must be stamped?"

"Must be. Absolutely. To not do that would mean

more than sacrificing my career. It would be a crime, and I'd land in jail. No thank you to that, either, Mrs. Fremont."

The two sat in silence.

"I've got it!" Jessie cried out suddenly. "You have to stamp the letters, yes? Do you do that here? On board?"

Wearily, the consul nodded.

"And the date, too? Do you stamp the date?"

"Certainly."

Jessie grinned. "So, you can put the San Francisco stamp on the letters, and postmark them all a month ahead! Or even two months! That way, you're giving out the mail to the right destination—and to men who'll be there when the date arrives."

The consul looked at her narrowly. "But that's still a breach of orders. In fact, it may be more illegal, because I would be fabricating the date and destination."

"But it'll work now, won't it?" Jessie cried. "Especially if you don't tell a soul except the people who actually stamp them. Just keep it a secret! The men won't notice. Even if they did, all you would have to do is point to the envelopes, and then it's their word against your postmark."

For a long while the consul sat in silence, looking off through the porthole and playing meditatively with his goatee.

"You know," he said finally. "I think you may have something."

Chapter 21

Two events made the next week one of the most memorable in Jessie Fremont's life. First, the mail had been distributed that very same day, and with it came the letter that Fremont had written to her from Taos. Secondly, two ships finally arrived in the harbor: the *Panama*, a huge clipper from New York that had rounded Cape Horn, and the *Californian*, down from San Francisco with a shanghaied crew.

The two vessels appeared in the harbor almost at the same time, and within an hour after they had set anchor, there was not a soul in Panama of any age or nationality who had not heard the wonderful news. There were also precious few who did not want to clamber aboard and make the trip, at any expense and any inconvenience, north to San Francisco.

By sunrise the next day, the waterfront was thronged with would-be passengers, each staking out a space as big as his bedroll and pairing up with someone else, so that when one went off to look for food or to relieve himself, the other might stand guard. There were gold diggers enough to fill twenty such ships, and that cast an ugly mood over all who waited.

A number of fights broke out that morning, most involving men from Panama, Venezuela or Colombia, and nearly all were instigated by Americans. Throughout the crowd, the fear of getting left behind had turned into focused annoyance at anything or anyone foreign.

From Madame Arce's balcony, Jessie watched the distant crowd with a sinking heart. How would she ever find a berth and get Lilly on as well? Given the situation, she decided to prepare herself for a long stay in Panama.

Below, she heard a knocking at Madame Arce's door. When no one answered, the knocking grew much louder. Finally, Jessie heard Madame Arce's soft, slippered footsteps. The door opened, and a murmur of voices wafted up. The stranger's voice was strong and insistent. Madame Arce's voice was gentle and surprised.

"Jessie? Jessie, there's a gentleman down here who knows you. A Lieutenant Fitzhugh Beale."

Jessie hurried down to throw her arms around one of her dearest friends. Lieutenant Beale had been born and raised in Missouri, and had often come to dinner at the Bentons' home in St. Louis when Jessie was growing up. The past few years had taken their toll on him. His hair was now silver, and his tight, military waist had broadened somewhat. But he looked healthy and happy, and to see him helped Jessie feel closer to her family and home again.

Upon his introduction the man with him proved to be even more of a surprise, for he was none other than Captain Mavis Owens of the *Panama*!

"You see, Jess, word got out to me that you'd be traveling over by Chagres," explained Beale, his eyes crinkling with amusement and affection. "From what I understand, you earn your passage when you go that way."

"I think, Fitz, that were I to do it again—which

I never shall, ever—I'd go by way of Cape Horn. It's safer, even if it is longer."

"You may be right, ma'am," the captain threw in. "But I'll tell you the God's honest truth, and I'm a sailor saying it—it has got to be the most boring, exhausting journey a man could make. And with hardly a woman aboard, and all those seasick—well, I'll be grateful to see my wife again in Frisco, that's all I can say."

Before the men had even been relieved of their hats and canes, Madame Arce announced that a lunch was prepared. So the conversation resumed around a buffet of chicken and dumplings and sassafras tea.

"I tell you, good people, it makes me feel awful to think of leaving men behind, but frankly I don't know how to avoid it," the captain declared. "Best thing I can think of is to hold a lottery and then take the hundred winners on up."

Jessie considered. "You might find yourself with a riot on your hands if you let anyone but Americans choose in the lottery."

"Well, you may be right," Captain Owens allowed. "But what can I do? Not let any Panamanians go, when I'm right here in Panama accepting their hospitality?"

There followed a battery of suggestions, but it was Lilly, finally, who came up with the obvious solution. "Why not make some people stay out on deck?" she suggested. "That way everybody'd fit."

This was exactly what Captain Owens decided to do. Some forty berths were filled by eighty Americans, all chosen at random, and the decks were given over to both Americans and foreigners, with every man taking only as much room as he needed to lie down. As for Jessie and Lilly, they were assigned to a berth near the captain's.

As soon as the ship was loaded the next morning, the *Panama* inched out of the harbor, propelled by a small steam engine, then raised its sails as it moved beyond the harbor's outlying point.

For Jessie, the movement of the ship provided a welcome tonic for the weakness of spirit that had descended upon her. It did not, however, prove to be of much help in staving off an attack of chills, which by the third day out had developed into a full-blown fever. The ship's doctor reassured her that it was not cholera, but only the result of poor diet and fatigue, so he told her to remain in bed for the duration of the journey.

Jessie was happy to oblige, for with the decks covered by gold diggers, there was precious little space to go wandering. But as she lay under the covers, sweating one moment and shivering the next, Jessie began to dream that her husband had lost his leg.

They reached the San Francisco harbor on a morning typical in that coastal town: cloudy and cool, with a hint that the sun would burn off the morning fog by noon.

A dozen other boats lay at anchor, all looking deserted. Through a telescope, one could discern luffing sails, loose rigging, even passengers' baggage. They had all been abandoned. Obviously, the passengers and crews alike had swarmed off into dinghies, rowed ashore and scrambled up past the town's empty waterfront houses to join the crowds in search of gold.

It was only March of 1849—the year the world would come to look on as the year of the Gold Rush. Already, though, San Francisco was a burgeoning place.

Ascending the town's surrounding hills was a shantytown of huts and tents stippled with clothes hung out to dry and plumes of bluish smoke that rose above campfires.

From the looks of it all, a passenger aboard the arriving *Panama* might have assumed the port to be teeming with people. In fact, the first flush of gold fever had half emptied the town. Houses had been abandoned. Families had packed up. With a pan in one hand and a shovel in the other, church-going settlers had hurried out to the hills, leaving their servants and a loyal militia behind.

Jessie, still delirious with what the doctor had decided was a purple brain fever, was convinced that her husband had perished. Racked by chills, she had envisioned him dying in a dozen different ways—always cruelly, and always painfully.

Now as the ship dropped anchor, Jessie felt extremely fearful of the news she was certain awaited her. She would step ashore, she thought, and hear that Colonel Fremont was dead.

From her sweat-soaked cabin bunk, she struggled up, swung her legs over and stumbled to the door. She was alone in this berth, for Lilly had been moved to another when her mother's fever had grown worse.

Resolutely, Jessie locked the door and staggered back into her bed. Footsteps rushed past her cabin, and men shouted about disembarking in an orderly fashion. Baggage was dragged by, scraping and bumping the walls.

Finally, a single pair of footsteps stopped in front of her door. Someone knocked, tentatively at first, then more firmly.

"Mrs. Fremont? Mrs. Fremont? You in there?"

Jessie recognized the voice. It belonged to a handsome young soldier named Joe Hooker.

"Mother? Are you awake? It's time to go," came Lilly's voice.

"You go on, honey. Leave me be. Joe, take her away. I'm not coming now."

"But why, Mrs. Fremont? We're in the harbor. Everybody's leaving."

Jessie choked back a sob. "I can't. I know what they'll tell me, and I don't want to hear it."

There was a murmuring outside as Lilly and Joe Hooker conferred about what to do. "Mrs. Fremont," said Joe, "I think you're getting this twisted in your mind. Your husband's fine. I'm certain of it. He's probably waiting for you right now, down at the dock."

"No!" Jessie cried out to him. "I know he's come to some terrible misfortune."

"All right, then, Mrs. Fremont. We'll go find out for you," Joe called in to her. The footsteps receded.

Jessie slipped into a painful sleep. She began to dream that her husband was scaling the highest peak of an ice-covered range, where a howling wind made it almost impossible for him to keep his hold. Then from above came an ominous rumbling. A rock slide! First one boulder, then another hurtled past him. Desperately, he dodged them, but his footing slipped . . .

"Mrs. Fremont, Mrs. Fremont?"

Jessie realized, as she forced herself awake, that the tumbling booms of the rock slide were only knocks at the door.

"Mrs. Fremont, your husband's all right! He's riding up from Monterey to meet you! He's all right, Mrs. Fremont. His leg isn't even frostbitten. Mrs. Fremont?"

Jessie felt as if some greater force had suddenly released its grip on all her muscles, letting them snap back to where they should have been. As the knocking persisted, she looked up to the ceiling with fever-blurred eyes and uttered a silent prayer of thanks.

* * *

From her room in the Parker House Hotel on Portsmouth Square, Jessie and Lilly had a view of the entire rough-and-tumble town and of the harbor, a wilderness of ships' masts. Due to the fact that their room cost seventy-five dollars a week, a price unheard of in St. Louis, Jessie did not consider the view a consolation.

But prices everywhere were incredible. The Parker House at least offered comfortable accommodations. Other lodging houses, at almost the same price, were not nearly as luxurious. Meals in the dining room downstairs were five dollars per person, and a drink cost a dollar. What little meat there was cost about three dollars per pound, and most of it was pork, pickled or cured, and always greasy. As for fruits and vegetables, they had become as rare as gold itself.

Though her fever had declined ever since she had received news that her husband was well, Jessie kept to her room and let Lilly go exploring with Joe Hooker. They came back with mud splattered on their clothes, caked on their boots and even splotched in their hair, for the streets of San Francisco, contrary to popular belief, were not paved with gold. They were not paved at all. And after a hard rain, they became quagmires.

Chapter 22

He came late in the day, a solitary figure on horseback with bedroll and pack. He sported a wide-brimmed hat, a frayed red shirt and baggy pants. His boots were crusted with mud. In fact, John Fremont looked like all the other gold diggers back from the hills with a stash of powder to spend. No one, though, could take a careful look at his deeply tanned face and fail to recognize the noble features, clear blue eyes and wavy blond hair.

"Mrs. Fremont! Your husband done got here at last!"

The porch-sitter who issued the cry drew the full attention of everyone in the square. With some embarrassment, Fremont slid off his horse and bounded up the hotel steps. Even as he did, a set of windows on the second floor opened out, and Jessie looked down to see his boots disappear beneath the porch roof. In her nightgown, she ran to the door and flung it open as footsteps clattered up the stairs.

In another moment, they were in each other's arms.

Not a word passed between them. Finally, Fremont stood back, his hands on her shoulders. Overwhelmed with love and concern, he gazed at her, saw

her wan complexion and felt her shoulder blades protruding.

"My darling," he whispered. "You've been ill. My
poor Jess."

Behind him, Lilly came up. Fremont turned to
sweep her up in a hug, then set her down on a nearby
chair. "When you didn't come," Lilly told her father,
"Mother almost died. And a lady downstairs says she
will die."

Fremont looked in shock from her to Jessie.

"What is she saying?"

Jessie smiled weakly. "I'm not going to die on
you, John Fremont. Don't worry."

For the next few hours, as the sky darkened into
night, the Fremonts traded stories of their last months.
John brought Jessie up to date on his trip out from
Taos, which had been uneventful except for the meeting with the first eastward-bound wagon train. When
Fremont had asked the mule drivers for news about the
coast, they had looked him over in stupefaction and
finally cried, "Gold, man! Gold everywhere!"

That, Fremont allowed with a sheepish smile, had
been his introduction to this gold rush madness. "Probably the last man in the country to learn of it," he
laughed.

Fremont had soon realized that the land he meant
to sell—the forty-three thousand acres of the rugged
Mariposa Forest—lay smack in the middle of gold rush
country. After recuperating in the Red River settlement
for a few weeks, he had ridden out with Gregorio in
late February, and, deed in hand, he had gone to Monterey to affirm his ownership of the property.

"How many of the others came, too?" Jessie
asked.

Fremont's face clouded. "None. I couldn't wait.
I still don't know about the men Godey went up to

rescue. It haunts me now. I did hear he got back to Taos, but I also heard not all of them made it. Godey's due in Monterey soon. We'll know more of it then, I expect."

A silence fell between them.

"But tell me about the land," Jessie exclaimed at last.

"So far, no one knows about the gold except the eight gold diggers from Sonora who're making exploratory digs all around the property. The first thing to be learned about this business is to keep quiet about what you find. And Lilly, that includes you. Not even a word that your father owns any land, let alone where it is, or what gets found there. Understand?"

Lilly nodded solemnly, her eyes wide with excitement. "Did you find any gold yet, Father?"

Fremont reached into his pockets and pulled out a handful of oddly shaped nuggets. Laughing, he gave one to Jessie and one to Lilly, then spread the rest over the bed. "You see? That's what it looks like."

The nuggets had an even luster all around.

"Clamp your teeth on it," Fremont smiled.

Jessie, obliging him, found the nugget bland-tasting, but it felt uniformly smooth and soft.

"Look," Fremont said, picking up one nugget that appeared to have been flattened with a hammer. "That's how you know it's really gold. Fool's gold will just shatter. Feels pretty gritty on the teeth, too. But this, my darling, is pure gold—and there's enough where this came from to make us rich the rest of our days."

"Oh, John!" Jessie cried. "I can't believe it. I mean, even if you've found a little bit of gold there, how do you know there's more?"

"We've already struck deposits in a dozen different places," Fremont explained. "The Sonorans are packing up the flakes and dust in hundred-pound buckskin sacks, and we've got two sacks already, each one worth twenty-five thousand dollars!"

In her already weakened condition, Jessie very nearly fainted. She reached out to her husband for support and felt his strong hands take hold of her. In a moment, he had carried her over to the bed, gathering up the nuggets as he did.

"Lilly, time for bed," Fremont whispered to his daughter. "It's been a long day, and we're all in need of some sleep."

"It scares me, John," Jessie said quietly when the girl had closed the door behind her.

"But why? It's the best news I've ever had to deliver in my life."

Jessie smiled. "Oh, I know, John. I know it's good. But look how wild they are for gold, all over this town, all over California. You know they'll find out sooner or later, and when they do, you'll have every starry-eyed gold digger in the state at your doorstep."

Fremont shrugged. "Maybe. I've got no right of ownership to any minerals found there under Mexican law. The Mexicans still think the land belongs to them —even after the war of '46. Technically, anyone can walk over the property and stake a claim. As long as he sticks to a hundred-square-foot plot, he's got a right to be there and take whatever he finds. But we've got a first say on which claims we want to stake, and by the time anyone else finds out, the Sonora men ought to have located the best veins around. They're good men, Jessie."

"Oh, I'm sure they are, but I've heard tell of what gold can do to good men. Who's to say they won't just steal the whole pile of it before you get back?"

"They won't," Fremont said firmly. "They have too much to gain by sticking with me. I've promised them a wage."

"Well, even still, how are we going to stay together if you've got to tend the property and oversee the digging? I'll have to stay here, John, while you go to Mariposa."

"No. I've already thought that through," Fremont said. "I don't have to go back for a while now. Everything's under control for at least a month, maybe more. After that, I could make a trip down once a month, or we could move down to Monterey. Monterey's only a hundred and forty miles from the tract."

"Monterey," Jessie repeated without much enthusiasm. "Lord knows, John, anywhere is fine. But if San Francisco is supposed to be the most civilized town in California, I'd hate to see what Monterey looks like."

"Much better," Fremont laughed, "if you prefer peace and quiet to gambling, drinking and carousing around in red silk camisoles and black garter straps."

Now it was Jessie's turn to laugh. "Well I don't know, John Fremont, I've never tried that. A bit of carousing might be fun. So might a gambling den. You certainly can't say that San Francisco is dull."

"Well, Jess, we'll be staying here awhile anyway. You've got to shake that fever and I have to do a little business."

"A little business?" Jessie asked, amused. "What does that mean?"

"It means buying a few things—for you, mostly. After all, I've got to spend this new money somehow, don't I?"

Jessie smiled good-naturedly and pulled him toward her.

"I don't need your money, John Fremont. I need you." She nestled his face against her shoulder. They lay quietly for a while in the comfort of each other's warmth. Then, when Jessie appeared to be falling off to sleep, Fremont disentangled himself and pulled off his boots.

Jessie, to his surprise, opened her eyes wide, and without saying a word, she slipped off her nightgown and slid between the covers to wait for him. Fremont blew out the gas lamp beside the bed as he lay down beside her.

"You've never been so quick to blow out the light before," Jessie teased him. "Don't you want to have to look at me?"

"Nothing like that, my darling. God, no. I'm just . . . frankly, I'm embarrassed, myself. I'm so thin now, so pale. I don't look the way I used to, Jess."

Jessie ran her hands over his body. "Hush up, John Fremont," she whispered. "Do you think I only love you when you're perfect?"

Over Fremont's protestations she added, "It's only me who looks such a waif. And feverish, too."

Lovingly, they comforted each other. For Jessie, the irrepressible happiness of holding her husband, her lover, the man of her life, was something she had always felt and would feel for the rest of her life. More than once, she had wondered how it would be to grow old with her husband, to cuddle up to him when he was fifty or sixty years old. Would they still feel as wonderful as they did now? Of course they would. She never doubted it.

Rarely were either of them too tired to make love, but when that occasion arose, there was never any need to speak of it. A gentle touch, or a kiss that said it better than words, was all that was needed. Now, Fremont gave Jessie a soft hug. Though he desired her more than he ever had, he was certain her fever had exhausted her.

Again he was surprised. Jessie's hands sought him out and ran the course of his body.

"But . . ." he whispered.

Jessie put her lips to his before he could say more, and with a sigh of pleasure, he held the kiss and pulled her close, her firm breast pressing against his chest. Finally, impassioned by each other's presence after the long separation, they made love.

The next day they moved from the Parker House into one of San Francisco's few elegant homes, that of the late vice-consul of the territory, Alexander Liedesdorff. The dignitary had left behind a staff of servants, and a *secretaire d'affaires,* who had heard of Fremont's arrival and had extended an invitation to him to stay at the house with his family as long as he should need to.

The move, thought Fremont, would do Jessie good, for she was still a bit feverish. It would also save them the maddening expense of the Parker.

Fremont used his time away from Jessie to shop for the myriad notions and fabrics, furniture and silverware, carpets and other accouterments that would make a home more gracious. The fact that he as yet had no home hardly deterred him. Over these last arduous months, Fremont had nursed such a vivid picture of the hearth he and Jessie would share that he felt it was already his and that he needed only the civilized touches of his imagination to complete it.

One afternoon he happened upon a plain, wood frame house that bore a sign which read: *"The Californian*—San Francisco's Best Read Daily." The windows of the house, however, were shut, and curtains drawn behind them. The door, upon inspection, turned out to be locked.

Curious, Fremont knocked.

There was no response.

He knocked once more, loudly this time. From

deep in the recesses of the house there grumbled an irritated voice, followed by rapid footsteps. In a moment the door swung open, and a young man, no older than twenty-five, stood before him, his thumbs slung in black suspenders that starkly contrasted with his neatly pressed white cotton shirt.

"Another creditor?"

Thereupon the man slammed the door in Fremont's face.

Amused more than insulted, Fremont knocked again.

The door promptly opened. "I paid all my bills, you see," the young man declared. "There's not another dollar to be had."

Fremont held up his hands. "I'm not a creditor, mister. Just curious is all. Thought I'd buy a paper, but I guess you're all closed up today."

The young man softened. "Closed up today and every day," he said. "This here paper is out of business."

"Hard to believe there's any lack of news around here."

"News? Hell, we got enough news to fill a dozen newspapers. In fact, there's so much news that my two reporters, my office boy, my secretary, my paper boys, they're all out covering it!"

"And they won't be coming back, eh?"

"You got it, my friend." The young man held the door open widely and bade Fremont to step in. "If you want to see something ridiculous, look in at this office. New desks and chairs, new office supplies and a new printing press right there in the corner."

The man pointed to a monstrous contraption that looked like a giant, open-faced metal sandwich. Beside it sat a high stack of rag paper and a row of ink-blackened rollers. Upon closer inspection, one side of the sandwich proved to contain eight long metal troughs with thin metal slugs of upraised type. The type ran backwards across each line. In one corner lay what appeared to be a wood-cut drawing. Both this and the upraised lines were covered with residual ink.

"Now this here, sir, is my pride and joy," the young man boasted. "This is my new printing press. Watch carefully, now."

Into a nearby tray he poured a spot of thick, black ink. Then he saturated a roller in the tray until it was evenly coated with the ink. The roller was fitted at one end of the sandwich side, which had the type on it, and rolled right over the type several times.

"Now comes the beauty of it," the young man said.

He took a large sheet of rag paper, placed it on the other side of the sandwich and closed the two sides together. When he pulled them apart again, the paper was printed and wet with ink.

Fremont took the drying sheet of printed paper, and studied it curiously. He had never really stopped to think about how a newspaper was made. For him, newspapers had always seemed little more than penny gossip sheets, casually acquired and quickly discarded. Those in which his own name and exploits had been discussed were sometimes amusing and sometimes annoying, but important only insofar as how many readers might believe whatever nonsense they propounded. That a newspaper might actually be printed by people who cared about it was a small revelation to Fremont.

"Collector's item," the young man said wryly, indicating the sheet Fremont held. "Our last edition. Week ago Monday."

"But why can't you find other people to help you put it out?"

"No one around! No one to write it, and no one

to read it. Every cotton-headed fool in San Francisco's gone up to the hills for gold. There's only two kinds of people left here in town—those that can't read and those I owe money to. Because you see, sir, all this wonderful equipment was bought just six months ago, when the paper started, and I'm up to my eyeballs in debt."

"But people can't stay up in the hills forever, can they? Pretty soon they'll come back down. This town's too big to die overnight."

"Exactly, exactly. They'll all come back. And if I had the money to sit 'em out, everything would be fine. But I don't. Invested all my money—and other people's, too—and that, sir, is the end of that."

Fremont reached in his pocket and pulled out a small sack of gold nuggets. "Fellow I knew was going to start a paper in San Francisco," he said, giving the sack to the astonished young man. "But he didn't make it out here. I'd like to see someone do it for him. Let me know how much you need. My name is John Fremont, and I'm staying at the old Liedesdorff house. Send a list of your debts over to me. I'll clear them up."

The young man stared at him, his mouth hanging open.

"Only one condition," Fremont smiled as he turned to go. "Make it an honest paper. An honest paper is what I want to see."

In the evenings, if the dirt streets were dry, the Fremonts would leave the Liedesdorff house, go wandering around Portsmouth Square, and amble down Telegraph Hill to promenade along the busy waterfront. To John Fremont's fears that the town was too wild for a woman, Jessie could only reply that after the Chagres River, nothing seemed wild.

It was wild, though, by anyone else's standards. Gunfire often cracked like fireworks across the town, and fights broke out on the streets at the slightest provocation. It was wilder indoors than out. Already, San Francisco boasted some two hundred bars and five hundred gambling dens. Here, both the men who had found gold early and those who had failed to find any at all packed into noisy, dimly lit rooms that reeked of cigar smoke. There was little to drink besides whiskey, but that was in great supply. The gambling went on every night. And every night, a few fortunes would be made, while many more were squandered with a single throw of the dice.

In this sprawling, tumultuous town, there were so few women that a crowd of lonely prospectors would often stage a mock-ball, where half of them would don dresses and bonnets to dance with the other half. Jessie, for amusement, spent a dinner hour counting all the proper ladies she knew of in San Francisco. Her total came to fifty. This figure, of course, did not include compliant waitresses and bawdy whores. The ranks of these were larger, though still sparse enough for a clever and attractive prostitute to make a comfortable living.

Fremont was often more outraged than Jessie when, as often happened, a plump, saucy streetwalker winked at him as he and his wife passed by. Did he look like the sort of man who would solicit a whore in the company of his wife? Or under any other circumstances?

"Oh, come now, John," Jessie would laugh. "She doesn't know you from Adam. All she knows is that every man from Adam on down has had a desire to sleep with a woman, and almost from the time of Eve, there have been women around to service that need for money. You should be flattered. She must think you're man enough to handle any number of women—at once, no doubt!"

It was on one of these promenading evenings that Fremont and Jessie came upon an angry crowd gathered in front of a three-story wood frame house known as the Chinese Hotel. The house itself was a local curiosity. It had been transported in finished pieces from China to San Francisco, and assembled by slipping the parts into place like the pieces of a puzzle, without using a single nail.

But what lay inside the house was, to many, more than curious. The Chinese Hotel was now the town's most thriving whorehouse. It had the greatest selection of women, the most reasonable prices and the coziest bed chambers. By its sheer size—it dwarfed other house for blocks around—and by the cavalier manner in which the ladies comported themselves, lounging scantily clad on the balconies and sashaying down the street in full, red-velvet dresses, the Chinese Hotel had become the symbol of a new decadence in San Francisco. For the more moral-minded citizens, it had become a blight.

They were gathered this evening, some two hundred strong, bearing placards that read: "Punish the Wicked!" and "Stamp Out Sin!" A few at the forefront were carrying torches. There was much shouting and fist-raising, and it was clear to Fremont that a confrontation would soon occur.

After a few minutes, an older, gaudily dressed woman appeared at the front door and shouted back at the crowd. At the sight of her, the crowd roared with rage. Only the barest thread of restraint prevented the front ranks from surging forward to tear the woman limb from limb. She, however, appeared to be undaunted.

"Let the fallen woman talk!" came a shout from the crowd.

On the wooden balustrades above, some of the whores now appeared, their hair mussed and their figures clad only in lacy underclothes and robes. A few were plainly frightened, and peered over the railings to see how far the torches remained from the house. Two of them, however, spat openly at the upturned faces below.

"Well, ain't you a bunch of upstanding citizens!" cried the madam at the front door. "Pure as the driven snow. And you're scared your little children are going to get tainted by a few whores. I wonder what those little children would think if they knew how many of their daddies in the crowd were regular paying customers, eh? Like Ned Claflin over there, for one."

An angry murmur ran through the crowd.

"Yes, and Old Doc Hubbard. Sure! The same Doc Hubbard who's holding that sign says 'Stamp Out Sin.' Ain't you, Doc?"

Now, from across the street, Fremont and Jessie could see a dozen or more men in the crowd turn their heads and duck away. One man at the fringes put his sign down and hurried off, turning his collar up as he went.

"And you, too, Thomas Sullivan!"

The man scurried around the corner and was gone.

Before the madam could call out anyone else's name, the crowd took up a chant of "Down and out! Down and out! Get the sinners down and out!" A half dozen burly, black-suited men leapt up on the front porch with pistols drawn, pushed past the madam and muscled into the house to roust out whores and customers alike.

Out they came, as motley a group as ever paraded together, garbed in black lace and dangling garter belts

and velvet boots. Behind them cowered a grey-whisk-
ered, portly man in his underwear. He clutched the
rest of his clothes in his hands. The younger whores
followed, some not even fourteen years of age.

The crowd pressed in and craned for a closer
look at the harlots and their customers, most of whom
drew hoots of recognition and cries of: "For shame!
For shame!" From where they stood, Fremont and
Jessie lost sight of the sorry parade, but they did hear
a loud voice of protest that struck Fremont as oddly
familiar.

"You got the wrong man here, good people, the
wrong man! I'm a preacher, not a pervert. And I
weren't in that house for no danged carnal pleasure. I
was savin' a soul in that sinful house, people, savin' a
soul for the Church of the Savior Jesus!"

It was Doubleback!

For a moment the crowd seemed undecided. Then
one man shouted, "Well, I never did see a minister
performin' holy rites in his long johns!"

Loud jeers met Doubleback as he tried to reply
and then he was swept on with the others in a short,
enforced march to one of San Francisco's two makeshift jails.

"Good Lord, Jessie, that's one of my men."

"Then why don't you help him?" Jessie cried. "He
doesn't sound much like a preacher, but no one de-
serves to be pilloried by this crowd of hypocrites."

Fremont led Jessie through the crowd and followed along well behind Doubleback as other passers-
by joined in to pick up the chants and have a laugh at
the hapless victims. With the torchbearers leading the
way, the parade wound around and down to a two-story
brick building with small, barred windows. The door
swung open, spilling a yellowish light onto the street,
and a tall, rangy man with criss-crossed gunbelts stood

framed in the doorway. From where Fremont watched, he could catch only snatches of the conversation that ensued between the lawman and the vigilantes.

"Well—hell, at this hour . . ."

". . . didn't give me no warnin'."

". . . food enough for ten is all . . ."

"Three to a cell, I guess . . ."

Finally, the prisoners were herded inside, and the crowd began to disperse. Some folks were solemn, but many laughed and slapped each other on the back. Two self-appointed leaders remained to debate with the jailer how long this mass incarceration should go on. The jailer insisted, more audibly now, that there was simply not enough food to hold the lot of them for more than a few days.

"That's all right," one of the men said. "By then, we'll have that house stripped bare and boarded up, and have a court date set up, too."

"Court date? Bah!" griped the other man, spitting in the dirt. "Lotta good that'll do. March 'em in one door and out the other. Judge'll just fine 'em five dollar a head and they'll be out on the streets next day."

"Well, Harry, you heard what the jailer said. 'Less they're murderers or bank robbers, they can't find the food to feed 'em. Just no money for it."

"Then we oughta go out and scare up the money," Harry declared. "So's we can keep 'em locked up till it does some good."

Finally, they went off, still arguing. As they turned a corner, Fremont and Jessie stole out of the shadows and hurried across the street to knock on the jail's big oak door.

"As if I ain't got enough trouble already," the jailer growled when he saw them. "What do you want?"

"Well sir, we'd just like to take a bit of trouble off

your hands," Fremont smiled. "What's the bail on each of the prisoners?"

"Bail?" The jailer scratched his head. "Hadn't given it much thought, to tell you the truth. You be wantin' a man or a woman?"

"One of the men."

"Well, in that case, let's say ten dollars. See, if you wanted a woman, I'd have to kinda tack on a surcharge, if you see what I mean."

The jailer went in to retrieve Doubleback. He appeared still clad in his long johns, with the rest of his clothes in one hand and his boots in the other. At the sight of Fremont, he turned scarlet and seemed almost as annoyed as he was embarrassed.

"Didn't have to help me none, Colonel," he said. "I can take care of myself."

"I know you can," Fremont said. "But you can do that a lot better outside of jail than in it."

"I suppose," Doubleback muttered, and spat a thin stream of tobacco juice past the jailer's feet. "Sorry to be leavin' you so soon, Tex. We was just gettin' acquainted."

They went for a block in silence. Jessie walked between the two men.

"Feels kind of strange to see you here, Colonel," Doubleback said at last.

"It's always that way," Fremont remarked. "You go through a rough spot with a fellow, and you almost don't want to see him again because it brings back the memory of that rough spot."

"Yeah, I guess that's it," Doubleback said slowly.

At the next corner, Fremont held out his hand. "You have a place to stay, Doubleback?"

"Me? Ah, sure, I'll be all right. Got a lady friend I'll go visit, I guess. Stay with her, for a while."

Jessie could not resist the jibe. "Let's hope this one doesn't cost bail money."

Doubleback laughed uneasily. "Nah, but she'll cost me enough, 'cause I got to buy her meals and such."

He tipped his hat good night and walked off without another word, his shoulders seesawing slightly as he receded into the dark.

Chapter 23

There was some talk, in those first weeks at the Liedesdorff house, of buying the place, or of building a house
that overlooked the bay. Fremont could make bimonthly trips down to Mariposa to supervise work on his
mines, and Jessie could enjoy not only the new friends
she was making, but also the great exhilaration of living
in this gold-crazed town. If life was something less than
civilized here, it was also less than boring. But as the
weeks wore on, it became apparent that Jessie's poor
health was not improving. While she had no fever now,
she was plagued by a racking, persistent cough that left
her weak and dispirited. Her condition was plainly ex-
acerbated by San Francisco's cold, foggy air. If she
were to regain her vigor, she would have to go south.

In at least one way that would be a boon. Fremont and Jessie could spend more time together. As
for Lilly, she would have to continue her education
under Jessie's tutelage, which suited her just fine.

They would travel by carriage to Monterey, the
coastal town closest to the Mariposa tract, and with
them would go Lieutenant Beale. Beale had received
yet another transfer, this time to San Diego, and was
visiting the Fremonts on leave.

The day they set out was a steamer day, and the

waterfront was thronged with prospectors awaiting the bimonthly arrival of the mail steamer. In a town where the slightest occasion was enough to justify a drink, steamer day was the most ardently celebrated among them. The man who got a letter had one reason to tie one on; the man who didn't had another. Now, as the Fremonts' mule-drawn carriage rolled through the rutted streets, a rousing cheer went up. The mail ship had just been sighted edging around the peninsula.

Only a few miles out of San Francisco, the dirt road narrowed to a winding horse trail, and the April countryside began to change. California's rolling hills assumed an even more graceful prospect, blanketed with fields of swaying oats, and dappled with evergreens. When the trail grew precipitous, Fremont and Beale would jump out and tie lariats to the carriage, walking along the uphill side and pulling it toward them to keep it from tumbling.

Though this was hardly a rigorous expedition, Jessie joked about finally getting to explore a trail with her husband. It was a joyful adventure for her, as restful and revitalizing as any medicine she might have tried. Mornings were wonderful, setting out on another day's twenty-five miles, basking in the warm California sunshine and being lulled by the clip-clopping rhythm of the mules. But evenings were also delightful. Fremont had brought along half of a sheep, a ten-pound sack of Spanish onions and a healthy supply of sweet red peppers. Lamb stew, or *guisado,* became the delectable nightly staple. Then, when all had eaten and the night sky had fallen around them, Jessie and Lilly would curl up to sleep under army blankets in the carriage. Fremont and Beale slept on the ground in the bedrolls nearby.

In such fashion the journey unfolded, one day as warm and relaxing as the next. Before long Jessie showed signs of recovering health. Her cough abated, her color improved and her strength returned. Fremont, too, felt revived, and as usual his skin turned a deep, rich bronze under the hot sun. His leg still bothered him, and he limped a bit, but it had improved considerably. Jessie teased him, saying it made him more attractive anyway. He had become, she stated grandly, her own Lord Byron.

Lulled by the sun and countryside, and dazzled by an occasional sweeping view of the blue Pacific below, the Fremonts were almost sorry to come upon Monterey one radiant morning. At first glimpse, Jessie felt sure they must be wrong, that the cluster of whitewashed adobe houses, nestled down around the next cove, could only be a tiny fishing village too small to even bear a name.

But it was indeed Monterey. As the Fremonts' carriage teetered down the last turns of the rutted horse trail, Jessie wondered in delight why this paradise had not been overrun with immigrants. Fewer than one hundred adobe buildings dotted the valley, most of which were ringed with neatly kept gardens. In back of the village were hillsides of pine trees, and above them, the vivid blue of the California sky, broken only by the brilliant white gulls that wheeled and keened in the air.

The carriage came to a stop before one of Montereys' most gracious dwellings, a two-story adobe with a wooden balcony and three chimneys, all set within high hedges and a lush, green lawn.

The woman who answered the ornately carved wooden door burst into a radiant smile as soon as she recognized Fremont. This was Senora Castro, wife of the well-known Mexican general who had remained in exile in Mexico after the recent war. Because of the part that Fremont had played in that war, and the dismal consequences it had held for Mexico, Jessie was astonished that the woman did not show great animosity. But as Fremont had promised, Senora Castro not only welcomed them into her home, she insisted on turning over a two-room suite to her guests for their temporary lodgings. Not until they found a home of their own or built one at Mariposa, she declared, would she let the Fremonts take leave of her hospitality.

After a fond parting from Beale, who went off to assume his new command, the Fremonts set about making their simple accommodations into a comfortable home. Much of this was left to Jessie, for after two days, Fremont was obliged to ride a fast mount the one hundred and forty miles to Mariposa. For Jessie, the greatest challenge of the first days was an unexpected one: how to do the laundry.

Senora Castro, as it happened, did her own, and Jessie was certainly not about to insult the woman by asking if she would do the Fremonts' as well. But Jessie was still too weak to think of washing any clothing herself.

In desperation, Jessie went down to the shore one morning and sought out the Indian women who did their wash along the delta where the mountain streams emptied into the sea. Armed with a fluency in Spanish, she explained her needs and elicited much laughter and sympathy. Finally, one of the women indicated to the others that they should gather up Jessie's wash. She motioned for Jessie to come along, and together the two walked through Monterey's clean-swept streets, gaily commiserating about the many trials of tending a home. For a pittance, the Indian woman agreed to come every week and do the Fremonts' laundry.

More imagination was needed to transform Monterey's only food staples into an agreeable diet. Other than rice and beans, only flour, cornmeal, sugar and fish were available. Virtually all the domesticated animals in the surrounding countryside had been bartered for and devoured by the waves of overland prospectors.

Still, with ingenuity and daring, Jessie concocted a number of original recipes. On the days Fremont stayed in Monterey, he made a great show of smacking his lips at many of these frontier delicacies but he still seemed to put away a meal of beans and rice fastest of all.

Few women would have enjoyed the hardships and turned them to her advantage the way Jessie did, and this was exemplified by her wardrobe. What clothes remained from her trip up the Chagres were badly frayed and torn and those she had purchased in San Francisco were in no better shape after their carriage excursion. Though her health had greatly improved, these garments still hung loosely on her, making her look even thinner than she was.

First, she had Fremont bring back rolls of fabric from a business trip to San Francisco. Then, since she had never sewn a dress in her life, Jessie took her cambric underclothes, used them as a pattern, and promptly made a dozen like them. She did the same with her one black silk dress. As for stockings, she labored in vain to knit a heel, until finally she abandoned the effort and knit them without. "It's a poor leg," she said to herself, "that can't shape its own stocking."

As the days turned into weeks, Jessie began to assume a new role for herself in Monterey. Because the town was situated just halfway down the coast, it now drew a swelling assemblage of prominent figures with political ambition.

Any fool, she thought, could see that California,

revitalized by the war's end and by the rush for gold, would now become a state. The only question in her mind was who should take the helm.

For any young man with the desire, there was no end of dreams to dream, and into Monterey crowded these men of promise, all gathering at Jessie Fremont's house. Here, more than anywhere else in that coastal town, a sense of what might come to pass hung vibrantly in the air. The rooms themselves still looked rough-hewn, having been furnished only with the goods that Fremont had carted down from San Francisco: Chinese matting for the floors, New England bedsteads, white curtain lace, a teakwood table, a set of china, spermaceti candles with tin candlesticks, and an impressive grizzly-bear skin on the floor.

The men who came to anguish over California's future saw in Jessie Fremont a person as fully informed as they were. For Jessie, it all added up to a new and exhilarating sense of being the *grande dame* of a frontier salon.

One frequent member of the Fremont salon was a young, sickly army captain named William T. Sherman. Quiet and consumptive, Sherman soon became one of Jessie's favorites. He could hardly cough without her getting up to heat a cup of medicinal herb tea or wrap him in Indian blankets. And another, Captain Henry Halleck, a gentle soul who claimed to be a harsh realist about the issue of slavery, always stirred the most protracted debates.

Meanwhile, Fremont attended to the mines. On the one hand, the work fascinated him. On the other, it was taxing and difficult. The Sonorans, more than a score of them, were the best workers a man could employ. They were honest, vigilant and incredibly tough. All day under a hot California sun, they would labor over the wooden Long Toms that Fremont had brought out for them. These were long sluices, down which a panful of watery sediment would be carefully poured. At the low end, the sediment swept through a perforated metal sheet, which the miners called a riddle, and into the ridged riffle box that would filter out any flakes or nuggets of gold.

But the Sonora gold diggers were not the only ones working the Mariposa tract. Every day, more miners flocked down to the rugged, stream-laced land to try their luck. Fremont would not have driven them off. He could not have if he wanted to. By Mexican territorial law, the mineral rights of a plot remained public property, even when a man had bought his acreage of land and put up fences around it. The only claim that man and government both respected was a placer claim, a plot actively worked by a miner who left his tools on the land to show ownership. On a poor patch of gold rush territory, a miner might stake a square mile. On a mineral-rich, glittering stretch like the Mariposa tract, the miners worked out equitable claim sizes among themselves: a hundred square feet, perhaps, or even less.

Every day, as more miners streamed onto his private land, Fremont found himself approached by newly rich businessmen who wanted to talk about making deals. Everything, Fremont discovered, was a "deal," whether it meant selling his land outright or sharing the gold rights with backers.

None of these options seemed at all appealing to him. But to dawdle as he had so far, while his loyal Sonorans worked their claims and saw other claims swallowed by interlopers, hardly seemed a better solution. Soon, he would have to shoulder the responsibility of becoming a serious businessman.

Perhaps knowing that this would come to pass made the present days seem even more delightful. In the early mornings, Fremont loved to awaken in the small log cabin he had built for himself, high above the stream where he had first found gold. His Sonorans, who preferred to sleep out under the stars, would be up ahead of him, already working the Long Tom, bringing back pails of sediment, shaking the sediment down the sluice, and working the riffle box to see what flakes and dust had been deposited. It was like this every day, and Fremont considered himself a lucky man.

But into this charmed life of love, gold dust and California sunshine arrived one dark cloud. Fremont was in Monterey, dining with Jessie, when a clip-clopping of hooves broke the quiet of the dirt street and stopped in front of their house. A rider dismounted and led the horse past the hedges, then up the flower-lined path. Curious to see which of their usual guests this might be, Jessie peered down through the curtains.

"Don't recognize the hat," she said.

There came a knocking at the door. Fremont listened to the murmur of voices below, then jumped up, his napkin still tucked in his collar. "Godey," he flung back at Jessie. He dashed out to greet his visitor.

Chapter 24

They met at the foot of the stairs, Fremont sweeping up the big man in a powerful bear hug. From the second floor landing, Jessie was struck by the silence between them. There was simply no need for words. They stood back to look at each other, Godey smiling through his big, black beard, Fremont grinning back.

"Took you away from dinner," Godey said finally, pointing to Fremont's napkin.

He pulled it off sheepishly. "You haven't eaten, I'll wager. Come on up, there's plenty."

Godey purposefully seated himself at Jessie's candlelit table and proceeded to polish off three heaping plates of rice and beans, washing it all down with two mugs of local beer. Throughout this performance, he said nothing, only nodding as Fremont and Jessie brought him up to date on the Mariposa property.

When he had finished and pushed his plate away, Jessie stood up to clear the table. With a smile, Fremont told her to sit, reaching for the plates himself.

"You cooked," he said to her. "I'll clean."

"Well, Colonel," Godey drawled. "I guess you took a lesson from old Kit there, didn't you?"

They all laughed. "You're absolutely right, Mr. Godey," Jessie put in. "John was a good husband before, but since that visit, he's been so diligent about pitching in with the chores that I've half a mind to hire him out around town."

"It's this china," Fremont said. "If Jessie starts throwing this stuff around, well, it's up to San Francisco to replace it."

Jessie then brought them coffee. They drank and talked for a while longer. It was Fremont who finally brought up the question that had haunted him for weeks.

"How'd it go back there with the rest of the men?"

Godey flashed a troubled look and returned to his contemplation of the candle flames. "Not so good, I guess. Not so good."

"Well, tell us. For God's sake, what happened?"

Godey cleared his throat. He looked hesitantly at Jessie, then at Fremont. "You both want to hear about this?"

"Yes, of course," Jessie spoke up. "Tell us, *please*."

"Well, after I saw you last, Colonel, that day in Taos with Baily, when we got the mules and provisions, I lit out with thirty mules, I think it was, all loaded up, and four good Mexicans. We made Red River that evening, stayed the night there and pushed on early the next morning."

Godey took a sip of his coffee and his eyes narrowed. "The first we seed was Vincenthaler and a few of the others near the Conjos River. Brattle, Martin and Bacon. They was in a terrible way. They'd been walkin' down along about three days without a thing to eat 'cept their own clothes, which they had already proceeded to do. I don't believe they would have made it on their own, Colonel, not all the eighty miles they had yet to go.

"Anyways, I gave 'em food and we set awhile,

and Vincenthaler told me what happened, at least from his side of the story. He said that when we all left to get help, he took command just like you wanted. And for four days he worked with the others to take baggage from up the stream down to where the rest of it was, and to move the whole lot of it into a cave where it might sit the winter.

"But they was out of food altogether by now. Nossir, not a speck or crumb to be had, and the men were desperately hungry. So first a couple of men began movin' down the river, thinkin' to meet the rescue party. They was Carver and Ducatel. Then a day later, the rest of 'em all started goin' down the river, too.

"The first one they lost was Joaquin. His feet was froze, and he wouldn't go on another step. Said he wanted to die, and he kept pleadin' with the others to shoot him right there. When they didn't, he turned around and walked off. For all the others knew, he was as good as dead.

"Then next day, Wise died as they were headin' down along the river. Vincenthaler says Wise just fell down on the ice, just like that. Starvation, most likely, but maybe also from hittin' his head, because he started bleedin' somethin' fierce, a big stream of blood that kinda followed after the men a bit before it froze.

"Next one to go was Carver. He just walked off screamin' like a crazy man, that's what Vincenthaler says. He'd been givin' out for days, I guess, gettin' spooked and laughin' and screamin', kinda like Creutzfeldt did. He just walked up the east bank of the river and kept on goin'.

"Now here's where Vincenthaler's story got a bit thin. He says that after that, the men was so hungry they was ready to eat whoever might die next, tear him apart from limb to limb. To keep that from comin' to pass, Vincenthaler set off at a faster clip with a few of the strongest men, leavin' the others to straggle along as best they could. But I don't truly believe that, Colonel, on account of what Kern said later.

"Now what we did, as soon as we gave those men food, was to push on up the river with Vincenthaler and his bunch. First men we had to find was Hubbard and Scott, who'd fallen behind. Both of 'em had kinda dropped in their tracks the day before, tellin' the others to go on ahead. Well, we found Scott first. He was still alive, though just barely. He was wrapped up in his clothes and huddled 'round a little fire the others had made for him. Hubbard wasn't so lucky, though. He was dead.

"From there we proceeded on up to find Kern and the rest of 'em. But the damndest thing happened. We'd missed 'em when we cut across a bend in the river to go the shorter distance. They was comin' right down that bend just as we cut up across it. But we did find two other men. That was Ferguson and Parker. Found 'em huddled up together, more dead than alive, one little blanket between 'em. Parker was dead, and Ferguson didn't even know it. He was so nearly froze and woozy with cold that he was kinda sleepin', and I guess he figured Parker was just sleepin' beside him. It took us awhile to make Ferguson realize what was goin' on, and that we was really there to save him. He thought we was a dream. Then when he saw Parker dead, he got awful upset. He was cryin' and carryin' on there, and sayin' he was the one who should have died 'cause Parker had a family and he didn't. He seemed to feel powerful guilty about it, as if it were his fault somehow. 'Parently he'd lost one of the blankets, and that's why he was sharin' the one they had left between 'em.

"Well, we took Ferguson with us, and left Parker where he was. We determined from what Ferguson told us that we'd probably missed the others. Sure enough, when we headed downriver, we found 'em, all in the most horrible condition. Kern told me all about it when they'd put some food in their gullets. Said Vincenthaler was a liar, that what had really happened was that he took the strongest fellows with him and left the weaker ones behind. Even a few days before that, when they shot an elk and brought it into the camp, they kept the weaker boys away from the meat until Vincenthaler and his boys had ate their fill, leavin' the others to pick and gnaw at the bones.

"Course, Vincenthaler was fit to kill when Kern started sayin' this. Hoppin' mad. And to tell you my opinion, Colonel, I think he was blusterin' around to hide the truth, 'cause later Cathcart said the same thing about him. Cathcart had stayed on with Kern, and he told the same story as Kern, every detail.

"What Cathcart and Kern said is that when Vincenthaler deserted 'em, they vowed they wouldn't split up any further, and that not one of 'em would leave another behind. Also, that if any of 'em died, there'd be no cannibalisin' betwixt 'em, and that if any real food was found, they'd share it as best they could.

"So a day passed, and Cathcart, one of the only men left who wasn't nearly blinded by the snow, set out to hunt up what he could. He came in with two grouse, which they proceeded to share. Then they stumbled across a dead wolf that was part ate up by other animals. So the men ate that, too. The only other food they could find was some bugs and some fungus, and every one they found they put together in a pile and divided amongst themselves.

"Those last days before we got up to 'em were 'parently about as bad as could be, and most of 'em was gettin' ready to die. Anderson did die, and Rohrer, too, day after him. And as for the rest, they sat around a little fire they kept goin' with bits of wood and

branches nearby. For about the last three days they had
no food at all. But they perked up pretty good when
we got down to 'em finally. Besides Anderson and
Rohrer, the rest was alive.

"Now the others rode down with the Mexicans on
the mules, but I kept goin' north a ways. I had plenty
of food and two good mules, and I figured I might try
to get some of the baggage—your pack in particular,
with all the instruments and logbooks and whatnot.
So when I got to the cave, why, there was one good bit
of news—Joaquin was up there, still alive, which surprised everybody. He had a fire goin', and was in pretty
good shape, 'cept for his feet, which was still all bunged
up. We came down directly, and brought your pack
with us, which I got outside. That's about it."

There was a long silence after he had finished.
Godey sat back. This was the most he had ever said at
one time in his life

"I had no idea . . ." Fremont murmured at last. "I
don't know what to say, except to thank you. I owe you
everything, Godey. You saved the rest of my men."

"Ah, hell, no," Godey exclaimed. "I mean, anyone could have ridden up there. And someone else
would have if I'd have stayed in Taos. Weren't nothin'
special about it."

Fremont smiled sadly. "I didn't, Godey. I stayed in
Taos."

"Why, of course you did, Colonel, you had no
choice. I mean, your leg was near froze right off. You
may not recall what you looked like down there, but I
do. You wouldn't have done nobody no good. Woulda
just been a damn fool thing to do, settin' up there with
me."

Jessie had been listening intently to Godey's story,
but at the mention of these last words, she stared in
amazement. "John—your leg—it was frozen?"

Fremont nodded reluctantly. He seemed to be in a daze. "Tell me," he said distantly to Godey. "What happened to them, the ones that made it? Are they still in Taos?"

"I'm not at all sure about all of 'em, Colonel. I know Cathcart said somethin' about havin' enough of the trail, and all. So as soon as he was fattened up a bit, he headed down to New Orleans and took a steamer up to New York. And guess where he figures to go from there?"

"Prussia."

Godey's jaw dropped. "Someone told you, then. Yeah, that's what he did, 'parently. Had some money back East, sold everything he owned and sailed to Europe."

"Nobody had to tell me, Godey. He was a man headed home. What about Kern?"

"Well Kern, he wasn't too eager to do any more travelin', and frankly, he wasn't too pleased toward you neither. He had a lot of harsh words to say. And I guess if he'd had some notion of pushin' on to California, he gave it up. As soon as he was fit enough to travel, he headed with Cathcart down to New Orleans, and was plannin' to take the steamer with him up to New York. Seems to have relatives up that way, and some kind of business. And I think a girl he was fixin' to marry."

"How about the others?"

"Well, the only ones I know about are Vincenthaler, Brattle and Old Bill. Vincenthaler, he set himself up in business in Taos, with some money that he got from his old daddy. Said he had a sure-fire way to make a million dollars. What he did was, he started buyin' all the pots and pans and whatnot that the settlers had brought out with 'em but didn't want to carry across the desert. The settlers was just goin' to throw it all away otherwise, so he got a good price. Only problem was, there wasn't anyone to sell it to. Indians had their own clay bowls and cups and their own home-made clothes. So did the Spanish. By the time I left, that damn fool had a store full of goods and not a dollar in his pockets. And may the Lord strike me dead, Colonel, but I weren't the least bit sorry for him either.

"As for Brattle, well, it was funny about him. We'd have figured if anyone was goin' to stumble around and make a mess of it, it'd be him, but from what I hear, that wasn't the way it worked out at all. 'Parently Brattle got himself a ride out to San Francisco, bought a shovel and washpan, and plunked himself down in some dadblamed riverbank that no one else had staked a claim in yet. Sure enough, it come up full of gold. So I guess Brattle had some brains after all."

Despite his great anguish over the rescue story, Fremont could not help but join in the laughter. It felt strange to laugh when his stomach felt so knotted and tight and sick with guilt and sorrow. "What about Old Bill? Did that worthless idiot go off and make his fortune as well?"

Godey shook his head. "Surprised you hadn't heard, Colonel. Old Bill's dead. And there ain't a man alive to say he didn't deserve it. After we all got down to Taos in May, Old Bill just spent all his time drinkin' and carryin' on with every woman he could wrap his tough old arms around. Then, once he was feelin' better, he went north to do a bit of huntin', mainly 'cause he had this idea he was gonna go up and retrieve the baggage from the expedition when the snow had melted."

"What? You mean to return it to us?"

"Hell, no. He was gonna keep it himself, sell it or whatever. There was a lot of supplies he could have sold, too. And he was always sure you had a bunch of money stashed away in one of them packs. Anyway that's what he told the Mexicans he took up with him. And so he got up there all right, early July, and somehow he ended up dead. Most figure his Mexicans killed him when they got to the baggage."

"Incredible," Fremont said, shaking his head. "So the baggage is gone, too?"

"It is, indeed. Gone and best forgot, Colonel. But as I say, I got your pack on my horse outside. Let me get it for you."

Godey clumped out of the room and down the stairs. Fremont sat in silence, staring at the candles. It was Jessie who spoke first.

"I know what you're thinking, John Fremont, and it isn't so. You did everything you could to save those men."

"But I didn't. I stayed in Taos."

"You can torture yourself about that till the day you die. It isn't going to change a blessed thing. You heard Godey. How were you going to save anyone in your condition? It doesn't make sense. In fact, the only thing that does make sense is that you made it alive, and so did most of the men."

"Out of thirty-three, ten are dead and one is insane," Fremont said quietly.

"Twenty-two are alive and well, though, John. Twenty-two men who have probably just lived through the greatest adventure in their lives. And what you never seem to remember about the men who died is that they signed on to do this. You always bat that thought away, but it's the God's honest truth. And they didn't die for nothing. They proved a railroad can cut across the country. There were eleven, yes, but how many lives are sacrificed in a war to keep a country free and growing? There have to be sacrifices, John."

"Perhaps."

Long into the night, after Jessie and Godey had both turned in, John Fremont stayed out on the front porch, reading through his trip logs and staring into the darkness. He felt utterly changed, as if he had lived a lifetime that very evening, and was now embarking on a new one. Feelings seemed to grow more complicated as life unraveled, until it seemed that wisdom was merely the seeing of different sides to the same shape at the same time. Tonight, he felt a bottomless sorrow at the story he had heard. It was a sorrow that would never entirely fade from his heart, yet he also felt a vast relief, and an eagerness to get on with the future.

It was a feeling that men had in the flush of triumph, and often in the face of defeat.

Epilogue

In the deepening autumn of 1849, John Fremont's tumultuous life took yet another turn, one that even Jessie, in all her pride for him, could not have predicted.

No one doubted any longer that California would soon enter the Union. In the last year alone, some eighty thousand emigrants had streamed across its borders, most with dreams of gold dust filling their heads.

Indeed, California's entry into the Union seemed so inevitable that the ambitious young men of Monterey began gathering as a legislative assembly to hammer out a government and jockey for positions as its representatives. For a meeting house they used the Colton Town Hall School, and on September 3, 1849, they met within its walls to open a statehood convention. Fremont had remained at Mariposa, for his mines now needed almost constant supervision. But Jessie attended as a prominent citizen in her own right.

That night a half dozen men threw their hats into the senatorial contest. Most were men who had propounded their political views for months in Jessie's salon: Captain Henry Halleck, for one, and William Gwin, and John Sutter, and a newspaper editor named Robert Sample. Fremont's name was also bruited

about, and, at last, most onlookers came to applaud
the choice. A few, of course, were bitterly resentful.
They criticized Fremont for the expedition and blamed
him for the many lives lost. They brought up the court-
martial and accused him of having mutinied against the
same government he would now presume to serve. And
they hinted darkly that Mariposa was an illegally gained
piece of land, purchased while Fremont was in the
army.

The most vitriolic of these critics finally banded
together to confront Fremont with a strongly worded
letter that demanded his views on political questions
and asked for a full account of the Mariposa purchase.
He replied in characteristic fashion—with blunt hon-
esty. He claimed to be a proud member of the Free-
Soil Party. He reiterated his long-standing opposition
to slavery, and he came out strongly for a central railroad to the Pacific, promising that if he were elected
senator, he would work for its implementation. And
he sent along inscribed copies of his land deeds.

To all but the most patently jealous observers,
Fremont's letter dispelled any lingering doubts and
floated his name to the top of the list of senatorial
candidates. The night a convention met in San Jose to
choose two men to become California's two senators,
Fremont attended the meeting, and then rode home
seventy miles through the rain to bring Jessie the wonderful news.

"I couldn't wait," he cried out at the door. His
blue eyes danced with pleasure and mischief. "I've
ridden from San Jose to be the first to greet Jessie
Fremont, Mrs. Senator from the state of California."

Christmas that year was a joyous occasion. Fremont brought gifts from San Francisco, including a
cashmere shawl for Jessie, and candy and a china doll
for Lilly. Even as the tree was adorned and a Christmas

feast prepared, Jessie was packing up trunks for the trip to Washington, where Fremont would take his seat in the Senate as soon as California was voted into the Union. The mines, meanwhile, would be worked by Fremont's faithful Sonorans, and overseen by a group of San Francisco businessmen he had come to trust.

They left on New Year's night, 1850, with a hard rain sweeping the streets of Monterey. Senora Castro's servants packed their carriage. The Fremonts piled in, and the coach clattered down to the dark waterfront, where their steamer awaited them. A ship's gun fired to announce the boarding, and onto the gangplank strode the senator's proud family.

From where they stood on deck, looking toward shore, John and Jessie Fremont felt their joy tainted with regret. Both knew, without speaking of it, that their lives would never be the same. The adventures they had endured would now slip into the past. Ahead lay a different life, full of different obstacles—not of the rugged frontier, but of politics and Washington. And who was to say which life was better? Whatever the answer, there was always the challenge of the future. And to John Fremont, there was nothing more important.

AMERICAN EXPLORERS #1

A cruel test, an untamed land and the love of a woman turned the boy into a man.

JED SMITH

FREEDOM RIVER

****

Arriving in St. Louis in 1822, the daring, young Jedediah Smith is confronted by rugged mountain men, trappers and bar-room brawlers. He learns all too soon what is to be expected of him on his first expedition into the new frontier up the Missouri River. Making lifelong enemies and fighting terrifying hand-to-hand battles, he learns how to live with men who will kill for a cheap woman or a drop of liquor. But he learns more. Far from the beautiful woman he left behind, in the arms of a free-spirited Indian girl, he discovers the kind of love he never thought possible. *Freedom River* is the historical drama of an American hero who opened the doors of the unknown wilderness to an exciting future for an expanding nation.